AMERICAN
DARK
COMEDY

Edvard Munch's *The Shriek* (lithograph, 1896). Courtesy of the Museum of Modern Art, New York.

AMERICAN DARK COMEDY

BEYOND SATIRE

Wes D. Gehring

Foreword By R. Karl Largent

Contributions to the Study of Popular Culture, Number 55

GREENWOOD PRESS
Westport, Connecticut • London

Library of Congress Cataloging-in-Publication Data

Gehring, Wes D.
    American dark comedy : beyond satire / Wes D. Gehring ; foreword
by R. Karl Largent.
        p. cm.—(Contributions to the study of popular culture,
    ISSN 0198-9871 ; no. 55)
    Includes bibliographical references and index.
    ISBN 0-313-26184-9 (alk. paper)
        1. Comedy films—History and criticism. 2. Tragicomedy—History
and criticism. I. Title. II. Series.
    PN1995.9.C55G42   1996
    791.43′617—dc20   96-154

British Library Cataloguing in Publication Data is available.

Library of Congress Catalog Card Number: 96-154
ISBN: 0-313-26184-9
ISSN: 0198-9871

First published in 1996

Greenwood Press, 88 Post Road West, Westport, CT 06881
An imprint of Greenwood Publishing Group, Inc.

Printed in the United States of America

The paper used in this book complies with the
Permanent Paper Standard issued by the National
Information Standards Organization (Z39.48–1984).

10 9 8 7 6 5 4 3 2 1

Copyright Acknowledgments

The author and the publisher are grateful for permission to reprint from
the following materials:

Wes D. Gehring, "A Charlie Chaplin Centennial: 1889–1989," *Journal of
Popular Film & Television* (Fall 1988), p. 130. Reprinted with permission
of the Helen Reid Educational Foundation, published by Heldorf Publications, 1319 18th Street, N.W., Washington, D.C. 20036-1802. Copy-
right 1988.

For Sarah & Emily

A CHARLIE CHAPLIN
CENTENNIAL:
1889–1989

Even a hundred candles
Can't make light of Charlie;
This streetwise survivor is
A regular road scholar.

Like evolution he is more
Than just monkey business,
Though his dance of Pan
Developed in leaps and bounds.

And because gold was the
Only thing critics hadn't panned,
This baggy pants prospector
Mimed a *Gold Rush* (Hollywood being a vein place).

Then like a ghost, he only
Worked when the spirit moved him;
But his tough & economical directing
Remained the same—give no quarter.

Long an enemy of talking pictures,
He avoided sound advice for years;
But eventually became verbal Verdoux,
A widow-shopping Bluebeard.

So toast this comic osteopath
Who doctors the public funny bone,
While showing if we spring from animals,
Some people didn't spring far enough.

CONTENTS

ILLUSTRATIONS

FOREWORD

I first met Wes Gehring at a writer's conference some ten years ago. An erudite and handsome young man, nattily attired, the possessor of a saber-quick wit, he most certainly did not look the role of a college professor. But there he was, complete with Ph.D. tucked neatly behind his name and the imposing title of Professor of Film on his credentials.

"Professor of film?" I questioned.

"A comedy historian," he clarified.

And so he has proven to be, not only recalling for our enjoyment, but often explaining, obtuse relationships between the antics on the screen and the mores of our time.

As I read an early draft of this latest book on black comedy, questions arose. Did I really understand what Lenny Bruce was saying? How much thought did I give (at the time) to *Dr. Strangelove?* Or, what was the real meaning behind Billy Wilder's *Some Like It Hot?* The answers to these questions (for me, at least) are lost in the musty convolutions of a mind that at the time was probably (I can't remember for certain) more obsessed with my glands than the real meaning of Frank Capra's *Arsenic and Old Lace.* I do remember thinking Lenny Bruce probably had to go to confession a lot (Catholics think that way), that Tony Curtis made a good looking filly, that Peter Sellers was funny, and that it would be cool to be as smooth as Cary Grant. Beyond that my thoughts were somewhat shallow.

Because I know Wes, and, if the truth were known that I'm a closet movie freak (I often watch old movies when I should be doing other things), Wes's latest effort, a foray into the world of black comedy, spurred me into going back and watching a few of the classics he both discusses and analyzes.

By golly, Wes is right. When Alan Arkin in *Catch-22* is arrested for a curfew violation after viewing a collage of violence and human baseness, it is "absurd." A re-viewing of the 1970 smash, *M.A.S.H.*, and the antics of Robert Duvall and Sally Kellerman are a commentary on the ludicrous way we view man's irrationality. In the harsh light (now) of a quarter-of-a-century of deteriorating standards of acceptable behavior, the egregious, the incongruous, and the arrant have become the norm. Most certainly it is a great deal more apparent than the trifling thought I gave it at the time.

So what is black comedy? Gehring gives us a real-world definition. In so many words, he tells us that black comedy is prophecy, a precursor to late twentieth-, early twenty-first century reality. It's all about our sexual perversity, *The World According to Garp*, our "anything at any cost" attitude that induces Blake Edwards to try to shock us by having his wife, Julie Andrews, go topless on *S.O.B.* (a long way from *The Sound of Music*).

Gehring says, "This man-made absurdity is the result of both general species incompetency and its perpetuation in human institutions." I couldn't have said it better. In fact, I couldn't have said it at all until Wes pointed it out to me.

If you enjoyed Gehring's ten other film comedy books, such as *Groucho & W. C. Fields: Huckster Comedians*, or *Screwball Comedy: A Genre of Madcap Romance*, you'll find his excursion into the often-disturbing world of black comedy equally risible and informative.

Or, as my late daddy might have put it, "Pull up a chair, sit down, shut up, and hang on. Welcome to the world of Black Comedy."

R. Karl Largent
July 20, 1995

[*Award-winning novelist R. Karl Largent is an author critics are heralding as the "new Stephen King."*]

PREFACE

When his [Tarantino] characters draw guns, as they so frequently do, one never knows if they're going to blow others'
heads off, make funny speeches (they often do both), have the
tables turned on them or make an honorable, peaceful exit.
　　　　　　　—*Variety* review of *Pulp Fiction* (1994)[1]

The mass of men lead lives of quiet desperation.
　　　　　　　—Henry David Thoreau, *Walden* (1854)[2]

As a child of the 1960s there was no escaping dark comedy. It was
a way of coping with the early promise of the decade, such as
President Kennedy's "New Frontier" and President Johnson's
"Great Society—fragmented by assassinations and open wounds
like Vietnam and civil rights. Then as now, political and social
events fed the arts, and vice versa. Consequently, one could note
director Stanley Kubrick's pivotal black comedy film *Dr. Strangelove: Or, How I Learned to Stop Worrying and Love the Bomb* (1964),
or novelist Kurt Vonnegut, Jr.'s equally dark and underrated *Slaughterhouse-Five* (1969). The former work chronicled man's inevitable
inability to avoid a nuclear holocaust; the latter novel found its
antihero forever time-tripping, yet never finding a civilized time.
Even the decade's musical masters of love, the Beatles, came up
with the song "Maxwell's Silver Hammer" (1969), which comically

chronicles the murders by medical student Maxwell Edison of anyone who proves bothersome.

On a more personal level, my interest in dark comedy was reawakened when writing my book *"Mr. B" Or Comforting Thoughts About the Bison: A Critical Biography of Robert Benchley* (1992). Indeed, I can even note the exact day: October 20, 1990. On that date I interviewed the late humorist's daughter-in-law Marjorie, executor of the Benchley papers at Boston University and widow of the humorist's eldest son, the gifted author Nathaniel. She shared with me one of Robert Benchley's Harvard College cartoons that the family had recently reacquired (see illustration 1). I had long enjoyed the humorist's occasional forays into dark comedy. For example, his famous essay "How to Watch Football," from *Pluck and Luck* (1925), and the namesake for Benchley's 1938 film short subject of the same title, paralleled a popular tendency of his criticism—reviewing the annoyingly disruptive audience. Both could provoke black comedy revenge. Thus, "How to Watch Football" suggests the humorist would soon be marketing folding pocket daggers, just as an earlier Benchley *Life* "Drama" column prescribes poison-stuffed marshmallows for doing away with the unruly audience member.[3] However, not until Marjorie shared this Benchley artwork was I aware of just how pervasive and long term his interest was in the genre. And my fascination with dark comedy was all the more piqued.

With these things in mind, Chapter 1 is a foundation for this genre of comic irreverence which flippantly attacks what are normally society's most sacredly serious subjects—especially death. This foundation is partly a literary overview, focusing upon key novels such as Herman Melville's *The Confidence Man* (1857) and Joseph Conrad's *Heart of Darkness* (1902), plus such World War I related works as Erich Remarque's *All Quiet on the Western Front* (1928) and Humphrey Cobb's *Paths of Glory* (1935). This war's terrible uniqueness to dark comedy came about because it was the first large-scale combat where twentieth-century technology came into conflict with nineteenth-century tactics. But it was not just tactical incompetence by the leaders. Many believed civilization could progress only if the lower (soldiering) classes were periodically purged. The result was a slaughter.

Chapter 1 also addresses World War II's impact upon the genre via both the Jewish Holocaust, which took six million lives in the

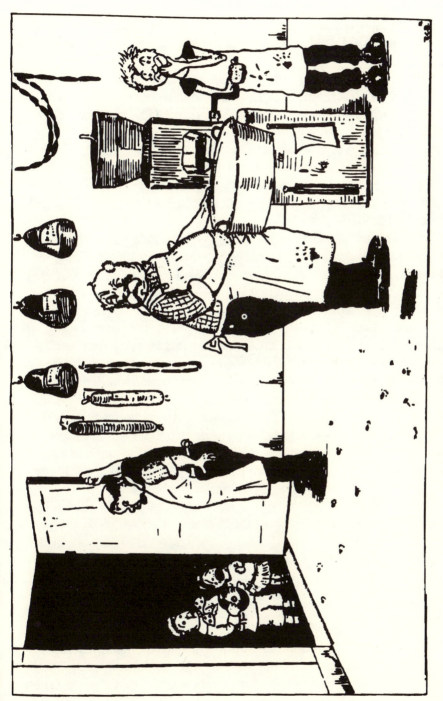

"Please, mister, have you seen our dog?"

1. Macabre college cartoon by Robert Benchley. Courtesy of Mrs. Nathaniel Benchley.

ugliest scenario of modern times, to a war that produced a weapon (the atom bomb) which gave people all the more reason to cope with comedy.

Chapter 2 examines numerous selected dark comedy films and three interrelated themes of the genre: man as beast, the absurdity of the world, and the omnipotence of death. The chapter begins with early black comedy precedents in the pre-1940 work of such comedy pioneers as Charlie Chaplin and Buster Keaton. The chapter then methodically surveys the history of American dark humor to the present, with four basic lessons to be learned or reaffirmed from the genre's obsession with death—the most dominant dark comedy theme.

The first lesson is that death itself is a terrible absurdity. How can a once vital, passionate, thinking human being suddenly be reduced to so much decaying garbage? Second, the casually random end-without-purpose unexpectedness with which death frequently occurs underlines both the world's absurdity and the insignificance of the individual. Third, the popularity of suicide in black comedies further accents man's earthly dilemma in several ways. For instance, suicide is that rare activity where the dark-comedy individual can initiate the event instead of being its random recipient. How ironically fitting for the genre that this act results in the total negation of the individual. The final basic lesson to draw from the genre's obsession with death demonstrates people's callousness to shock. While viewers tend to be surprised, in-film dark comedy characters often have the worn-down "and so it goes" attitude of *Slaughterhouse-Five*'s central character, Billy Pilgrim.

Chapter 3 addresses three pioneering works of dark film comedy: the Leo McCarey directed the Marx Brothers' film *Duck Soup* (1933), Charlie Chaplin's *The Great Dictator* (1940), and Ernst Lubitsch's *To Be or Not to Be* (1942). The trilogy warrants special status for three reasons. First, while each is now an acknowledged cinema classic, their vanguard status within the genre is still not fully recognized. For instance, *The Great Dictator* is swallowed up by the unique status of its writer, director, producer, and star—Charlie Chaplin. A second explanation of why the trilogy qualifies for additional attention is the shared subject matter—misguided leaders and the inevitability of the wars which follow them. The final reason this threesome merits more study is to examine how a much earlier era dealt with a still-controversial genre.

Chapter 4 addresses the coming-of-age movie, such as *Harold and Maude* (1972), and its ties to black comedy. While one would be foolish to deny the strong links between the cynicism of age and dark humor, there is also a propensity for youthful comic nihilism, especially since the late 1960s. Youth often have great impatience to change things and especially wish revenge against snobby in-crowd peers and/or unsympathetic parents. As critic André Bishop suggests, in America we are encouraged that "our dreams not only *can* come true, but *should* come true, and that if they don't someone or something is to blame."[4] This chapter examines a pivotal coming-of-age example of the genre for each of the three final decades of the century. This includes the aforementioned *Harold and Maude* (1971), *Heathers* (1989), and *Natural Born Killers* (1994).

Chapter 5 examines the close ties between the genres of dark comedy and film noir. But unlike Chapter 4's coming-of-age movie, which occasionally slides into black humor, the noir film is more predisposed to be overwhelmed by dark comedy. To better demonstrate this phenomenon, I first critique a movie on the black comedy bubble, *Chinatown*, especially because it is considered a modern noir classic. Despite that noir status, even here there is a strong argument for labeling it a dark comedy. Once this precedent is established, two more readily acknowledged black comedies (though not without noir overtones) are examined—*Pulp Fiction* (1994) and *The Player* (1993).

Chapter 6 is a brief summing up, both a reiteration of some pivotal points and a few closing reflections on a work that has been several years in the making. If someone requested a single antidote to be drawn from this study I would note George Orwell's comments on H .G. Wells's inability to believe people could be so irrational as to follow Hitler: "Wells is too sane to understand the modern world."[5]

NOTES

1. Todd McCarthy, *Pulp Fiction* review, *Variety*, May 23, 1994.

2. Henry David Thoreau, *Walden and Other Writings of Henry David Thoreau*, ed. Brooks Atkinson (1854, *Walden*; repr. New York: Modern Library, 1965), p. 7.

3. Robert Benchley, "How to Watch Football," in *Pluck and Luck* (New York: Henry Holt and Company, 1925), p. 137; Robert Benchley, "Drama: Inventory," *Life*, December 7, 1922, p. 46.

4. André Bishop, "Preface," in Stephen Sondheim and John Weidman's *Assassins* (New York: Theatre Communications Group, 1991), p. xi.

5. Paul Fussell, *Thank God for the Atom Bomb and Other Essays* (New York: Summit Books, 1988), p. 90.

ACKNOWLEDGMENTS

I wrote this book during an especially trying period of my personal life. Inadvertently, I became living proof of one key thrust of this study—dark humor can help one get through traumatic times. And though I would hardly wish this sort of test on anyone, it is comforting to know this genre can be a catharsis for pain. Due to this difficult time, my acknowledgments are all the more heartfelt.

Since the germination period for this book has covered many years, there is hardly space to thank everyone individually, but a few people stand out. My department chairperson, "Dr. Joe" Misiewicz, assisted with both securing release time for me and facilitating university financial help. Novelist R. Karl Largent took time from a busy schedule to write an amusingly thoughtful foreword. Janet Warrner, my local copyeditor, was forever available and helpful, with Jennifer Ellis doing the computer preparation of the manuscript. The comments of friends were often helpful, especially those of Joe Pacino and Conrad Lane.

Research for this text involved several important archives and their invariably helpful staffs, including the New York Public Library System, especially the Billy Rose Theatre Collection at Lincoln Center; the Museum of Modern Art (New York), especially the Film Stills Archive; the Library of Congress; the Margaret Herrick Library at the Academy of Motion Picture Arts and Sciences (Beverly Hills); and Ball State University's Bracken Library (Muncie, Indiana).

With the many mini-crises that constitute writing a book, my daughters Sarah and Emily provided both emotional support and technical reference assistance. Of the many dark comedy screenings they sat in on, *Pulp Fiction* (1994) proved to be their favorite. They were invaluable analysts.

HISTORICAL LITERARY OVERVIEW

If there's anyone out there who can look around this demented
slaughterhouse of a world we live in and tell me that man is a
noble creature, believe me, that man is full of bullshit.
> —Newscaster Howard Beale (Peter Finch) to
> his television audience in the Oscar-winning,
> Paddy Chayefsky script for *Network* (1976)

It's all about flights of fantasy. And the nightmare of reality.
Terrorist bombing. And late night shopping. True Love. And
creative plumbing.
> —Ad campaign for *Brazil* (1985)

At its most fundamental, black humor is a genre of comic irreverence that flippantly attacks what are normally society's most
sacredly serious subjects—especially death. In fact, death is both
the ultimate black comedy joke and its most pervasive. Comedy,
traditionally about optimistic new beginnings, frequently is symbolized by endings that celebrate a marriage and/or a birth. Thus,
deathly black humor is sometimes described as "beyond a joke,"
or anticomedy. And like the avant-garde films of old, such as Luis
Buñuel and Salvador Dali's *Andalusian Dog* (1928) which features
an eye being sliced, the humor is geared for shock effect,
juxtaposing comedy and terrifying chaos, from individualized

graphic violence to nuclear apocalypse. The student of comedy theory would do well to link shock to the humor hypothesis that credits surprise as the most pervasive explanation for laughter. Only here the laughter is of a nervous, "should I be responding in this manner?" nature. Fittingly, black humor also has been called "comedy of terrors."

The genre's ability to personalize in the viewer a jumble of conflicting emotions is meant to reflect the on-the-edge absurdity of modern life. The commonsense platitudes of any updated Yankee cracker-barrel philosopher are now inadequate. As critic Hamlin Hill observed at the height of the Cold War, the antihero is "incapable of inventing homespun maxims about hundred-megaton bombs, or of feeling any native self-confidence in the face of uncontrollable fallout."[1] And while the Soviet Union has since self-destructed, world problems have not. Consequently, it should come as no surprise that another critic, with tongue firmly in cheek, christened black humor "Yankee Existentialism."[2]

Dark comedy resignation is nicely captured in Kurt Vonnegut, Jr.'s repetition, in *Slaughterhouse-Five* (1969), of "And so it goes" for every sorry event which afflicts his antiheroic Billy Pilgrim. Along similar lines, Joseph Heller's "catch-22" expression, from the 1961 novel of the same name, has become synonymous with life's inherent absurdity. Going beyond satire, black humor's message is that there is no message, so audience members had best steal a laugh before they are too dead to do even that.

Black humor is the midnight world of the comic antihero who is the foundation for screwball film comedy. This is best demonstrated by Cary Grant's absent-minded professor in the definitive example of the genre, *Bringing Up Baby* (1938), later loosely remade as *What's Up Doc?* (1972).[3] But the absurdity of screwball comedy hardly registers on the chaos scale. It merely plays comically with its victims. Screwball comedy is a humor of frustration, not fatalities. In black comedy, however, absurdity has become predator. Thus, even the modest daydream victories of James Thurber's antiheroic Walter Mitty are taken away, unless one translates them into the often shocking time-tripping of Billy Pilgrim (becoming "unstuck in time") or the ultimate mind-game escape—black humor's "kind" offer of insanity. This is the surprise fate of Jonathan Price's character at the close of *Brazil* (1985). To borrow a metaphorical title from dark humorist Franz Kafka, life is an ongoing "trial" of nightmare proportions.

Even a mainstream humor journalist like Pulitzer-prize-winning Dave Barry now holds a theory of comedy with which Kafka would be comfortable. In a July 3, 1989, *Time* interview, Barry stated that humor is based in the "fear that the world is not very sane or reliable or organized and that it's not controlled by responsible people. Anything can happen to you, and you have no say in it, and it could be bad."

There is nothing inherently new about dark humor; it can be found in the work of Aristophanes (448–385 B.C.), or Jonathan Swift's (1667–1745) baby-eating premise for "A Modest Proposal." (Director Oliver Stone has compared the shock effect of his controversial 1994 macabre film comedy *Natural Born Killers* to Swift's essay.[4]) American literature boasts such pioneer dark humorists as Edgar Allan Poe (1809–1849), Herman Melville (1819–1891), Ambrose Bierce (1842–1914?), and the late work of Mark Twain (1835–1910).

Maybe the most provocative example from these authors is Melville's 1857 novel *The Confidence Man*, which boasts a desperate, Poe-like character in a minor role. Melville suggests that life is a costume party where all the disguised guests should be prepared to play the fool. To do any less (sans costume and a sense of humor) makes one a burden both to self and to the party. Moreover, to shun the masquerade (the title character undergoes several metamorphoses) suggests an eventual inability to survive. But to play the devil's advocate—and with whom better than the sometimes Lucifer-like Confidence Man—a more troubling interpretation of the costume-party metaphor might suggest that behind one's many masks lies no real identity. And what is survival if the individual is lost?

Melville scholar Hennig Cohen suggests the novel's ongoing problem is "how to live in a world in which nothing is what it appears to be, in which the only thing knowable is that nothing can be known, and the only thing believable is that nothing can be believed."[5] Cohen might just as well be defining the world of black comedy.

Dark humor was also pushed more to the center stage by the writing of Charles Darwin (1809–1882) and Sigmund Freud (1856–1939). Comparison of their importance, in the terms of the decen-

tralization of the individual in the grand scheme of things, could
be made to Copernicus's then-heretical discovery in the sixteenth
century that God's earth and creations merely orbited the sun, and
not vice versa.

Darwin's shocking claims for man's haphazard evolution from
lesser beasts rather derailed the comfortable noble claim of being
made in His image. Darwinism's long-term effects reduced mankind's sense of uniqueness to something less than heroic. His
writing on evolution still qualifies as probably the most radical
change in image mankind has ever had to address. Serious doubt
was cast, for the first time, on the literal truth of Christianity. As
with later theories of Freud, Darwin's work might fundamentally
be labeled naturalism, in that it leads one away from the super-
natural. Coupled with the oppression of the nineteenth-century
Industrial Age, belief in a God-centered rationalism was rapidly
failing. Here was fertile ground indeed for dark comedy.

While Darwin shook claims to some heavenly heritage, Freud's
pioneering work in psychoanalysis effectively called into question
the possibility of even being in control of one's own mind. Freud's
influence on twentieth-century literature was immense. He was
the first guide to the dark powers of the unconscious—a cinema of
the brain forever serving up unexpected shocks.

Add to this Freud's emphasis on the then-taboo subject of
sexuality and one has a solid foundation for black comedy.

Fittingly, Freud was fascinated by dark humor, ranking it at the
top of all comedy types. He was especially taken with the tale of
the fellow heading to the gallows who asked for a neckerchief to
guard against taking a cold.[6] Freud felt such humorous moxie
represented a "greatness of soul." For him it was a way to use
comedy as a defense mechanism against the inevitable—death.

Freud believed man was largely motivated by the dark side,
which is the basic premise of black humor. His work does much
to metaphorically decipher what might be called the first twentieth-century novel—Joseph Conrad's pioneering dark comedy *Heart
of Darkness* (1902), that was later the foundation for film director
Francis Ford Coppola's controversial *Apocalypse Now* (1979). Both
Freud and Conrad were groundbreakers in stressing man's irrational elements. The latter's novel traces the narrator's (Marlow's)
trip up the Congo River in search of the mysterious Kurtz—once
the most idealistic of men. What has turned him into a sadistic

killer? The further Marlow advances into the jungle, the clearer it becomes that Kurtz has shed his veneer of civilization. Marlow feels the same temptation of his dark side. Thus, *Heart of Darkness* is a story about survival in both a physical wilderness and the moral wilderness of one's mind. This naturally also involved the implications of Darwin's work, from his "survival of the fittest" premise to man's implied loss of moral confidence with the negation of a religious base.

In addition, Freud's exploration of the mind also led to surrealism. This early twentieth-century artistic movement attempted to express the workings of the subconscious by fantastic imagery and incongruous juxtapositioning of subject matter. Surrealism is often linked to dark humor. For example, Buñuel and Dali's aforementioned shock effect, *Andalusian Dog*, is considered to be the first surrealistic film. However, the main difference between black comedy and surrealism is one of frightening vulnerability. As defined by humor historian Max F. Schultz, surrealism keys on "internal disorder" of the subconscious mind, while dark humor generally suggests that disorder is now the external, *real* state of things.[7] Certainly, a pivotal element in black humor moving to center stage in the chaotic 1960s was based on the fact that surrealism was more and more becoming the day-to-day norm.

The Vietnam War was a major catalyst for the post-1960s dark humor phenomenon. But World War I (1914–1918) was the initial armed conflict that gave dark humor fertile ground for growth. With this war "writers began to encounter the almost insurmountable difficulties of giving literary . . . expression to such a cataclysmic conflict. Courage, honor, dignity, and other traditional values became meaningless."[8] There were two reasons for this war's terrible uniqueness—it was the first conflict where twentieth-century technology came in conflict with nineteenth-century tactics. Foot soldiers were asked to rush machine gun nests, cope with poison gas, and ward off such new inventions as the airplane, the flame-thrower, and the tank. "Suicidal offenses nurtured a . . . resignation to death. A military historian has likened this apathy to the passivity of inmates facing extermination in Nazi death camps."[9] It was, in part, this upper-echelon failure to recognize the new technology of atrocity that would result in over four million military casualties alone. (See historian Alan Clark's 1961 case against the British High Command of World War I detailed in *The Donkeys.*[10])

When soldiers responded realistically to insane directives by falling back, there was still a possible death threat from the nineteenth-century mindset of their commanders. Novelist Humphrey Cobb's *Paths of Glory* (1935) focuses on one such case of "mutiny" that actually occurred. When a French division made no headway in an ill-advised attack late in the war, the commanding generals concocted a scenario of patented absurdity. A man randomly chosen from each company would be run through a rubber stamp court martial for cowardice and executed: "Discipline is the first requisite of an army . . . one of the ways of doing it is to shoot a man now and then. He dies, therefore, for the ultimate benefit of his comrades and of the country."[11] Artists have little need to invent black comedy situations when thinking like this exists.

The second reason for World War I's terrible uniqueness was more frightening than mere tactical incompetence. It also helps explain why those in command seemed to perpetuate the same high casualty war plans year after year. Many European intellectuals of the time, particularly those in Italy, Germany, and France, believed that civilization could progress only if periodically purged of the lower-class rabble. "War and slaughter would conveniently get rid of this worthless mass."[12]

This philosophy was largely an outgrowth of "Futurism," a literary and artistic movement that flourished in the 1910s and 1920s. Its pivotal architect was Italian poet F. T. Marinetti, who glorified war as the only health giver of the world. The flamboyant poet lectured frequently and caused a sensation in England just prior to World War I when he coupled his readings with a militaristic cadence, such as imitating the sound of a machine gun, or having a drum beat offstage to accent his words. Fittingly, the feelings of a general in *Paths of Glory* are described by the narrator, "Where there were no casualties, there was no fighting. . . . The smell of the dead reassured him on this point."[13] Such thinking anticipates *the* dark comedy scene in *Apocalypse Now*, where Robert Duvall's commander orders a helicopter attack as coverage for a surfing show. His character ultimately observes, "I love the smell of napalm [death] in the morning."

Between archaic battle tactics and a belief that the blood of the lower classes would oil the progressive machinery of civilization's future, it is no wonder that the great literary works of World War I are peppered with dark comedy. For example, Englishman Robert Graves' memoir *Good-bye to All That* (1929) quotes two soldiers apologizing to their commander about accidentally shooting their company's sergeant-major. When he asks if they thought he was a spy, they baldly reply, "No, sir, we mistook him for our platoon sergeant."[14] This is the stuff of such black comedy classic novels as Heller's *Catch-22*, or Jaroslav Hasek's *The Good Soldier Schweik* (1930) with a title character who survives World War I by being the most successful of wise fools.

In Hemingway's novel *A Farewell to Arms* (1929) his central character is an American ambulance driver for the Italians, then battling the Austrians. Since there were a large number of casualties, his friends kid about dining on dead Austrians, with the topper comment being the old World War I joking refrain, "The white meat is from officers."[15] Earlier in the book, Hemingway's American is decorated for a wound he received while "eating cheese."[16] One is reminded of the *Catch-22* scene where antihero Yossarian and the entire bombing squadron are decorated for killing fish.

German author Erich Remarque's *All Quiet on the Western Front* (1928) is often considered both the greatest book on the conflict and *the* anti-war novel of all time. Appropriately, it contains more dark comedy references than any of the celebrated World War I literature thus far mentioned. For instance, one soldier says to a friend "they will have a job with Hans Kramer's body at the Judgment Day, piecing it together after a direct hit."[17] Consistent with this plethora of black humor, Remarque's main figure offers up a timeless survivor perspective on the genre: "The terror of the front sinks deep . . . we make grim, coarse jests about it; that keeps us from going mad . . . If it were not so we could not hold out . . . our humor becomes more bitter every month."[18]

Even for those whose survival was assisted, in part, through dark humor, such as Remarque, Hemingway, Graves, and Cobb, theirs was to be called a "lost generation." But Remarque's terse opening notes on *All Quiet on the Western Front* are more frightening: "It will try simply to tell of a generation of men who, even though they may have escaped its shells, were destroyed by the war."

A further irony for the returning veterans was that even after the war, some writers continued to romanticize the conflict. For instance, Willa Cather did just that with her Pulitzer Prize winning novel *One of Ours* (1922). This false perspective might have contributed to the fact that World War I is often considered the catalyst of the anti-war novel.

Appropriately, director Richard Rush's highly acclaimed black comedy *The Stunt Man* (1980) takes as its subject a filmmaker (Peter O'Toole) shooting *the* anti-war movie and using World War I as its focus. O'Toole's director observes, "Why did we pick World War I in the first place, [because it is] the ultimate romantic insanity." That is, lingering nineteenth-century misconceptions about the glories of battle butt heads with the twentieth-century horrors of modern warfare. And argumentatively, the best British and French dark comedy about the absurdity of war also takes World War I as its subject—*King of Hearts* (joint production, 1966).

Historian John Keegan has drawn a provocative analogy between those soldiers who did not survive World War I and the Holocaust victims of World War II—another pivotal tragedy which has had a major impact on the study of black humor. Keegan suggests that the British trenches of the July 1916 first day Somme Offensive (which futilely left twenty thousand dead on both sides) "were the concentration camps of the First World War . . . young men . . . plodding forward across a featureless landscape to their own exterminations inside the barbed wire."[19]

The student of Holocaust literature has long been aware of dark humor as a Jewish psychological defense against Hitler's "final solution." Radically different approaches to this modern horror story still come back to laughter. The young teenager diarist Anne Frank wrote, "There's *one* golden rule to keep before you: laugh about everything and don't bother yourself about the others!"[20] After the war, concentration camp prisoner Dr. Viktor E. Frankl wrote a classic psychiatric text on survival which also counsels laughter: "Humor, more than anything else in the human make-up, can afford . . . an ability to rise above any situation. . . . "[21] On the sly, Frankl would train fellow prisoners to better utilize their sense of humor. But on a more macabre note, he also mentions instances, such as entering a shower room that might be a gas chamber, where black comedy was an automatic reflex: "most of us were overcome by a grim sense of humor. We know that we had nothing to lose except our so ridiculously naked lives . . . we all tried very hard to make fun."[22] Even before the actual liquidation potential, victims were referring to dark humor as "Jewish novocain."

With some Holocaust literature one need not move beyond the title for the dark humor message. The immediate post-war Auschwitz stories of Tadeusz Borowski are entitled *This Way for the Gas, Ladies and Gentlemen* (1959).[23] And the name of Steve Lipman's 1993 study is even more direct: *LAUGHTER IN HELL: The Use of Humor During the Holocaust.*[24] Probably the greatest irony of black—sick—humor is that it is *the healthiest survivor outlook to take*.

Lipman's book also addresses dark comedy as a resistance technique, a way to undermine the morale of an oppressor. In this way, it is reminiscent of a 1942 pioneering academic study on the genre, Antonio J. Obrdlik's "'Gallows Humor'—A Sociological Phenomenon." The following is a classic Obrdlik example of a black comedy resistance act which Lipman later recycles: "In a village the Gestapo men found a hanged hen with the following inscription fastened to her neck: 'I'd rather commit suicide than lay eggs for Hitler.'"[25] Jokes such as these, which author "George Orwell called 'tiny revolutions,' were considered a direct attack on the [Nazi] government, and violators were subject to harassment, arrest, imprisonment, or death."[26]

Unfortunately, such "tiny revolutions" gradually disappeared as Hitler's liquidation plans for the Jews accelerated. Jewish dark humor often turned to a self-deprecating slant: "Dear God, for five thousand years we have been your chosen people. Enough! Choose another one now!"[27]

The twisted black-comedy tendencies of the Nazis are often forgotten in the Holocaust equation. For instance, the deadly gas at Dachau was transported in Red Cross vans and the killing chambers were called Bathhouses. The words "Arbeit Macht Frei" (work gives freedom) were placed over the entrance to Auschwitz. This chilling statement possibly inspired the Big Brother Party slogans of Orwell's *1984* (1949):

WAR IS PEACE
FREEDOM IS SLAVERY
IGNORANCE IS STRENGTH[28]

Regardless of the situation, such semantic manipulation makes truth and reality completely relative. In fact, director Terry Gilliam's *1984*-inspired dark humor film *Brazil* (1985) puts this even more graphically when it simply includes the "obscene" wall graffiti "REALITY".

Before most of the Nazi crimes against humanity took place, the specter of Hitler was still used as the subject of a pioneering black comedy film—the Charlie Chaplin movie *The Great Dictator* (1940). This was most fitting, since his *Shoulder Arms* (1917) had been the only film during the 1910s to comically explore the darker side of World War I. When Chaplin was attacked in print for making the *Dictator*, his response sounds remarkably modern, "There is a healthy thing in laughing at the grimmest things in life, laughter at death even."[29]

There was a macabre further twist in the appropriateness of Chaplin's comically bludgeoning Hitler. This most terrible of men wore a toothbrush mustache that made him somewhat resemble the world's greatest clown. Such a black comedy juxtapositioning was not lost on persecuted Jews of the 1930s. Fifth-columnist jokes such as the following quietly circulated among them: "Charlie Chaplin is indignant. 'I don't complain that Hitler has my small mustache; it's all the same to me that [German Propaganda Minister] Goebbels [who moved with a limp] imitates my walk; but it makes me very angry that [the obese Field Marshall] Goering gets more laughs then I do.' "[30]

World War II would also inspire darkly comic literature, such as Heller's acclaimed *Catch-22* (see illustration 2) and Vonnegut's *Slaughterhouse-Five*. But these novels appeared late enough that their impact on the genre is best equated with the center-stage emergence of black humor in the 1960s. Indeed, although set in World War II, their comic anti-war statements were generally interpreted as pertaining more directly to the controversial war then being fought in Vietnam. Literary critic Alfred Kazin went one step further, suggesting that "they are really about the Next War [a nuclear holocaust], and thus about a war that will be without limits and without meaning, a war that will end only when no one is alive to fight it."[31] (Both novels will be addressed later in the text.)

The greatest and most frightening legacies of World War II, as they pertained to dark comedy, would be the Holocaust and the atomic bomb. The former gruesomely showcased just how evil man could act. The latter (which some have interpreted along similar lines, despite contributing wartime pressures for a hasty end to the conflict) revealed that mankind had the power to generate its own

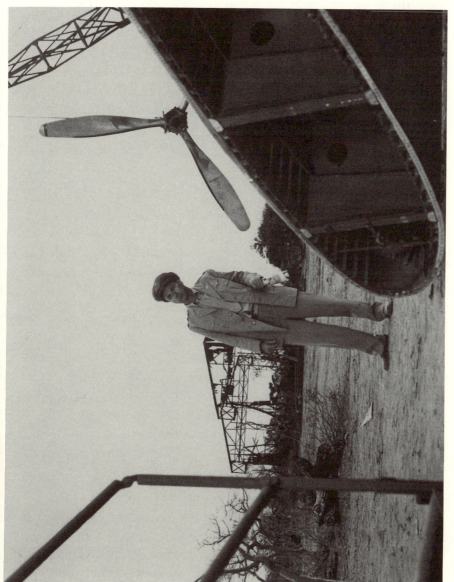

2. Alan Arkin in *Catch-22*.

earth-ending apocalypse. With the atomic bomb came the added horror that man's ethics had seldom kept pace with his intelligence. Would he now be any more successful as the keeper of *the bomb*? Plus, there was an "increasing gap . . . between our technological capacity for perpetrating atrocities and our imaginative ability to confront their full actuality."[32]

Black humor was also influenced by the post–World War II philosophy of Existentialism. As with any school of thought, this approach has splinter groups. The branch best linked to dark comedy is attributed to Jean-Paul Sarte and Martin Heidegger, who posit that man is alone in a godless irrational world. Moreover, one cannot depend upon other human beings, and anguish is a universal phenomenon.

Before reaching the all-important 1960s black comedy explosion there are also numerous roots in the mislabeled "Happy Days" of the 1950s, from the cartoons of Jules Feiffer to Lenny Bruce's shock approach to stand-up comedy. Feiffer's gift to the age of the bomb and the "box" (TV) was a series of cartoons called *Sick, Sick, Sick*. It addressed everything from a public becoming blasé over an atomic holocaust, to countless variations on conformity. Dark humor critic/historian Tony Hendra addressed the deeper irony to be found in Feiffer's title for the cartoons: "You say we are sick, and we are, but the reasons lie outside us as much as in ourselves . . . those whom orthodoxy labels sick . . . [and] who behave rebelliously . . . are healthier than those who condemn them."[33]

Lenny Bruce's initial foray into comedy abandonment was far from the cerebral quality of Feiffer. Bruce, working as an early 1950s strip-club emcee in sleazy Los Angeles night spots, was competing for attention with naked women and an audience not interested in interruptions. Through blue language (and ultimately stripping once himself—the last thing his male spectators wanted to see) he received little attention. But he did not become the Bruce we celebrate today until his act evolved into "stripping" away at moral issues, from the specifics of words and racism, to what he saw as the hypocrisy of the American dream. His work remained controversial, because like a darkly comic Socrates he continued to poke at sacred apple-pie topics like religion and the judicial system. But unlike another pivotal period comic, Mort Sahl, Bruce lobbed his metaphorical bombs with profanity, trying to shock audiences into recognizing unpopular reality. Moreover, he was so good at portraying the "animals" he abhorred that some people mistook him for the enemy. For example, influential period commentator Walter Winchell dubbed him "'America's Number One Vomic,' confusing Bruce's brilliant depiction of Northern bigotry with endorsement of it."[34] Bruce wanted people to learn the truth, not what should be the truth. Consequently, his work goes beyond Sahl's satire. Like a true dark humorist, his material was based in what he often called "destruction and despair."[35]

Despite this survey of generally non-cinematic dark comedy roots, the genre is still considered more of a post–1960s phenomenon. Indeed, the general acceptance of the term black humor/comedy (as opposed to references such as "gallows humor" or "sick humor") came into acceptance during that decade, where the phrase was frequently applied to the fiction of several authors then gaining critical recognition. Black humor theorist/historian Mathew Winston has noted two especially significant 1965 publications: a *Time* magazine article entitled "The Black Humorists," chronicling the emergence of novelists like Joseph Heller, John Barth, Terry Southern, and Bruce Jay Friedman; and a Friedman-edited anthology of such works called *Black Humor*.[36] Winston might also have included black-comedy author Conrad Knickerbocker's pioneering 1960s essay on the genre, "Humor with a Mortal Sting" (1964).[37] While it does not have "black" in the title, it begins immediately with a broad comparison of white (traditional) and black humor. Regardless, "black humor became an aspect of the libertarian, idol-shattering side of the sixties."[38] Dark comedy is about confronting taboos. Once-controversial language and themes were now increasingly surfacing in mainstream sixties art forms such as film and fiction.

Despite the genre's ties to foreign isms and authors, America seems to have had a corner on the market. As Japanese humor scholar Kōji Numasawa observed in his essay "Black Humor: An American Aspect," "American writers on the whole appear to be more articulate about it, and American audiences more susceptible to the form."[39] Central to this American–black-humor connection was the social unrest of the 1960s, when the idealistic Great Society itself was failing—fragmented over issues like Vietnam and civil rights. The shocking violence so common to black humor was also a regular staple of the decade, from political assassinations (especially Jack Ruby's live television assassination of an alleged assassin), to the medium's evening-news "body counts" from Vietnam, which eventually numbed themselves into being just another optionally-noted box score. One social critic found the body count "the perfect symbol of America's descent into evil. What better represents the . . . grotesque competition . . . characteristic of the overall American crime of the war in Vietnam?"[40]

Black humor theorist/historian Douglas M. Davis has suggested this American affinity for the genre is an outgrowth, ironically, of the nation's unique ties with what might best be called the hopeful populism of anything-is-possible—but "These beliefs do not stay the course. [The early promise for the 1960s goes unfulfilled.] They are rigid and break when they fall. Therein lies an invitation for black comedy."[41] Added inspiration for depictions of dark comedy absurdity was to be found in the American governments's "unshakable insistence that black was white, that [Vietnam] escalation was really the search for peace, and that the war was being won."[42] Again, it was a posture of semantic word games of which George Orwell might have been proud.

NOTES

1. Hamlin Hill, "Modern American Humor: the Janus Laugh," *College English*, December 1963, p. 174.

2. Douglas M. Davis, *The World of Black Humor: An Introductory Anthology of Selections and Criticism* (New York: E. P. Dutton 1967), p. 14.

3. See my *Screwball Comedy: A Genre of Madcap Romance* (Westport, Conn.: Greenwood Press, 1986).

4. Jerry Carroll, "Oliver Stone on His 'Natural Born' Overkill," *San Francisco Chronicle*, syndicated in the *Muncie Star*, August 28, 1994, p. 10–B.

5. Hennig Cohen, "Introduction to Herman Melville," *The Confidence Man* (1857; repr. New York: Holt, Rinehart and Winston, 1964).

6. James A. Thorson, "A Funny Thing Happened on the Way to the Morgue: Some Thoughts on Humor and Death, and a Taxonomy of the Humor Associated with Death," *Death Studies*, 9 (3–4), 1985, p. 204.

7. Max F. Schultz, *Black Humor Fiction of the Sixties* (Athens: Ohio University Press, 1973), p. 71.

8. Leslie M. Thompson and William R. Cozart, "The Technology of Atrocity," *Forum* (Ball State University), Autumn 1984, p. 64.

9. Alfredo Bonadeo, *Mark of the Beast: Death and Degradation in the Literature of the Great War* (Lexington: University of Kentucky Press, 1989), p. 101.

10. Alan Clark, *The Donkeys* (1961; repr. New York: Award Books, 1965).

11. Humphrey Cobb, *Paths of Glory* (New York: Viking Press, 1935), p. 174.

12. Bonadeo, p. 70.

13. Cobb, p. 80.

14. Robert Graves, *Good-bye to All That* (1929; repr. with revisions. Garden City, N.Y.: Doubleday Anchor Books, 1957), p. 109.

15. Ernest Hemingway, *A Farewell to Arms* (1929; repr. New York: Scribner's 1957), p. 174.

16. Ibid., p. 63.

17. Erich Remarque, *All Quiet on the Western Front* (1928; repr. Greenwich, Conn.: Crest Books, 1964), p. 86.

18. Ibid., p. 87.

19. As quoted in Bonadeo, p. 101.

20. Anne Frank, *Anne Frank: The Diary of a Young Girl* (1947; repr. New York: Pocket Books, 1958), p. 227.

21. Viktor E. Frankl, *Man's Search for Meaning* (1946; repr. Boston: Beacon Press, 1992), p. 54.

22. Ibid., p. 29.

23. Tadeusz Borowski, *This Way for the Gas, Ladies and Gentlemen* (1959; repr. New York: Penguin Books, 1986).

24. Steve Lipman, *LAUGHTER IN HELL: The Use of Humor During the Holocaust* (1991; repr. Northvale, N.J.: Jason Aronson, 1993).

25. Antonin J. Obrdlik, "'Gallows Humor'—A Sociological Phenomenon," *American Journal of Sociology*, March 1942, p. 715.

26. Lipman, p. 25.

27. Ibid., p. 140.

28. George Orwell, *1984* (1949; repr. New York: New American Library, 1961). The slogans occur frequently—for instance, pp. 7, 17, 87.

29. "Mr. Chaplin Answers His Critics," *New York Times*, October 27, 1940, Section 9, p. 5.

30. Lipman, p. 96.

31. Alfred Kazin, "The War Novel: From Mailer to Vonnegut," in *Viewpoint*, ed. Burton J. Fisherman (New York: St. Martin's Press, 1972), p. 110.

32. Robert Jay Lifton, "Beyond Atrocity," in *Viewpoint*, p. 55.

33. Tony Hendra, *Going Too Far* (New York: Doubleday, 1987), p. 92.

34. Ibid., p. 122.

35. See the John Cohen–edited *The Essential Lenny Bruce* (New York: Ballantine Books, 1967) for an excellent overview of the comedian's work and philosophy.

36. Mathew Winston, "Humor Noir and Black Humor," in *Veins of Humor*, ed. Harry Levin (Cambridge, Mass.: Harvard University Press, 1972), p. 273; "The Black Humorists," *Time*, February 12, 1965, pp. 94–96; Bruce Jay Friedman, ed., *Black Humor* (New York: Bantam Books, 1965).

37. Conrad Knickerbocker, "Humor with a Mortal Sting," *New York Times Book Review*, September 27, 1964, pp. 3, 60–61.

38. Morris Dickstein, "Black Humor and History: The Early Sixties," Chapter 4 in *Gates of Eden: American Culture in the Sixties* (New York: Basic Books, 1977), p. 117.

39. Kōji Numasawa, "Black Humor: An American Aspect," *Studies in English Literature* (University of Tokyo), March 1968, p. 177.

40. Lifton, p. 60.

41. Davis, p. 20.

42. Dickstein, p. 117.

2

SELECTED AMERICAN DARK COMEDY FILMS AND THEMES

This is developing into a very bad habit.
>—Mortimer Brewster (Cary Grant) describing his
aunts' policy of knocking off lonely, unattached
elderly men in *Arsenic and Old Lace* (1944)

Numbers sanctify.
>—Title character Charlie Chaplin suggesting to the court in
Monsieur Verdoux (1947) that murder is only acceptable
to society if done in a big way, such as a war

PIONEERING WORKS

Chapter 1 examined the pivotal 1965 *Time* magazine article "The Black Humorists." When the article moved from print medium to film, it fittingly began with *Dr. Strangelove: Or How I Learned to Stop Worrying and Love the Bomb* (1964). This film was described as "treating the hydrogen bomb as a colossal banana peel on which the world slips to annihilation."[1] The British production was produced and directed by American expatriate Stanley Kubrick and was co-scripted by acknowledged black comedy novelist Terry Southern. *Dr. Strangelove* remains an important dark humor archetype, though the genre's mainstream emergence in American cinema started at the end of the 1960s.

Of course, earlier black humor film precedents exist. One could go back through American cinema history and find numerous movies with dark comic undercurrents, beginning with the pioneering works of Mack Sennett. But that is usually what they are, simply undercurrents. There were some legitimate pre-1960s black comedy antecedents, such as the comic attacks on Hitler and Nazism by Charlie Chaplin and Ernst Lubitsch, respectively, in *The Great Dictator* (1940) and *To Be or Not To Be* (1942). (See Chapter 2.) But for every one of these, there are countless other movies which, while showcasing the characteristic occasionally, are best categorized in other more traditional genres. For example, Chaplin's *The Gold Rush* (1925) (see illustration 3) features scenes of cannibalism comedy that were inspired by the tragic Donner Party's very real cannibalism. And the darkly comic wall-screen intrusions of the factory boss in Chaplin's *Modern Times* (1936) inspired the Big Brother screens of George Orwell's *1984*. Although early films feature a dark humor side, they are best defined as personality comedies. Other Chaplin contemporaries (whose clown personae sometimes embraced black comedy) include cynics Buster Keaton, W. C. Fields, Laurel and Hardy, and the Marx Brothers. (The unique status of Groucho and company's 1933 *Duck Soup* will be addressed in Chapter 3.)

Since Keaton was the first of the aforementioned comedians to achieve film success, his work will be used briefly to exemplify a dark humor "undercurrent." Keaton provides tombstone closes to both *Cops* (1922) and *College* (1927), films which otherwise showcase Keaton successes, such as eluding an army of policemen and winning his university girlfriend's hand. In contrast, the ending of *Frozen North* (1922—he awakens from a dream) defuses an otherwise dark comedy spoof of western star William S. Hart, with Keaton casually shooting an innocent couple. But such comic violence is unusual for the comedian. More typical is the stoic pessimism he brings to a scene in *Daydreams* (1922). In this metaphor for the treadmill nature of life, Keaton is caught in whirling boat paddlewheel and climbs ever faster to avoid becoming a victim. The scene embraces a basic tenet of black humor; at best, life is a holding pattern. Still, Keaton's ongoing persistence in this Sisyphus world, despite frequent frustration, also embraces an unconquerable spirit which is a moral victory all its own . . . possibly the only one available in the modern world. Moreover, his

3. Charlie Chaplin in *The Gold Rush*.

ability to accomplish the seemingly impossible often puts him one leg up on most black comedy heroes. One example is his adaptation of an ocean liner's galley equipment—designed for large numbers—scaled down for two in *The Navigator* (1924).

Pre-1960s examples of a black humor "undercurrent" could also surface in the movies strongly linked to other genres. This is often true of films directed by Howard Hawks, such as his classic gangster picture *Scarface* (1932). Dark humor shrouds those scenes highlighting the life and death of title character Paul Muni's private secretary Angelo (Vince Barnett)—the intense little man who does not know how to write, yet always takes calls during major gun battles.

Hawks's *His Girl Friday* (1940) quite literally incorporates "gallows humor," as the story revolves around an impending execution by hanging. But its interaction of character, especially with the constantly befuddled Ralph Bellamy, more logically places the film in the screwball genre (see my book *Screwball Comedy: A Genre of Madcap Romance*, 1986). Other precursor directors whose works frequently contain black comedy elements include Billy Wilder and Alfred Hitchcock. The culmination of this tendency for Wilder would be his use of two musicians witnessing a mass gangster execution, the St. Valentine Massacre, as the basis for his inspired comedy *Some Like It Hot* (1959). Elements of black comedy are even more pervasive in Hitchcock, especially starting with the film that established him in the American film market, *The 39 Steps* (Great Britain, 1935). This thriller might have been subtitled "Screwball Comedy Meets Murder Mystery." Fittingly, one prominent review of Lubitsch's *To Be or Not To Be* made reference to the picture having a touch of Hitchcock.[2]

Bona fide dark humor films, or even ones supporting an undercurrent of these tendencies, have invariably been controversial. This was especially true of American movies during the 1940s and 1950s. One has only to read the 1944 reviews of *Arsenic and Old Lace* (see illustration 4). I make this selection for three reasons. First, the film was a major critical and commercial success. Second, the story is innocuous. Third, because it was adapted from an equally successful stage version, one can briefly discuss the black comedy genre in relation to another medium.

The story finds two sweet little old ladies from Brooklyn welcoming lonely unattached elderly men into their boardinghouse

4. Cary Grant and Priscilla Lane flanked by crazy aunts Josephine Hull and Jean Adair in *Arsenic and Old Lace.*

only to slip them some elderberry wine . . . with a touch of arsenic. The philosophy of these delightfully demented women is that the men will be happier when the troubles of this world are over. A nephew living with the women thinks he is Teddy Roosevelt. Consequently, he buries the gentlemen in the cellar—thinking them victims of yellow fever during the digging of the Panama Canal.

The movie's solid reviews still had many critics feeling awkward about the subject matter. For instance, the *New York Sun*'s Eileen Creelman observed, "The movie is fast , funny, but unlike the play, somewhat gruesome. . . . There are moments when the sight of a insane family rushing corpses around the drawing room called for shudders rather than laughs."[3] Creelman went on to hypothesize that the film was darker "because the camera makes any scene more intimate."[4]

She might have been speaking for the film's director, Frank Capra, because this was precisely his reason for eliminating two different endings for *Arsenic*. As in the play, Capra shot the closing scene where the Happy Dale Sanitarium director (Edward Everett Horton) has come for "Teddy Roosevelt," only to fall victim to the elderberry wine. But at the first preview the audience was demonstratively upset with losing beloved character actor Horton's Mr. Witherspoon. Consequently, Capra gave the figure a reprieve: "On the stage there was distance between the audience and the players, but a closer film medium has a way of making everything seem realistic. I'm sure the movie audience was right about Horton."[5]

Even before the preview Capra had eliminated the play's comically macabre curtain call on similar grounds. While the curtain call is a device normally associated with the theater, it is not unheard-of in film, especially if there is a comic twist. A period example would be Orson Welles's movie adaption of *The Magnificent Ambersons* (1942), where Welles individually introduces the cast at the close of the film. But since he did not appear, when it is his turn for a bow, all the camera presents is a mike . . . with no one in sight.

Interestingly enough, the curtain call Capra had planned to carry over from the stage production was just the opposite of Welles's surprise. One had expected to see Orson and did not. At the theater close of *Arsenic* the play's many formerly unseen corpses (the sisters had been busy for some time) solemnly rose from their cellar resting places to take an unexpected mass bow with the principal performers. (This dark-comic shocker of a close was referred to as a "howler" by period theater critics.) Capra had proceeded to restage the curtain call. But the director dropped the sequence even before the preview, and for precisely the same reason as previously noted—film made such dark humor too intimate . . . at least by 1940s standards.[6]

This added cinematic realism/intimacy would be even more shockingly effective for the genre in American film's post–censorship-code 1970s; witness the graphic reproduction of surgery near a war front in *M.A.S.H.* (1970). Moreover, this camera intimacy further heightens the quick emotional swings of dark comedy. For instance, "Capra said *Arsenic* was a demonstration of the fact that comedy is closely allied to tragedy and that it doesn't take much of a push to send the dramatic see-saw from tears to giggles and back again."[7]

This is a provocative Capra quote for three reasons. First, the tragedy—comedy dichotomy he evokes would seem more applicable to his melodramatic populist films, such as the ups and downs of George Bailey in *It's a Wonderful Life*. To have Capra apply it here is to broaden one's perspective of him as a humanist. Second, though one would seldom equate *Arsenic* with tears—unless they were tears of laughter—there is the potentially tragic slant of aging and euthanasia. Third, for such a gifted and celebrated mainstream American director—architect of so many feel-good, middle-class movies—to embrace this dark comedy subject is to suggest the future increasing visibility of the genre.

One such pivotal 1940s example is Charlie Chaplin's *Monsieur Verdoux* (1947) (see illustration 5). The comedian's title character, the first complete break with his Charlie-the-tramp persona, makes a business of marrying and then murdering little old ladies. The film was inspired by the "career" of Frenchman Henri Landru, better known as the "modern Bluebeard," who was guillotined in 1922 for liquidating ten of his girlfriends. Orson Welles had originally approached Chaplin about the role of Landru in a series of simulated documentaries the young director was contemplating. But Chaplin's often-macabre sense of humor was more drawn to the comic potential of the material. Cannibalism of the snowbound Donner Party had inspired some of the most poignantly

5. Charlie Chaplin in *Monsieur Verdoux*.

funny scenes in *The Gold Rush* as had Hitler's Nazism in *The Great Dictator*.

If one is to use *Dr. Strangelove* as a signpost of the 1960s arrival of black humor, *Monsieur Verdoux* merits similar archetypal status as a genre starting-point of sorts. There had been earlier dark comedy films, but none so directly addressed the murderous ethics, or lack thereof, for the genre. Celebrated period critic James Agee's *Time* review credited Chaplin with having "borne down on moral complexity, terror and irony with an intensity never before attempted in films."[8] Certainly, there were no such intellectual mind games going on while watching the daffy, dear sisters of *Arsenic and Old Lace*. And while Chaplin had done *The Great Dictator* (see Chapter 3), black humor undercutting dictatorship was much more palatable to 1940s viewers than was *Monsieur Verdoux's* warning about the murderous inclinations of big business: Chaplin's character paraphrases the famous observation by Prussian general and military theorist Karl Von Clausewitz (1780–1831) that "War is the logical extension of diplomacy," stating, "The logical extension of business is murder."[9]

Beyond the provocative nature of the subject matter, here was cinema's most memorable comedy artist—then and now—abandoning film's all-time most beloved character for an engaging yet undeniable murderer. This was a great artist pushing the envelope, refusing to play it safe.

Monsieur Verdoux also received high visibility because of the public nature of Chaplin's private life. For example, despite the tongue-in-check richness of the often woman-plagued comedian becoming a "Lady Killer" (the working title of the script), much of the film was written during actress Joan Barry's messy paternity suit against him. And *Monsieur Verdoux* was hurt financially by the ongoing controversies associated with his left-wing political sympathies. In America's growing post–World War II paranoia over the threat of Communism (which would culminate in the McCarthy witch-hunting 1950s), Chaplin's liberalism was a decided liability. Consequently, in some areas the film was banned and/or picketed by organizations such as the American Legion.

Regrettably, other than for a few critics—especially James Agee's *Nation* essays and Robert Warshow's *Partisan Review* writing—the film was not immediately appreciated for the watershed work it was.[10] When re-released in 1964 it was universally acclaimed as a classic dark comedy, with critic Judith Crist calling it "the prototype of the lovable-murderer comedy."[11]

Crist's compassion for Verdoux—"the murderer [who] has won our hearts"—hits upon the key departure from the later *Dr. Strangelove* model of black humor.[12] While *Monsieur Verdoux* also focuses upon an absurd, predatory world, the movie's dark comedy comes from a sympathetic individual who is given some justification for his deeds. Chaplin explained Verdoux's motivation by saying "He is protecting his home [and family], he thinks, just as a soldier using a flame-thrower in a war believes he is protecting his home."[13]

Chaplin's character is merely paying back a harsh world in kind. Moreover, though the viewer only "meets" a single victim, her less-than-pleasant nature is presented as the norm, especially when coupled with another victim's comically dysfunctional family, who assist in the eventual capture of Verdoux. That one should not be concerned about the demise of these women is further underlined by the case of Martha Raye's character, the only wife Verdoux fails to liquidate. Her nouveau-riche loudmouth literally has the viewer rooting for her demise, though circumstances always intervene. Even period critics otherwise bothered by the film's dark story enjoyed the stand-off with Raye's Annabelle. For instance, the *Christian Science Monitor*'s John Beaufort repeatedly bemoaned the loss of the tramp figure, but he did welcome the funny but futile efforts to murder an indestructible lady (indestructibly played by Martha Raye)."[14]

The comedy secret of their inspired confrontations is the clash between the cultured manner of the French Verdoux and the coarseness of the American Annabelle. This humor is further heightened by Verdoux's finding her easily the most unbearable of all his "business" wives, yet still having to play the loving husband.

This Verdoux model—black comedy emanating from a sympathetic character—was the pre-1960s norm, and it has continued to appear. The film was immediately appreciated in Europe, influencing the 1949 British black humor classic *Kind Hearts and Coronets*. The latter movie follows the same patern, with Dennis Price superbly playing a wrongly disfranchised member of a titled family. With comic coolness, Price methodically kills those less-than-sympathetic relatives (all played by Alec Guinness) who stand in the way of his becoming a duke. More recently, the Blands (Paul Bartel and Mary Woronov) get back at a victimizingly sick world by killing sex "perverts" throughout *Eating Raoul* (1982). In 1987, Danny DeVito had an excellent reason to *Throw Momma From the Train*, with Anne Ramsey getting an Oscar nomination for her parent from hell role. And 1989's *Heathers* plays upon the dream of every high school outcast—knocking off the snobbishly dreaded "popular" classmates.

An examination of a number of black comedies, with *Monsieur Verdoux* and *Dr. Strangelove* as the poles of the genre (the sympatheic small-time murderer versus the large-scale establishment operation), disclosed three interrelated themes: man as beast, the absurdity of the world, and the omnipresence of death.

Dark humor operates on a decidedly less-than-idealistic view of people. Through the years director Kubrick, after giving the world films like *Dr. Strangelove* and *A Clockwork Orange* (1971), has repeatedly been asked his view of mankind. His chilling reply has ramained the same: despite the world's ongoing senseless violence and wanton sexuality, he is always surprised that things are not worse. Kubrick firmly believes the species is capable of much more heinous crimes.

Director Arthur Penn's 1970 adaptation of Thomas Berger's *Little Big Man* put it most boldly when the story's only collection of positive people, the adopted Indian tribe of the central character (Dustin Hoffman) ironically call themselves the "Human Beings." This revisionist black-comedy look at the white man's attempted genocide of the Indian, an indirect commentary upon the genocide then occurring in Vietnam, was most focused in its celebrated topping of the legend and heroic aura surrounding General George Armstrong Custer and his defeat at the Little Big Horn. While other black comedies seldom have such a dramatic historic figure as Custer to showcase man as beast (excepting the Hitler-inspired works), the beast metaphor is central to the genre. Visually, it is most dramatically presented in *Catch-22* (1970), when Alan Arkin's Yossarian is out after curfew. That night he witnesses a cross-section of human depravity in the streets: aberrated sexuality, children robbing a drunk, vicious beatings (of man and animal), and the aftermath of a murder—a young, raped girl lying dead on the cobblestones. The black comedy send-up of all this is that no one is arrested except Yossarian—for breaking curfew.

Man as beast is given a psychedelic twist in Oliver Stone's *Natural Born Killers* (1994) when an odyssey of killing is presented through an avalanche of film stocks and formats, peppered with everything from slow motion and unrealistic rear projection to superquick close-ups and heavy-metal animation. This over-the-top dark comedy centers on Mickey and Mallory (Woody Harrelson and Juliette Lewis), an attractive young couple who simply kill for the crazy love of it. They become media heroes to a TV society raised on tabloid "news" which swallows violence like so many comedy pills. The ultimate man-as-beast scene occurs when an Australian tabloid host (Robert Downey, Jr.) is so exhilarated by the violence that he joins the killing as Mickey and Mallory escape from prison. However, director "Stone has touched a nerve here, because his film isn't about violence, it's about how we [the feeding-frenzy fans of *Geraldo*-type shows] respond to violence, and that truly is shocking."[15] (See Chapter 4.)

To fully compile and chronicle both the genre's depiction of man's inhumanity to man and the insignificance attached to human life would take a platoon of movie ushers. But certainly, one of the most definitive examples would be General "Buck" Turgidson's (George C. Scott) argument in *Dr. Strangelove* for a full-scale nuclear attack on the Russians: "I'm not saying we wouldn't get our hair messed. But I do say no more than ten to twenty million killed, tops—depending upon the breaks."

Comically shocking, yet one is reminded of the real-world revelations of *The Atomic Café* (1982), a rather black-comedy documentary compilation film of America's often-shocking approach to the nuclear age prior to *Dr. Strangelove*—for instance, the World War II decision to drop the atomic bomb on "virgin targets" (ones having suffered little previous war damage) like Hiroshima to better "see the total bomb damage." And as one critic later observed, *The Atomic Café*'s "chilling" collection of 1950s misleading government educational films on the atomic bomb, such as the "duck and cover" drills taught to adults and children alike (supposedly to protect them during a nuclear attack), nicely prepared the way for the subtitle of Kubrick's *Dr. Strangelove*: "*How I Learned to Stop Worrying and Love the Bomb.*"[16] (As a child growing up in 1950s Omaha, home of America's Strategic Air Command, I "learned" through numerous "duck and cover" drills that an atomic war could be no more dangerous than the occasional tornado . . . which also had a drill.)

Going hand in hand with the reality shock effect of *The Atomic Café* has been the United States government's ongoing 1990s internal investigation of its own Cold War–era human radiation experiments. The most sinister documentation thus far declassified involved intentional radiation fallout: "from 1948–52, [when] at least a dozen secret tests were conducted in the populated areas of Los Alamos, New Mexico; Dugway, Utah; and Oak Ridge, Tennessee, to see how radioactive fallout would travel."[17]

Such revelations showcase how life imitates Cold War art—it is the stuff of *Dr. Strangelove*'s secret military agendas. Indeed, with the late 1980s collapse of the Soviet Union, equally provocative information is now being released about the former Communist state. One such bombshell has direct links to *Dr. Strangelove*. In the film American nuclear warheads are mistakingly sent winging toward Russia. Unfortunately, the Soviets have a doomsday machine set to retaliate automatically—destroying the world, which is how the movie ends. It now appears that the Soviets actually had such a system, called "Dead Hand."[18] Kubrick once described *Dr. Strangelove* as "a fantasy which tries to stay within the realms of believable behavior."[19] Frighteningly, the director's work seems to be more realistic with each passing revelation.

I am reminded of critic Roger Ebert's *Natural Born Killers* comment, "Maybe Stone meant his movie as a warning about where we were headed, but because of [the O. J.] Simpson [case], it plays as an indictment of the way we are now."[20] Fittingly, director Stone credits *Dr. Strangelove* as having had a major influence on his work.[21]

The shock value of black comedy (such as the sudden mushroom cloud culmination of *Dr. Strangelove* or the graphically portrayed U.S. cavalry massacre of Indian women and children in *Little Big Man*, 1970) is the genre's trademark manner of undercutting any concept of man's nobility. However, there is a more pervasive example—portraying his obsession with sex. This sexual negation of man has four variations. First, it is difficult to attach any significance to man's lofty ideals when serious subjects of concern are constantly displaced by sex. For example, the world ends at the close of *Dr. Strangelove* with the lecture of the title character (Peter Sellers in one of his three parts) on postwar survival's having digressed to a scenario of ten women for every man. Even with an approaching apocalypse, the mere thought of sex reduces man to the most base and selfish of animal needs.

Such weakness also includes those black comedy characters initially shown as being made of purer stuff—such as Robert Duvall's overly religious Frank Burns in *M.A.S.H.* (1970). Burns comically pays for his hypocrisy by having his sexual activities with another hypocrite (Sally Kellerman's "Hot Lips") broadcast over the base intercom system. In *Little Big Man*, Faye Dunaway's character makes a startling switch from parsonage wife to brothel prostitute. And in *Harold and Maude*, the priest, while counseling teenager Harold (Bud Cort) against a relationship with the seventy-nine year old Maude (Ruth Gordon), inadvertently reveals his own sexual desire for the young man.

Director Blake Edwards provides pointed commentary on this sexual vulnerability in *S.O.B.* (1981, with its fitting black comedy title) when his in-film director-producer makes a hit from a failed film with pornography and the bared breasts of its formerly goody-goody star. Added shock comes from Edwards's casting of wife Julie Andrews (with her equally goody-two-shoes Mary-Poppins image) as the star.

Sex also represents an absence of self-control, consistent with man's plight in black comedy. This breakdown is most comically presented in the bug-eyed panting of Yossarian (Alan Arkin) and his *Catch-22* company after they meet the sexy companion of visiting General Dreedle (Orson Welles)—completely ignoring their bombing mission briefing. One is also reminded of Major King Kong (Slim Pickens) happily astride a falling, phallic-shaped atomic bomb called Lolita, whooping his way to world oblivion (see illustration 6). As Luis Buñuel, the most acclaimed foreign director of black comedy, observed, "In a rigidly hierarchical society, sex—which respects no barriers and obeys no laws—can at any moment become an agent of chaos."22

Sex as chaos is at its most chilling in the dark comedy film-noir classic *Chinatown* (1974, see also Chapter 5). Wealthy, manipulative civic leader Noah Cross (John Huston) has had an incestuous relationship with his daughter (Faye Dunaway). When she tries to escape him to protect the now teenage daughter born of this liaison, Dunaway's character is killed and Cross's granddaughter/daughter falls under his custody. Her fate and all the other heinous crimes for which the ironically named Cross is responsible are frighteningly explained earlier in the film. Jack Nicholson's Sam Spade/Philip Marlowe–like private eye asks Cross how he can live

6. Slim Pickens in *Dr. Strangelove*.

with everything from incest to murder. Cross's disquieting answer is that unlike many men he is "capable of anything." Incest was just one more example of how he could not only break society's laws and survive, but also prosper . . . even to be seen as a pillar of society.

A less ominous suggestion of possible incest occurs at the close of *Where's Poppa?* (1970). George Segal plays a repressed lawyer saddled with a live-in, senile mother played by Ruth Gordon. Segal's character is attempting to honor a family promise to keep her from a nursing home. But her presence has curtailed any possible sex life for him. He is already so desperate that early in the film he dons a gorilla costume and attempts to scare her to death. (The movie would later be re-released as *Going Ape*.) At film's end, with one more girlfriend lost because of mother, he falls in bed beside her. The implication is that he will be replacing the long-time-dead "Poppa."

In addition, black comedy frequently makes direct links between sex and death—the ultimate lack of control. Indeed, biographer Deborah Crawford's *Franz Kafka: Man Out of Step* (1973) chronicles that the suicide of George in "The Judgement" was linked in Kafka's mind to the sensation of a violent sexual ejaculation. Fittingly, in the dark comedy film *Heathers* (1989) the sexual cliche "Is this as good for you as it is for me?" actually refers to murder . . . several of them.

The most popular black film humor link between sex and death is the Bluebeard variety, and *Monsieur Verdoux* is a prime example. Chaplin pushes the dark comedy envelope here by implying all the victims are burned . . . and this so soon after the Holocaust revelations. But death can also appear as an ironic commentary on man's self-destructive lifestyle, such as Bob Fosse's *All That Jazz* (1979). The latter film is the most direct about the subject—literally casting death as a sexy and flirtatious lady ironically dressed in white (Jessica Lange). The film's central character is a workaholic stage director (Roy Scheider) killing himself with self-centered absorption in his art. He is also a womanizer, and Lange's sexy figure of death is the perfect metaphorical grim reaper for this artist. The dangers of one's art being coupled with sex are also played out in *The Stunt Man* (1980). The film's title character (Steve Railsback) seems to be hurtling toward his death in a stunt gone wrong when the film cuts to his simultaneous orgasm with his lover (Barbara Hershey). The sounds of death and ecstasy are indistin-

guishable. And near the close of *A Clockwork Orange,* Malcolm
McDowell's character lies moaning in a hospital bed. What sounds
like another patient's similar cry turns out to be a nearby doctor
and nurse reaching sexual climax.

Sex and death in black comedy can be a commentary upon man's
sexual perversity. Witness the *Eating Raoul* (1982) victims who were
attracted by an advertisement promising kinky favors, or Marcy's
(Rosanna Arquette) description of her *After Hours* (1985) husband
as a Wizard of Oz freak who used to scream "Surrender, Dorothy!"
at the moment of orgasm. The gag in the underrated *Weekend at
Bernie's* (1989) finds the dead title character, thanks to the wonders
of rigor mortis, providing his unknowing airhead of a girlfriend
with the sex of a "lifetime." And the fulfillment of *Brazil*'s (1985)
central character's sexual fantasy also begins with a necrophilia
joke.

Probably the most elaborate dark comedy suggestion of a necrophilia scene occurs in *M.A.S.H.* (1970). Painless Pole the dentist
(John Schuck) decides to commit suicide when an experience of
impotency creates fears of latent homosexuality. His friends provide him with a coffin and what he thinks is a lethal black capsule.
But it is merely a sedative which allows them to transfer him from
the coffin to an equally somber setting—what appears to be a dead
Painless laid out in bed. Then an attractive nurse, who initially
thinks the Pole is deceased, is convinced she should sexually help
bring him back to life.

One is also reminded of the pornography theater conclusion of
John Landis's *An American Werewolf in London* (1981). It is fascinating that the film's final transition of the title character (David
Naughton) to the beast should occur in a Triple-X theater (with the
animalistic urges associated there with), and that the cries of pain
that accompany his change should be indistinguishable in the
darkened theater from the sexual moans emitted from both screen
and audience.

Historically, death and sexual perversity often found their way
into Buñuel's films. This even occurs as early as the still-startling
Andalusian Dog (1929), "when the man caresses the woman's bare
breasts as his face slowly changes into a death mask."[23] In Kubrick's
A Clockwork Orange (1971), Alex (Malcolm McDowell) murders one
woman victim by metaphorically raping her with a large sculpture
of a penis (see illustration 7).

7. Malcolm McDowell in *A Clockwork Orange.*

The fact that sex frequently symbolized the only solace even for the genre's nominal good guy is a further comment upon the pitiful condition of modern man. This is best showcased by sorry Billy Pilgrim's (Michael Sacks) lovemaking scenes with voluptuous movie star Montana Wildhack (Valerie Perrine) in the human zoo on the planet of Tralfamadore in *Slaughterhouse-Five* (1972).

Even when the genre uses sex as a positive story device, a sense of the comically shocking and unnatural remains. An example is the consummation of the loving and meaningful relationship between title characters Bud Cort and Ruth Gordon in *Harold and Maude* (1972), where a sixty-plus-year age difference exists.

In George Roy Hill's adaptation of John Irving's *The World According to Garp* (1982), sex as an act of necessary closure results in tragedy . . . and a perversely comic injury. Garp's (Robin Williams) wife (Mary Beth Hurt) has been having an affair with one of her college students. When it threatens her marriage, she breaks it off. But the devastated young lover begs her to perform one last act of oral sex. Hurt's character reluctantly does this in a parked car on the secluded drive of the Garp family residence. It is a dark, rainy night and her husband and children are gone. However, Garp and the two boys return early and Williams' figure plays the longstanding family game of turning off the car lights as they enter their long driveway. This movement through the dark simulates the freedom of flying, an ongoing theme of the work. But this time they slam into the parked car, killing one of the boys and causing their mother inadvertently to bite off her student's penis.

Dark comedy directors often implicate the viewer as well as the film characters in showcasing people's extreme vulnerability towards all things sexual. Robert Altman's *The Player* (1992) is particularly manipulative along these lines. The film's obligatory steamy sex scene is shot and cut in such tight close-up that while there in no question of what is going on, one sees no provocative full-figure nudity. Ironically, an earlier nonsexual hot tub scene has visually left nothing to the viewer's imagination.

The always chain-pulling Altman once related the story that after an early sneak preview of *The Player*, Paul Newman came up to him and observed, "I know what this picture's about. It's about getting to see the tits of the girl whose tits you don't care about seeing, and not getting to see the tits of the girl whose tits you want to see."[24] A tongue-in-cheek Altman replied, "You're absolutely right." But while the movie does much more than that, this genre seldom lets the voyeurist viewer get away feeling innocent. (See Chapter 5.)

Consequently, sexual references abound in dark comedy, be it the large number befitting an archetype like *Dr. Strangelove* (which moved one film critic to devote an entire article to the subject[25]), to the meandering philandering of Tom Conti's Scottish poet in the excellent but more modest black comedy *Reuben, Reuben* (1983). A sadly funny final commentary upon sex and people occurs in *The World According to Garp*. Garp's mother (Glenn Close) has herself impregnated by a dying war pilot whose injuries have reduced him to a vegetable state . . . but an ever-erect penis. And the only thing he says during his hospitalization, besides his name, occurs after this intercourse. The pilot says "Good." How appropriate for the genre that man can still perform the sex act without a mind; the sexual organ always seemingly displaces the cerebral organ anyway, even when the brain is functioning.

The second dark humor theme, after man as beast, is that it is an absurd world, where the individual counts for very little. This absurdity is most obviously shown by the fact that the genre's antiheroes often are not so much participants as they are unwilling spectators in a terrible, ongoing joke called life. This leaf-in-the-wind charaterization is best presented in the adaptations of *Little Big Man*, *Catch-22*, and *Slaughterhouse-Five*. But countless other examples exist, such as Steve Railsback's fugitive in Richard Rush's *The Stunt Man* (1980), where a devil-like director (Peter O'Toole) and the tricks of filmmaking forever add to the antihero's vulnerability. What this stunt man as well as other dark comedy antiheroes have to deal with might best be articulated by the omnipotent comments of O'Toole's figure, "If God could do the tricks we can do, he'd be a happy man."

Black humor absurdity is usually presented in two ways—through the chaos of an unordered universe and through the flaws of mortal man. The first and most fundamental simply has man being victimized for merely trying to exist. For instance, in Martin Scorsese's *After Hours* Griffin Dunne's Mr. Normal character meets a beautiful stranger, Marcy (Rosanna Arquette). But the "after hours" (when new rules seem to apply?) ends up a Kafkaesque nightmare. It is seldom a good sign when your date commits suicide early, but things actually do get worse for Dunne. As he runs around (flees?) late-night New York City, he has comically frightful encounters with a myriad of strange characters, from a vigilante-type ice cream lady to Teri Garr's equally lethal Monkees groupie. And one should not neglect the story's interweaving of petty criminals Cheech and Chong, who exist as a rather offbeat comic-chorus reminder that yes, this is a comedy, a black comedy (see illustration 8). Or, as Dunne's Paul eventually observes, "All I wanted to do was go out with a girl and have a nice time. Do I have to die for it?"

As if in anticipation of this impending comedy of terrors, early in the film Paul makes reference to Edvard Munch's anguishing Expressionistic lithograph *The Shriek* (1896; Expressionism was a movement, like black humor, which often used the shock effect to draw attention to life's darker side). See this book's frontispiece.

The Shriek portrays a figure on a nighttime bridge whose carica-ture-like face is caught in a terrible scream. The hollow cheeks and staring eyes remind one of death's skull. Lithographs sometimes illustrate dark comedy works, especially the writings of Kafka, a contemporary of Munch. Along those lines *The Shriek* could be interpreted as a visualization of the writer's metaphor for life as an ongoing "trial" ended only by death.

The catalyst for Paul's *After Hours* reference to this Expression-istic piece is the sculpture of Marcy's roommate Kiki (Linda Fiorentino). She creates lifesize plaster-of-Paris versions of tor-mented, *Shriek*-like men. Although this is not the most reassuring artistic slant for your date's friend to take, it is pivotal to the story. As Paul's evening from hell progresses, he becomes more and more like a Munch man. Eventually, his life depends upon literally becoming a Munch-like art object. Another sculptress (Verna Bloom) conceals him from his now legion of enemies by plastering him into a figure like Kiki's art.

The implication here is that even in safety life freezes you into something you are not. And the *After Hours* absurdity only contin-ues as the Cheech and Chong characters soon come along to steal Paul the art object. With night finally over, what appears to be real escape occurs when the living sculpture falls out of the burglars' van. Freed from the shattered plaster, Paul ironically finds himself in front of his hated place of employment . . . just in time for the start of work. He has merely traded one form of encasement for another. Munch and Kafka would have been pleased.

8. Griffin Dunne flanked by Cheech and Chong in *After Hours*.

Seeing Dunne (who produced *After Hours*) as the ongoing victim of the world's absurdity also reminds one of his role in *An American Werewolf in London*. His character dies early in the film but continues to comically appear (in ever more graphic stages of physical deterioration), with the message that his friend must take his own life or else become a werewolf. Truly, this is not your run-of-the-mill comic chaos.

Jeff Daniel's naive young consultant has an extended *After Hours*-type experience in Jonathan Demme's *Something Wild* (1986). Only this time, he is the one picked up—or, more comically correct, kidnapped—by a sexy but strange character (Melanie Griffith), who for a time sports both a Louise Brooks wig (bobbed black hair) and the Brooks nickname Lulu.

Of course, one need not leave the neighborhood in search of absurdity. It can always move in next door, as happened to John Belushi in the 1981 adaption of Thomas Berger's *Neighbors*. Or, it can pop up in the high school of *Teachers* (1984), where the best instructor is an escaped crazy and the worst teacher's in-class death goes unnoticed.

Another black comedy example of the dangerous randomness of life is the slow-witted Mafia hit-man (Jack Nicholson) falling in love with a rival hit "man" (Kathleen Turner) in *Prizzi's Honor* (1985). This results in the genre's definitive "romantic" question—"Do I ice [kill] her, or marry her?" *Reuben, Reuben* seems about to close on an upbeat note: Tom Conti's poet has decided not to commit suicide (though he is still standing on a chair with neck in noose), and his years-long writing block has ended. Ah, but then life's randomness hits, and the neighbor's big, friendly dog Reuben lumbers in, accidentally dislodges the chair, and a saved poet is lost.

For all the comic frightfulness of an unordered universe, man has been a strong contributor to the absurdity of the black comedy world. *Pogo* cartoonist Walt Kelly capsulized this nicely with his delightful pun of a famous axiom, "We have met the enemy and he is us." This manmade absurdity is the result of both general species imcompetence and its perpetuation in human institiutions.

Dr. Strangelove fairly shouts species imcompetence, as do most Kubrick films, but it is often showcased in an institutionalized package. The film is a catch-all for nearly every type of absurdity (including the chance occurrence of a person in power, like Sterling

Hayden's General Jack D. Ripper, going crazy and playing God),
but the overall point is that man is incapable of controlling what
he has created. The irony is heightened by the fact that the scientific
knowhow needed to initially construct the bomb was immense; it
is just that with humans in control, there can be no real fail-safe
system. Leadership has never matched the technical strides made
in science. And beyond the imcompetence of major-power leaders
trying to indefinitely juggle the bomb, there is an army of other
uniformed homo sapiens who could contribute to a nuclear apol-
calypse, from the third-world intervention of *The Mouse That
Roared* (1959) to a high school whiz-kid accidentally tapping into
the system in *War Games* (1983). In dark comedy, as is so often the
case in science fiction, to wear a uniform is to be a liability.

Species incompentence does not, of course, have to focus on
state-of-the-art nuclear holocaust. Man has been unable to get along
with man since the beginning of time. One is reminded of the scene
in Kubrick's *2001: A Space Odyssey* (1968) which moves from
cavemen creating the first crude weapons to an immediate transition to the space age arsenal of the future. This endless involvement
in war is man's greatest tribute to incompetence—and a major
ingredient of the absurd world he helped create. Vonnegut paid
ironic tribute to this endless, insane legacy when he noted what
one critic of antiwar books had advised as an equally productive
subject—"Why don't you write an anti-*glacier* book instead?"[26]

Fittingly, black comedy often focuses on war, be it Billy Wilder's
Stalag 17 (1953) or Robert Altman's *M.A.S.H.*, because war is the
perfect symbol for every person's ongoing battle for day-to-day
survival. *M.A.S.H.* captures this dual-nature absurdity (of shooting
war and war as metaphor for life). First, what could be more
fundamentllay absurd about real war than the policy of medical
miracles which save lives—only to send them right back into battle?
(One receives a sense of this in Ernest Hemingway's *A Farewell to
Arms*, since the central character is an ambulance driver.)

M.A.S.H. does not show us the actual fighting—only the casualties—as the doctors mix humor and the graphic realism of the
battlefield operating room. The plight of the civilian casualty of an
absurd world follows a similar scenario. One does not witness the
individual, internalized war most thinking human beings experience; it only comes to attention when someone is psychologically
"wounded." As Henry David Thoreau observed in *Walden* (1854),

"The mass of men lead lives of quiet desperation. What is called resignation is confirmed desperation."[27] Psychological casualities do not mend so easily—though, like the recovered soldier, they too find themselves back in the fray. (Of course, in a nuclear war, everyone would be on the "front lines.")

M.A.S.H. further accents the warlike nature of the civilian sector when it devotes considerable time to the football game between American army units. As more and more commentators on the American scene have noted, football represents an excellent microcosm of this violent, competitive society. Propononts of this perspective range from Lenny Bruce's acknowledeged stand-up comedy protégé George Carlin to university professor Michael R. Real.[28] Director Peter Davis drew just this analogy in his Academy Award–winning Vietnam documentary *Hearts and Minds* (1974). Of course, Altman underlines his football-as-metaphor-for-America by the comically aggressive, anything-for-a-victory attitude taken by both *M.A.S.H.* teams.

This interchangeable approach to war and life is also borne out by the extended meaning to come out of Heller's phrase "Catch-22." As originally applied, it meant that combat flyer

Orr was crazy and could be grounded. All he had to do was ask; and as soon as he did he would no longer be crazy [concern being a rational mental process] and would have to fly more missions. . . . If he flew them he was crazy and didn't have to , but if he didn't want to he was sane and had to.[29]

Quickly, this absurdity-of-war phrase was embraced by the general public—*before* Vietnam was an issue—and was applied to the homo sapiens-influenced absurdity of the world. It was even neatly classified in civilian dictionaries everywhere (an added tribute to man's absurdity—the need to organize his chaos), with dictionary crispness: "catch 22 n. (slang) a dilemma from which the victim has no escape."[30]

Paddy Chayefsky's script for *Network* (1976) is more direct and earthy about manmade absurdity. Newscaster Howard Beale (Peter Finch) explained why he had planned to commit suicide: "I just ran out of bullshit. . . . Bullshit is all the reasons we give for living." This brings one to the second chief source of man-made chaos—institutionalized absurdity. Finch, who won a posthumous Oscar for his role, moves from personal bullshit to indicting religion, "If we can't think up any of our own [bullshit], we always have the God bullshit."

The often absurd actions/policies of establishment institutions like the church or the military are constantly under attack in black comedy. Their star target status is because they routinely propagate the lie, or "bullshit," that it is a rational world, and then their onging implemenation of this lie results in mass dehumanization and/or death.

Harold and Maude presents a triple threat attack on institutions. Whenever teenage Harold displays any atypical behavior, his mother sends him to one of three misguided counselors: the family priest, career army officer Uncle Victor, and a psychiatrist. Each is comically frightening, especially his uncle, the former "right-hand man" of General Douglas MacArthur. This bit of information is especially memorable, since the viewer's initial sight of Victor finds him actually lacking a right arm . . . black comedy's commentary on the benefits of being highly placed in the military. The empty, starched sleeve does, however, have a mechanism which allows Uncle Victor to make the most surreal of salutes. This is genre homage to Peter Sellers's zany interpretation of the *Dr. Strangelove* figure (with his comic malfunctioning—"heil Hitler"—artifical arm). Fittingly for dark comedy, Uncle Victor recommends that going to war would be the best thing for his troubled nephew.

Besides *Harold and Maude's* broadsides against the institutions of religion, medicine, and the military, the teenager's constant encounters with his domineering mother are an onging comic deflation of the most basic of institutions—family. Still, the single most chilling indictment of institutionalized power comes in a fleeting moment the morning after Harold and Maude have made love. There is a brief glimpse of a number tattooed on her arm. Suddenly, with the concentration camp implication, all the film's warnings about institutions are given added credibility.

Institutionalized absurdity, therefore, means man's chaos-making abilities can attain irrevocable steamroller proportions, as in the Holocaust. Such absurdity is further fueled by additional goofs and/or greed—big-business style. The first, for which *Dr. Strangelove's* less than fail-safe system is the ultimate example, remains the most popular norm in the institutuionalized absurdity category.

In *Brazil* the state so flippantly executes its alleged enemies that a simple misspelling, caused by a squashed bug in a typewriter (a "bug in the system"), leads to an innocent man's death—the event upon which the whole film turns. Other black comedy examples of institutional incompetence range from Woody Allen's CIA in *Bananas* (1971), which sends military support to both sides in an insurrection to guarantee inclusion with the winners, to the core travesty of *Slaughterhouse-Five*—the firebombing of the nonmilitary target city of Dresden (which actually occurred during World War II).

The big-business approach to institutionalized absurdity finds craziness a byproduct of the profit motive. *Catch-22*'s enterprising Milo (Jon Voight) is the perfect example of this phenomenon. His creation and direction of "M and M Enterprises" turns World War II into the most profitable of businesses, and the source of much of its planned absurdity. These enterprises range from his taking all the camp parachutes because he could obtain a good price on silk (Alan Arkin's Yossarian only discovers this when he opens his pack to find that his chute has been replaced by two shares of M and M stock), to a Milo deal which has Americans bombing their own base in exchange for the German enemy's helping Milo liquidate his unloadable stockpile of cotton. Fittingly, late in the movie Voight's character paraphrases the famous old General Motors big-business axiom—"What's good for M and M Enterprises is good for the world."

This *Catch-22* model of organized and bankable absurdidty is nicely complemented in the civilian world by *Network*—which chronicles the live television murder of a newscaster because he had "lousy ratings." (The murder also represented an excellent lead-in for a network program shot and produced by revolutionaries!) Early in the film network owner Arthur Jensen (Ned Beatty) puts this all in perspective when he observes, "There is no America, no democracy, there is only . . . [names corporations after corporations]. Those are the nations of the world." As if the metaphor needed further expansion, he goes on to say, "The world is a business; it has been since man crawled out of the slime."

Even the less global black comedies frequently play on this analogy, be it Chaplin's killing of little old ladies to maintain his stock portfolio in *Monsieur Verdoux*, or the casual frying pan murders of *Eating Raoul*, where money is being raised for a restaurant while ridding the world of sex perverts. And in *Raising Arizona* (1987) the father of a kidnapped child turns the ensuing press conference into a commercial for his unpainted furniture business that promises the lowest possible prices "or his name ain't Nathan Arizona" . . . it later turns out to be Nathan Huffhines.

The genre's showcasing of absurdity is frequently reinforced by a fragmented narrative of less than linear proportions. At its extreme, such as in *Slaughterhouse-Five*, central character Billy Pilgrim is constantly time-tripping through events in his past, present, and future. Editing, which forever juxtaposes these worlds, makes the transitions as startling for the viewer as for the aptly-named Pilgrim, thus reinforcing dark comedy's theme of absurdity. The *Catch-22* flashbacks keep one scrambling for the narrative, especially the art film–like repetitions of Yossarian's discovery of the dying Snowden. Quentin Tarantino's *Pulp Fiction* (1994) is like a collection of cinema short stories connected by a cross-weaving of a few pivotal characters, particularly John Travolta's Vincent. This charcacter dies in the second of three main plot lines but reappears in the third when the viewer finds himself returned to an earlier time.

Writer/director Tarantino has said, "I like things unexplained."[31] Thus, his mindset is consistent with the genre's fragmented narrative—keep the audience off balance. But it also enables Tarantino to maintain another component of the genre: avoid sentimentality. Just as we are about to mourn the death of a likable character, Tarantino is "plugging our emotions. . . . It may be a cold and cunning way to cut [edit] a movie, but it's urged on by a serious desire to stop any schmalz creeping through."[32]

As with the formalistic editing, black comedy's self-conscious use of music is an additional commentary on the theme of absurdity. The mushroom cloud close of *Dr. Strangelove* is ironically accompanied by Vera Lynn's sentimental, romantic World War II song "We'll Meet Again." *Brazil* takes its title from the upbeat, breezy 1930s Ary Baroso song of the same name, a song which frequently punctuates this dark comedy. Kubrick's *A Clockwork Orange* follows this same model by juxtaposing violence and "Singing in the Rain."

Black humor is one comedy genre where formalistic techniques, such as self-consciously elaborate editing and music, reinforce theme. Life has no plot in dark comedy. And if any attempt at making sense of the genre's fragmented formalism were made, one might embrace the Cubism of Picasso. That is, traditional perspective and illusion are abandoned in favor of analysis of a subject from numerous perspectives at once. And this is one more way black humor can alienate an audience.

The genre's self-consciousness is also borne out in the tendency to include scenes of film parody. It is as if to say that dark comedy attacks all "institutions," including celebrated auteurs and genres of its medium of expression, from the brief take-off on Sergei Eisenstein's "Odessa Steps" sequence (*Battleship Potemkin*, 1925) near the close of *Brazil*, to the more lengthy Major "King" Kong's (Slim Pickens) preparation of his *Dr. Strangelove* bomber crew for its mission.

In the latter case , much of what King says in ludicrous (such as his comments on their survival kit in case they bail out—what would they be jumping to?). Yet Kubrick so slickly apes the standard men-into-action scene of the war film, including "When Johnny Comes Marching Home Again" on the soundtrack, that the viewer ironically is tempted to root for success, despite what that would mean. Once again black comedy has put the viewer's emotions at cross-purposes.

The third theme of the genre focuses upon the awful finality of death. To borrow a Vonnegut metaphor, also echoed in the earlier quote from *Network*, everyone is headed to the slaughterhouse. In black comedy, death means THE END, also the title of Burt Reynold's underrated 1978 stab at the genre.

To paraphrase a popular axiom of the genre, "Life is awful, and then you die." Though not a black comedy, Woody Allen expresses an expanded version of this dark moral in the opening monologue to *Annie Hall* (1977): life is "Full of loneliness and misery and suffering and unhappiness and it's all over much too quickly." Any way one defines it, in black humor death is the final joke of futile life. The genre merely obtains more mileage out of a terrible dilemma (death) by laughing at it.

There are few *final* happy endings, as Buñuel implies with the title of his autobiography—*My Last Sigh*.[33] The related taboos are those sacred things black comedy attacks that attempt to give meaning to death (religion), and reveal the less than dignified elements of pitiful life, from body functions to the sorry state of the body after death. Laughter itself becomes a comfortingly cynical "religion" in this genre. The portrayal of black comedy

death is also a compendium for the genre's themes (man as beast
and the absurdity of life).

There are four basic lessons to be learned or reaffirmed from
the genre's obsession with death. First, death itself is a terrible
absurdity. How can a once vital, passionate, thinking human
being suddenly be reduced to so much "garbage" in death? Yet
that is a central black comedy revelation. It is borne out by the
conclusion of Yossarian's pivotal repeated scene with wounded
and dying Snowden in *Catch-22*, where his insides ooze to the
floor. Poor Snowden's terrible secret is that "Man was matter. . . .
Bury him and he'll rot like other kinds of garbage. The spirit gone,
man is garbage."[34] Literary critic and black comedy theorist
Sanford Pinsker calls this, rather than "Catch-22," the "heart of
the novel" (something that applies equally to the film adaption),
while academic critics like Leslie M. Thompson and William R.
Cozart term the scene the "ultimate description of technological
atrocity."[35]

By the time of *Eating Raoul*, Snowden's dark humor secret is a
secret no more—Mrs. Bland's comment to her murderer husband
as he experiences a modicum of guilt is a casual "He [the victim]
was a man, now he's just a bag of garbage." It is gruesomely
appropriate that in a genre where the individual is insignificant,
he should also be physically destroyed.

Second, the casually random end-without-purpose unexpectedness with which death frequently appears underlines both the
world's absurdity and the insignificance of the individual. For
instance, the sudden execution in *Slaughterhouse-Five* of the caring
former teacher Edgar Derby because of a misunderstanding about
a glass figurine, the even quicker propeller slicing in half of Kid
Sampson during a *Catch-22* prank, and the death of a Garp child
during the lightless car game of *The World According to Garp* all
document the transitory nature of man's stay on earth. That such
events should also occur during moments of joy, be they comic
pranks or Derby's initially happy surprise at finding a figurine like
one from home in the rubble of Dresden, underline all the more
the absurdity of life and death.

Such cruel randomness reinforces the genre's denial of a God
and any rational plan for the earthy world. Indeed, to minimize
death, as this genre does (or as the undertaker does by applying
rouge to the corpse), by necessity minimizes God. Black comedy

is one response to His silence. In this genre people are often just so many laboratory mice scrambling ludicrously in an experiment gone awry. If there is some omniscient scientist/God present, He is merely a silent observer to the frantic movement in the maze. The ways of the people and those of God are irreconcilable. The silence continues.

Third, the popularity of suicide in black comedies, from the multiple stagings of the act in *Harold and Maude*, to Monsieur Verdoux's indirect suicide by way of letting himself be caught, further accents man's earthly dilemma in several ways. It dramatically demonstrates that the genre's disregard for life begins with the individual, even by the indirect manner of working oneself to death, as in *All That Jazz*. Suicide is that rare activity where the black comedy individual can initiate the event instead of being the random recipient. How ironically fitting for the genre that this act results in the total negation of the individual. Third, life is full of pain, and suicide provides a way around this, as the title to *M.A.S.H.*'s theme song dramatically shows: "Suicide Is Painless." That this escape has always been an alternative to life's suffering is underscored by Lubitsch entitling a pioneering black comedy film with Shakespeare's celebrated wording for suicide—*To Be or Not To Be*. Even Malcolm McDowell's ultimate nasty character in *A Clockwork Orange* attempts suicide after the government reprograms his brain: "I just want to die peacefully, with no pain."

On a metaphorical level, suicide is an apt phrase for the literal implementation of the death-wish-like tendency of modern man to seemingly rush toward an apocalypse of his own making, such as the inevitable mushroom cloud conclusion of *Dr. Strangelove*. Suicide is a modest example of something black comedy frequently showcases on a broader and more terrible scale—man playing God. Examples range from *Little Big Man*'s Custer and Chaplin's Hitler-inspired Great Dictator to Strangelove himself—whose ironic name is so fitting for these pain-producing "Creators."

Black comedy suicides, or the attempt, often also reveal that randomness is just as strong in suicide as in the frustrating lives it seeks to end. Thus, *Reuben, Reuben* documents an accidental suicide, after Tom Conti's character has decided to live; Sissy Spacek's Babe MaGrath comes closest to death in her various *Crimes of the Heart* (1986) attempts at suicide after she decided against it, only to accidentally knock herself out trying to remove her head from the oven. *S.O.B.* works a variation on suicide and chance when the in-film director (Richard Mulligan) continually fails at suicide, while a nearby heart attack victim seeking help dies. Later when Mulligan's character has something to live for, he is shot and killed.

A final manner in which suicide further underlines man's dark plight is how this ultimate personal surrender can be reduced to the latest fad. This is the message of *Heathers* (1989), where the high school characters played by Winona Ryder and Christian Slater kill several teens and stage the murders to look like suicides. The vacuous adults and most of their equally empty-headed kids are all too ready to buy into the angst-ridden stereotype of suicide victim . . . especially when it means fifteen minutes of fame during the ever-present media coverage.

The *Heathers* catalyst for using suicide as a cover for murder came through a passing reference to a real life angst-ridden case: Sylvia Plath. The Cliff Notes to her autobiographical cult novel *The Bell Jar* (1963), about the 1950s crack-up of an overachiever, are seen near the body of the first *Heathers* victim. Plath's work is now often defined through her suicide. And within the context of *Heathers*, reference to Plath provides further literary correctness to suicide as fad. Woody Allen's *Annie Hall* (1977) provides a sardonically appropriate black humor slant on Plath: "Interesting poetess whose tragic suicide was misinterpreted as romantic, by the college-girl mentality."

The fourth basic lesson to draw from the genre's obsession with death demonstrates people's callousness to shock. While viewers tend initially to be surprised, in-film black comedy characters often have the worn-down "and so it goes" attitude of *Slaughterhouse-Five*'s Billy Pilgrim. Or they have the ho-hum complacency with which the Hitchcock characters treat the corpse in *The Trouble with Harry* (1955) and the even more subdued response of Bud Cort's screen mother to his seemingly very real "suicides" in *Harold and Maude*. This in-movie complacency reaches dark comedy extremes with the cartoon-like grizzliness of *Beetlejuice*'s (1988) afterlife characters.

Part of any audience's first-step shock, therefore, is a response to this nonchalant behavior toward the horrible. Any shock, in-film or not, if sustained, eventually produces a numbing effect. Faye Dunaway's character in *Network* addresses just this point when she describes the 1970s American public as "clobbered on all sides by Vietnam, Watergate, the inflation, the depression, they've turned off, shot up, and fucked themselves limp and nothing else helps." Thus, black comedy's graphic portrayals of death are forever trying to produce new shocks for the viewing public, and occasionally even for the film characters themselves.

This "turned off" audience complacency could also be demonstrated in mainstream non-dark comedy entertainment. Dean Martin's popular period television variety show is a prime example. Mick Tosches' critically and commercially acclaimed biography of the entertainer observed, "Dean was the American spirit at its truest: fuck Vietnam, fuck politics, fuck morality, fuck culture and fuck the counterculture, fuck it all. We were here for but a breath; twice around the fountain and into the grave: fuck it."[36] The language of Tosches's praised book, moreover, is in keeping with popular culture's ongoing embrace of shock effect, whether in the startling death scenes or other taboo-breaking examples. For instance, Robert Altman satirizes the *Last Supper* in *M.A.S.H.* (borrowing from Buñuel's *Viridiana*, 1961) and the *Catch-22* nurses run human excrement back through the 100 percent bandaged body of a wounded flyer, simply by reversing his intake/outtake bottles. If one were to include the cult, underground, pre-*Polyester* (1981) films of John Waters in the genre, examples such as Divine's (Glen Milstead) downing of real dog excrement at the tacked-on close of *Pink Flamingo* (1972) would be further prime evidence of shock effect. Fittingly, Waters entitled his 1981 autobiography *Shock Value*.[37] Black comedy is a genre that respects nothing, including the values of its audience.

These, then, have been the three interrelated central themes of dark humor—man as beast , the absurdity of the world, and the omnipresence of death—all terrible realities that belie the veneer of rationality that "civilized" man too often accepts as the norm. The genre screams *Think about it!* as it scrambles one's complacency by juxtaposing humor and horror. Of course, "thinking about" the unanswerable is another application of Catch-22, but it does allow the individual to make his own separate peace . . . or to surrender.

As this chapter has demonstrated, the genre embraces a wide cross-section of films. As Freud saw humor in terms of sexual taboos—laughter being an acceptable way of addressing a subject

which many found difficult to discuss—dark humor applies that
principle to the complete gamut of unmentionables that seem now
to happen daily. The black comedy umbrella finds worthy topics
in everything from nuclear apocalypse to the latest mass murderer
(or is that redundant?) . . . whatever is the tragedy of the day.
Possibly perverse coping, but coping just the same. As Clint
Eastwood's character observes in a film not even of the genre (*A
Perfect World*, 1994), "Gallows humor . . . without it we'd all be
losing our lunch."

NOTES

1. "The Black Humorists," *Time*, February 12, 1965, pp. 94–96.

2. *To Be or Not To Be* review, *Christian Science Monitor*, March 6,
1942, in the *To Be or Not To Be* file, Billy Rose Theatre Collection, New
York Public Library at Lincoln Center.

3. Eileen Creelman, *Arsenic and Old Lace* review, *New York Sun*,
September 2, 1944, in the *Arsenic and Old Lace* film file, Billy Rose
Theatre Collection, New York Public Library at Lincoln Center.

4. Ibid.

5. Victor Scherle and William Turner Levy, *The Films of Frank Capra*
(Secaucus, N.J.: Citadel Press, 1977), p. 192.

6. The "Frank Capra" segment of A&E's *Biography* program, broadcast July 25, 1994.

7. *Arsenic and Old Lace* review, credit citation missing, in the *Arsenic
and Old Lace* film file, Billy Rose Theatre collection.

8. James Agee (unsigned), *Monsieur Verdoux* review, *Time*, May 5,
1947, p. 100.

9. "Veterans," *Time*, February 3, 1947, p. 43.

10. See James Agee, "Monsieur Verdoux," in *Agee on Film*, vol. 1
(New York: Grosset and Dunlap, 1969), pp. 252–262. (Originally ap-
peared in *Nation*, May 31, June 14, and June 21, 1947.) Robert Warshow,
"Monsieur Verdoux," in *The Immediate Experience* (1962; repr. New York:
Atheneum, 1972). (Originally appeared in the July–August 1947 edition
of the *Partisan Review*.)

11. Judith Crist, "Mirth and Murder," *New York Herald Tribune*, July
26, 1964, p. 27.

12. Ibid.

13. John Beaufort, "An Assault from Mr. Chaplin," *Christian Science
Monitor*, April 19, 1947, p. 8.

14. Ibid.

15. Roger Ebert, "'Killers' a Biting Indictment of Society" (Universal Press Syndicate), syndicated in *Cedar Rapids Gazette*, August 26, 1994, p. 7-W.

16. "Atomic Cafe" entry, in *TV Movies and Video Guide* (1987 edition), ed. Leonard Maltin (New York: New American Library, 1986), pp. 43–44.

17. Rae Tyson, "Radiation Testing Shown in Documents," *USA Today*, December 21, 1993, p. 2-D.

18. "Life Imitates Cold War Art," *Newsweek*, October 18, 1993, p. 51.

19. Eric Lefcowitz, "'Dr. Strangelove' Turns 30. Can It Still Be Trusted?" *New York Times*, January 30, 1994, Section 2, p. 13.

20. Ebert, p.7-W.

21. Lefcowitz, Section 2, p. 13.

22. Luis Buñuel, *My Last Sigh*, trans. Abigail Israel (1982; repr. New York: Random House, 1984), p. 14.

23. Ibid, p. 15.

24. "Robert Altman on *The Player*," *Film Comment*, May–June 1992, p. 26.

25. Anthony F. Macklin, "Sex and *Dr. Strangelove*," *Film Comment*, Summer 1965, pp. 55–57.

26. Kurt Vonnegut, Jr., *Slaughterhouse-Five* (1969; repr. New York: Dell, 1974), p. 3.

27. Henry David Thoreau, *Walden and Other Writings of Henry David Thoreau*, ed. Brooks Atkinson (1854, *Walden*; repr. New York: Modern Library, 1965), p. 7.

28. George Carlin, "Baseball—Football," on the album *An Evening with Wally Londo* (Los Angeles: Little David Records, 1975). Michael R. Real, "The Super Bowl: Mythic Spectacle," in *TELEVISION: The Critical View* (third edition), ed. Horace Newcomb (New York: Oxford University Press, 1982).

29. Joseph Heller, *Catch-22* (1961; repr. New York: Dell, 1968), p. 47.

30. Eugene Ehrlich, Stuart Berg Flexner, Gorton Carruth, and Joyce M. Hawkins, eds., *Oxford American Dictionary* (1979; repr. New York: Avon Books, 1982), p. 131.

31. Peter Biskind, "An Auteur Is Born," *Premiere*, November 1994, p. 100.

32. Anthony Lane, *Pulp Fiction* review, *The New Yorker*, October 10, 1994, p. 96.

33. Luis Buñuel, *My Last Sigh*, trans. Abigail Israel (1982; repr. New York: Random House, 1984).

34. Heller, p. 47.

35. Sanford Pinsker, "The Graying of Black Humor," Chapter 3 in *Between Two Worlds: The American Novel in the 1960s* (Troy, N.Y.:

Whitston Publishing, 1980), p. 23. Leslie M. Thompson and William R. Cozart, "The Technology of Atrocity," Ball State University Forum, Autumn 1984, p. 69.

36. Nick Tosches, *DINO: Living High in the Dirty Business of Dreams* (1992; repr. New York: Dell, 1993), p. 386.

37. John Waters, *Shock Value* (New York: Dell, 1981).

3

DISMANTLING DICTATORS: "MARXIST" OR OTHERWISE

> What he [Jack Benny's mediocre in-film actor] did to Shake-
> speare we're [Nazi Germany] now doing to Poland.
> —Colonel Ehrhardt (Sig Rumann) in *To Be*
> *or Not To Be* (1942)

Before examination of several pivotal dark film comedies in the post—*Dr. Strangelove* (1964) flowering of the genre, a trilogy of pioneering works merit analysis: *Duck Soup* (1933), *The Great Dictator* (1940), and *To Be or Not To Be* (1942). None were fully appreciated at the time of their initial release. Indeed, the disastrous commercial and critical reception *Duck Soup* nearly ended the Marx Brothers' screen career. However, this trilogy now warrants special attention for three reasons.

First, while each is now an acknowledged cinema classic, their vanguard status within the dark comedy genre is still not fully recognized. This celebrated nature is more a result of the auteur aura which envelops them. *Duck Soup* is seen as the quintessential Marx Brothers film, besides being their only outing with a brilliant director—Leo McCarey. *The Great Dictator* is swallowed up by the unique film status of its writer, director, and star, Charlie Chaplin. And *To Be or Not To Be* is the product of acclaimed director Ernst

Lubitsch, whose "signature" on a movie was so distinctive that it came to be known as the "Lubitsch touch."

A second reason the trilogy qualifies for additional attention is the shared subject matter—misguided leaders and the inevitability of the war which follows them. Though still a popular dark comedy scenario, in the early cinema days of the genre, when the world was not always seen as irrational, government and war were more likely to be accepted as subjects of absurdity. Moreover, there are direct links between these films and later examples of the genre. For instance, the paranoia of Groucho Marx's Rufus T. Firefly in *Duck Soup* has direct ties to General Jack D. Ripper's (Sterling Hayden) psychotic obsession that the Soviets are about to overrun America in *Dr. Strangelove*, a parallel that will be addressed shortly.

More generally, *The Great Dictator* and *To Be or Not To Be* use Hitler and his then only beginning grizzly legacy for their humor. This is still the stuff of dark comedy, from *A Clockwork Orange*'s (1971) Alex (Malcolm McDowell) being subjected to Nazi concentration camp footage while being reprogrammed, to Mel Brooks's propensity to lace his parodies with dark comedy Nazis. In fact, Brooks's greatest film, *The Producers* (1968, originally entitled *Springtime for Hitler*), is a black comedy. It revolves around the attempt to produce the world's worst play—a musical comedy "romp with Adolf and Eva [his mistress] at Berchtesgaden [Hitler's mountain retreat]."

The Producers presents the viewer with a provocative reflective exercise in dark comedy. One watches the in-film theater audience applauding the exercise in poor taste called *Springtime for Hitler*. Brooks gives the screen viewer an in-your-face dose of the ambivalence inherent to dark comedy—the nervous laughter about horrors such as the Holocaust that can be assimilated into comic art. Yet this awkward, on-the-edge quality defines the genre. Black humor is about being politically incorrect. The ideal patron of this genre, however, uses such art to both cope with past human atrocities and help prevent them from occurring again. In those oblivious to yesterday, this controversial art (that even now appears in such mainstream mediums as the poignant cartoon books of Art Spiegelman) should encourage historical awareness and responsibility. Fittingly, Brooks's fascination with this subject resulted in his remaking *To Be or Not To Be* in 1983. As if in tribute to Lubitsch, the film follows the original almost scene for scene.

The third reason the trilogy merits further attention is to examine how a much earlier era dealt with a still controversial genre. And this also involves other period variables, such as that *The Great Dictator* received a better critical and commercial response than Lubitsch's *To Be or Not To Be*, having been released before America's 1941 entry into the war.

DUCK SOUP

That the Marx Brothers frequently excel at black comedy and the surreal, particularly in *Duck Soup*, should come as no surprise to the student of their childhood. The best slant at the dark side of these New York City children of immigrants was the straight-talking autobiography of the cinematically silent Harpo (1888–1964):

When I was a kid there really was no future. Struggling through one twenty-four-hour span was rough enough without brooding about the next one. You could laugh about the past, because you'd been lucky enough to survive it. But mainly there was only a present to worry about.[1]

Getting around the city was like traveling in a war zone. The young Marx Brothers fell back on several different huckster techniques. These ranged from the most bold of cons—assuming the ethnic dialect of the gang whose space had been violated—to carrying some expendable trinkets with which to bribe one's way out of trouble.

It was a period (early twentieth century) when American literature was discovering "naturalism" (muckraking realism), with subject matter often focused on the plight of this country's more recent immigrants. While the Marx family was not straight out of Upton Sinclair's *The Jungle*, times were not easy; and Harpo's autobiography sometimes has a matter-of-fact naturalism about it that can be shocking. For example, his description of what might be labeled the East River breast-stroke—the "pushing away" motion of your hands—was "the only way you could keep the sewage and garbage out of your face" when swimming.[2]

The poverty-stricken Marx homefront was, moreover, depleted by a fifth columnist within their midst. Young Chico (1887–1961) had a lifelong gambling addiction which resulted in his pawning anything in, or out of, sight. Groucho (1890–1977) observed that the local pawnshop had more Marx family items than their flat.[3] To safeguard possessions, Chico's habit inspired surreal acts of defense by his brothers. For instance, Harpo made a cherished pocket watch Chico-proof by removing its hands. Thus, unlike the nightmare symbolism of a handless clock in Ingmar Bergman's art-house *Wild Strawberries* (1957), Harpo's action was an offbeat comic victory of life —perfectly in keeping with the later surrealism of the Marx Brothers films.

The dark comedy catalyst in their movies is the dominating, fast-talking Groucho, with his other-worldly greasepaint mustache and eyebrows. In real life the most moody of the brothers (thus his name), he was the odd boy out as a child. Like the young Jewish Franz Kafka, Groucho was a bookish loner haunted by his inability to receive adequate attention from his mother.

Part of Groucho's less-than-favored position with Minnie Marx was based in appearance. Older brothers Chico and Harpo had decidedly Germanic looks, with light hair and fair complexions. Also Germanic in appearance, Minnie thought of herself as more German than Jewish, and as her older boys' light hair darkened with age, she kept it light with peroxide. Groucho's prominent nose, dark, coarse hair, and dark complexion favored the family's Jewish heritage. His bookish nature added to the estrangement with his mother, who nicknamed him "der dunkeler" (the dark one) because he was somehow melancholy or suspect for reading. Ironically, this label also reinforced the fact that he looked more Jewishly dark than the favored Chico and Harpo.

Kafka biographer Frederick Karl blamed the writer's alienation in part on being a German-speaking Jew in the increasingly nationalistic Czech Prague of pre–World War I Europe—a phenomenon Karl likened to being an immigrant to America during the same period.[4] Whether or not one makes this one more connection with Groucho, both young men felt that their Jewishness made them outsiders, both aspired to be writers, and both were acutely aware that language (like life) was not always what it seemed.

Unlike Kafka, however, Groucho was able to vent his frustrations in the most public of forums—motion pictures. While Kafka was the thinly veiled antihero/victim of his fiction (such as central character "K" of *The Castle*), Groucho's film persona made comic mincemeat of threatening authority figures. Though Kafka died before Groucho and his brothers entered film, he certainly would have enjoyed the antics of the mustachioed one, especially since Kafka was a great movie fan of the iconoclastic Chaplin. This Prague writer saw Charlie's rebellious Tramp "as the spokesman against the machine world, in which men could no longer manage to do what they liked with their lives."[5]

Interestingly enough, the reason *Duck Soup*, the nihilistic attack on the absurdity of government, was a critical and commercial failure was its overly dark comic approach to a then vulnerable establishment. Sociological film historian (and now screenwriter and director) Andrew Bergman insightfully expands upon this unfortunate timing: "After a year of Roosevelt's energy and activism [e.g., the flurry of New Deal legislation], government, no matter what else it might be, was no absurdity."[6] In 1993 Dick Cavett and I disagreed about this point on Arts and Entertainment's nationally broadcast cable *Biography* episode on Groucho. Cavett felt period viewers would not have walked out on *Duck Soup* simply because it undercut the government. But this misses the real thrust of the Bergman position (with which many historians, myself included, concur). The tenor of the times was such—"Give the new president a chance"—that most potential patrons avoided theaters showing *Duck Soup* in the first place.

Paradoxically, while Groucho thumbs his nose at authority, he often operates from a seeming position of establishment power. This is best demonstrated by his Dictator Rufus T. Firefly in *Duck Soup*. As the leader of mythical kingdom Freedonia, Groucho's character is abrasively direct in his plans. For instance, Firefly baldly asks Margaret Dumont's high-society snob Mrs. Teasdale, "Will you marry me? Did he [her late husband] leave you any money? Answer the second question first." Besides such self-serving directness, Firefly is constantly blitzing Teasdale with in-your-face comic insults, such as, "Married! I can see you now bending over a hot stove, but I can't see the stove."

Though Dumont's character is an ongoing target in *Duck Soup* (and other Marx Brothers films), Groucho addresses everyone in this assault manner. In *Horse Feathers* (1932) he tells the Huxley College president his character is replacing, "Why don't you go home to your wife? I'll tell you what. I'll go home to your wife and outside of the improvements she'll never know the difference."

Despite such nastiness, it is hard to resist him. I was reminded of this conflict (affection for a comedian whose shtick puts new emphasis on the cliché "I killed them") when recently reviewing the in-your-face lethal style of Billy Crystal's film character Buddy Young, Jr. in *Mr. Saturday Night* (1992). For example, there is Buddy's historical footnote, "As Mrs. Einstein said to her husband, Albert, 'What the hell do you know?'" Here is brutal humor that also complements the often misogynous nature of Groucho's persona. One can imagine him enjoying Crystal's film.

The fact that most Groucho "subjects" just accept his verbal steamrolling, or are oblivious to it, is an interesting commentary on the then-modern citizen. This is especially true when one considers how Firefly's comic dictatorship in *Duck Soup* parallels the rise of Hitler in Germany. Most period reviews were too close to the events to make the connection, though a few critiques did not ignore the foreign ties. To illustrate, *New York Sun* critic John S. Cohen, Jr., found the film's eventual comic war "highly pertinent, looking at the volatile 1930s map of Europe."[7]

This Groucho phenomenon of people loving him regardless of what he does to them is not limited, of course, to *Duck Soup*. What makes this movie unique, as well as its black comedy reason for being highlighted here, is that *Duck Soup* is the only time Groucho's huckster has a chance to gamble with lives. And gamble he does. Early in the movie his Firefly sings that anyone not cutting him in on the graft will be executed.

Later he takes Freedonia into a war just for the hell of it. As Firefly leads the country's cabinet in "The Country's Going to War," a big production number peppered with several musical styles and an inspired satire of how patriotism can be cranked up among the people to make armed conflict seem like a day in the country, Groucho's mesmerizing comedy presence has a frightening side. One need only substitute any number of real charismatic despots who have manipulated their citizens into war. His anti-establishment, anti-stuffed-shirt tendencies do not prevent him from comically abusing the power his movie character has or to which he aspired.

Fittingly, *Duck Soup*'s "actual war cruelly burlesques all the horrors of 1914-18 [World War I]."[8] (See Chapter 1 for more on the appropriateness of this conflict being satirized.) The greatest horror of the war was poor leadership. And what qualifies with more dark humor than Firefly mistakenly machine-gunning some of his own soldiers? Prepared to give himself the "Firefly Medal" for heroism when this error is brought to his attention, he slickly covers the mistake with a bribe, which he immediately gets back. It is such an apt moment because 1930s critics often noted his "machine gun" verbal patter that metaphorically tore people apart. How appropriate, then, that he should use the real weapon in his most over-the-top, dangerously comic role. Moreover, despite the World War I foundation, "Groucho's appearing in every [war] scene with a different uniform, from a Davy Crockett hat to a poilu's [French soldier, 1914-1918] tin helmet, becomes not simply a spoof of history, but a matter of 'The Universal Soldier [victim].' "9

Firefly gets Freedonia into war because he is a periodic victim of runaway paranoia. Normally Marx Brothers films present this comic slant in everyday situations. For instance, there is his secretary's omission in *Animal Crackers* (1930) of a dictated "Hungerdunger" from correspondence to the law firm of Hungerdunger, Hungerdunger, Hungerdunger, Hungerdunger, and MacCormick. Groucho is bent out of shape by the mistake: "You've left out a Hungerdunger! You left out the main one, too! Thought you could slip one over on me, didn't you, eh?"

Again, what puts *Duck Soup* in a special Marx Brothers category is that Groucho's paranoia here leads to life-threatening black humor extremes. His looniness over the intentions of a rival nation's Ambassador Trentino (Louis Calhern) is the ultimate cause of war between their two countries. The scene in question is innocently initiated by Margaret Dumont's figure:

Mrs. Teasdale, you did a noble deed! I'd be unworthy of the trust that's been placed in me if I didn't do everything within my power to keep our beloved Freedonia at peace with the world. I'll be only too happy to meet Ambassador Trentino and offer him, on behalf of my country, the right hand of good fellowship. [happy] And I feel sure that he will accept this gesture in the spirit in which it is offered. . . . [less than happy] But suppose he doesn't? A fine thing that'll be! I hold out my hand and he refuses to accept it! That'll add a lot to my prestige, won't it? [angry] Me , the head of a country, snubbed by a foreign ambassador! Who does he think he is that he can come here and make a sap out of me in front of all my people? Think of it.

The scene continues as a comically indignant Groucho paces about, waiting on Trentino. His Firefly soon explodes to Teasdale, "I hold out my hand and that hyena refuses to accept it! Why, the cheap, four-flushing swine! He'll never get away with it, I tell you." Naturally, when Trentino does enter, the totally lathered Firefly verbally lambastes him before the astonished man can say a word: "So! You refuse to shake hands with me, eh?" Firefly then slaps Trentino with his gloves. Not surprisingly, this leads to war. Marx Brothers scholar Martin A. Gardner, in an unpublished dissertation on the team, has insightfully connected Groucho's paranoia here to American historian Richard Hofstader's suggestion that this country's foreign policy has often been based on a psychotic preconception that an evil foreign conspiracy is out to do dastardly deeds.[10]

In terms of film history, Groucho's *Duck Soup* interpretation of a persecution complex anticipates the even darker paranoia of *Dr. Strangelove*'s General Ripper. Played by Sterling Hayden, Ripper starts an apocalyptic atomic war because he believes the fluoridation of America's post–World War II water supply to be an evil plot hatched by the Soviet Union to communize this country. Although *Dr. Strangelove* does not offer the viewer a case history of Ripper's paranoia, one need not be Sigmund Freud to suggest this is the action of a sexually frustrated individual. It seems that Hayden's character links his impotence to fluoridation and the violation of his precious bodily fluids. He becomes the ultimate antihero; in attempting to exert his manhood he extinguishes mankind.

The General Ripper sexual-frustration scenario makes for a provocative analogy with Groucho. Given the mustachioed one's dirty-old-man persona, a regular "King Leer," this might at first seem comic blasphemy. But when teamed with Thelma Todd in *Monkey Business* (1931) and *Horse Feathers* (1932), there is the suggestion that Groucho's sexual screen bravado is mere show. Unlike Margaret Dumont, who is neither physically attractive nor frequently mentally attuned to Groucho's amorous innuendo, Todd is both inviting and *inviting*. During their cabin scene from *Monkey Business*, she seems to be on the same steamy wavelength as Groucho. She even quotes from an earlier delightful bit of his dialogue, a comic anthem to hot-bloodedness: "I want excitement. I want to ha-cha-cha-cha." She then breaks into dance, as Groucho did after uttering these lines. That he does not take her up on the "ha-cha-cha-cha" (period film censorship not withstanding) is an interesting calling of Groucho's sexual bluff. Moreover, as a 1930s studio publicist for the team later observed, "Todd always gave the appearance of being far too worldly and conniving a woman ever to be taken in by Groucho's wooing."[11] Appropriately, the wedding that closes *Horse Feathers* has Todd marrying Groucho *plus* Chico and Harpo.

Though given little screen time, a variation of the Thelma Todd character also surfaces in *Duck Soup*. The sexy Vera Marcal (Raquel Torres), accomplice to Trentino, catches Groucho's attention by suggestively murmuring that maybe they could dance some time. But he seems intimidated by the possibilities. Groucho later reconsiders, after she places a hand on his chest and risquély asks, "Oh, Your Excellency, isn't there something I can do?" He provocatively replies, "Yes, but I'll talk to you about that later." Yet nothing comes of this. Maybe Groucho's sexual bravado is a search for a metaphorical mirror— a woman who would simply reflect back how fascinating he attempts to be. But each open invitation of a sexy Todd or Marcal breeds antiheroic frustration: he cannot perform. No wonder he seems more secure around Dumont.

And like the later General Ripper, the rest of Groucho's activity as *Duck Soup*'s dictator has him waging war. His Firefly leaves no sexually frustrated notes pertaining to fluoridation at his battlefield post, but even here there are reference to such antiheroic moments. To illustrate, in one scene he gets a huge vase stuck on his head and observes "The last time this happened to me I was crawling under a bed." Marx critic Allen Eyles calls this scene "another glimpse of the thwarted Casanova."[12] Regardless of how you read it, Groucho's dark comedy persona has a certain sexual vulnerability to it, despite (and possibly better explaining) the showy swagger. In addition, it provides a fresh slant to other scenes, such as the dialogue between Groucho and Dumont as they board the ship in *A Night at the Opera* (1935). Her Mrs. Claypool innocently asks, "Are you sure you have everything, Otis?" In a much too defensive manner he replies, "I've never had any complaints yet."

Unlike the democratic film populism of Marx Brothers contemporary Frank Capra, Groucho needs no reason to instantly turn on a character. Therein lies the dangerous attraction of his persona, for he is forever stuck in the attack mode—often, but not always, for the good. Thus, one might make a Groucho–Capra comparison to reiterate the sometimes disturbing potential of the mustachioed one.

Both *Duck Soup* and Capra's *Meet John Doe* (1941), though in decidedly different comedy manners, provide a warning against fascism. But whereas Capra's somewhat tarnished populist (with all-American Gary Cooper in the title role) still plays the honest hero eventually, in *Duck Soup* Groucho's Firefly *is* the danger, however entertaining. After *Duck Soup's* concluding Freedonia victory, one would assume it will be back to crooked government business as usual.

Of course, Groucho's extreme dark-humor tendencies in *Duck Soup* are softened through victimization by Chico and Harpo (see illustration 9). For instance, Groucho's Freedonia leader is recklessly dangerous but Chico's character (Chicolini, the one-time peanut vendor) is a spy, and briefly a soldier, for the opposing army. In the spirit of the Marxes, one is tempted to pun that while President Franklin D. Roosevelt gave 1930s Americans a "New Deal," in *Duck Soup* Groucho and company provided a comic false shuffle. The praise is earned, as long as one does not forget the question posited by comedy historian Gerald Weales: "Where are these Piped Pipers [Groucho and company] leading us?"[13] That is, with the mustachioed one there is forever the danger that he will take us over the precipice . . . the ultimate accenting of "to die laughing." Such a trait is best showcased in *Duck Soup*.

Humor theorist Neil Schmitz offers a final slant on the Marxes as dark comedy artists. During the production of *Duck Soup*, writer and team friend Herman Mankiewicz kiddingly described Groucho's brothers as a "mute" (Harpo) and a "Guinea" (Chico), a generally derogatory slang term for an Italian.[14] Schmitz then observes that three of the alleged identities of the mysterious title character in Herman Melville's watershed black humor novel *The Confidence Man* (1857; see Chapter 1) are a fast-talking hustler (a capsule definition of Groucho), a mute, and a "Guinea"—though in this case the term referred to a black person from the West African area of Guinea.

Schmitz's link might seem like a long shot, but it translates as another argument for the Marxes to be seen as dark film comedy transition-figures. *The Confidence Man* showcases the ultimate huckster as existing in any number of forms—matching the many scam vulnerabilities of man. The Marxes merely represent modern

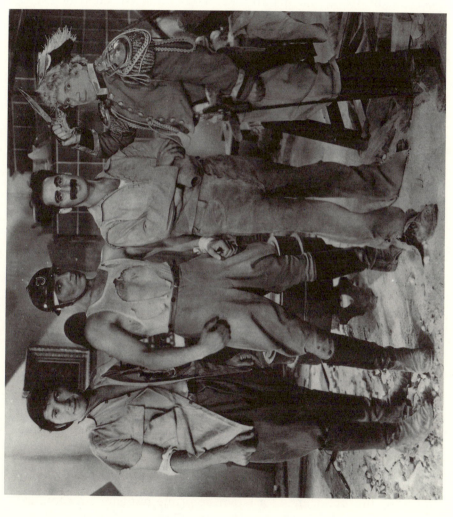

9. Left to right, Chico, Zeppo, Groucho, and Harpo Marx in *Duck Soup.*

actualizations of three Melville types: Groucho's machine-gun talker, Harpo's surrealist mute, and Chico's ethnic wise fool.

Moreover, the team as led—or misled—by Groucho personifies the dark-side readings of Melville's novel by modern critics. Just as the culminating identity of Melville's confidence man has been seen as the devil, the life-and-death–wielding Groucho of *Duck Soup* is a fellow three out of four fallen archangels would follow. Reviewers during the early 1930s saw it this way, when Groucho and his brothers were periodically labeled "comedemons."[15]

THE GREAT DICTATOR

The childhood of Charlie Chaplin (born 1889) was even more desperate than that of the Marxes. His alcoholic father abandoned the family very early on, and his mother, Hannah, had trouble supporting Charlie and his brother Sydney. In 1896 the family was forced to enter the Lambeth Borough Workhouse in London. Chaplin painfully notes in his 1964 autobiography that they were considered "inmates of the 'booby hatch,' the slang expression for workhouse."[16] And for a time Charlie was in London's Hanwell School for Orphans and Destitute Children.

The family would occasionally reunite on its own. But Chaplin's mother's mental health had begun to deteriorate, and she would be institutionalized before Charlie was nine. There would later be a temporary recovery, but she soon suffered a breakdown from which she would never recuperate. The now often child of the streets would eventually find modest security as a touring performer before he became a teenager. But this Dickensian childhood would forever haunt his later work, as would his propensity for dark comedy.

Fittingly, Chaplin also had a Victorian fascination for the macabre. His autobiography reflects the comedian's interest in grizzly tales: the murder scene of a Japanese prime minister, an acquaintance who developed leprosy, a clinical examination of what the electric chair does to its victim, often vivid descriptions of the suicides of several friends, a chance meeting with a man condemned to hang, the story of a Buddhist monk who, because he had spent a lifetime floating in oil, allegedly had skin so embryonically soft that a finger could be put through it, and on and on.

Charlie Chaplin, Jr. (from the comedian's marriage to second wife Lita Grey) suggests in his affectionate biography *My Father, Charlie Chaplin* (1960) that the comedy star's interest in the subject was very much like that of Charles Dickens, and invariably the elder Chaplin's bedtime stories were extracts from the novelist, with a "macabre cast to them."[17] Later this son theorizes that his father's favorite fiction writers were Dickens and Guy de Maupassant "because of the peculiar combination of the humorous and the macabre in their works."[18] Interestingly, though Charles, Jr. does not take the analogy any further, each of the other fiction favorites he notes of his father—Edgar Allan Poe, Oscar Wilde, and Mark Twain—also specializes in black comedy.

This son adds that his father's close friendship with Dr. Cecil Reynolds, who later committed suicide, was largely based on the fact that Chaplin, Sr. was "attracted to the macabre, and as a surgeon, Dr. Reynolds had plenty of this kind of fare to serve him."[19] These observations are also consistent with those of the comedian's prodigal son (from his marriage to fourth wife Oona O'Neill) Michael Chaplin, in *I couldn't smoke the grass on my father's lawn* (1966), right down to more comically grizzly bedtime stories— except that now the tales are of Chaplin's own invention and fall under the general heading of the "Nice Old Man" stories. One of Michael's favorites ends with a baby falling in the sea and the "Nice Old Man pushing the pram in after him and went [sic] off to spend the money the parents had given him to look after the baby."[20] Chaplin was a great fan of Luis Buñuel's often shocking surrealist films. Geraldine Chaplin, the comedian's oldest child by Oona, has said that her father enjoyed playfully frightening his children by describing moments from these movies. Geraldine shared this with me and other Chaplin scholars at a 1989 Paris gathering celebrating the 100th anniversary of her father's birth.

It seems appropriate, moreover, that the darkest story in Chaplin's autobiography manages to briefly find its way back to the comedian's most praised work, *The Gold Rush* (1925). The tale in question involves the ill-fated Donner Party, a group of mid-nineteenth-century American pioneers who resorted to cannibalism when snow stranded them in the mountains. Chaplin drew heavily upon this real-life tragedy for the movie, sometimes called the greatest of all film comedies. His screen persona Charlie plays a starving miner in the frozen North, with an equally hungry partner who hallucinates that the "Little Fellow" is a chicken. Charlie must do darkly comic battle for his life. An initial delaying process involved cooking and eating one of Charlie's shoes. This celebrated and much film-anthologized scene drew from the fact that some members of the Donner Party had eaten their moccasins.

Unfortunately, Chaplin's autobiography spends little effort on his interest in mixing the macabre and the comic, beyond observing the paradox "that tragedy stimulates the spirit of ridicule. . . . We must laugh in the face of our helplessness . . . or go insane."[21]

Regardless, one need not focus on Chaplin signature scenes (like the boot-eating routine) to showcase black comedy elements in his work. He liberally peppered most of his films with examples, such as comic violence in *Easy Street* (1917), trench warfare laughs in *Shoulder Arms* (1918), or fleeting thoughts of pitching an abandoned baby down the sewer in *The Kid* (1921). Indeed, the tramp's view of man at the start of *The Kid* is less than positive. Having just had second-story tenement garbage accidently rain down on him as he walks through an alley, his first assumption upon seeing the child is that she, too, had been discarded from above. (For more on dark comedy victims as garbage, see Chapter 2.) Even Charlie's "east-west" feet were based on the real life deformity of a turn-of-the-century London cabdriver, just as *The Great Dictator* was drawn from history's ultimate madman.

Maybe the most perverse dark-comedy slant on Chaplin doing a Hitler film is that the two men had several things in common besides that little mustache. Without going into the detail of some Chaplin biographers (such as Julian Smith's *CHAPLIN*, 1984), there are numerous parallels between the director and the dictator, from being born a mere four days apart to having alcoholic fathers, and mothers they worshipped. Both managed to survive childhood poverty and fears of family histories with insanity. And both were control freaks easily reduced to childish behavior if things did not go their way—a situation often minimized by surrounding themselves with yes-men.

While the watershed dark comedy status of Chaplin's *Monsieur Verdoux* (1947) has been examined in Chapter 2, *Dictator* was his first full embrace of the genre. And as illustrated at the start of this chapter, *Dictator* merits further study along black humor lines. The period response to the picture is also provocatively important, especially since it proved to be Chaplin's greatest box office hit versus the initial commercial fiasco of *Duck Soup*.

A central theme of dark comedy is portraying man as beast. And what could be a more apropos example than Chaplin's darkly comic rendering of a beast-like Hitler in *The Great Dictator*? This is never more apparent than in the film's initial presentation of Hynkel (Chaplin) the dictator. The scene is a delicious travesty of Hitler as an orator, with its "Demokratien shtunk!" and "Frei Sprecken Shtunk!" allowing Chaplin to showcase his exceptional talents for both verbal mimicry and pointed political satire. This acclaimed performance of German gibberish (echoed in the name Chaplin gives the dictator—Adenoid Hynkel) is complemented by the comedian's ongoing ability to give his work numerous levels of comedy richness. Thus, while one first laughs at Chaplin's parody of German's guttural sounds, the speech gradually disintegrates into an angry tirade of incoherent scene which manages to be simultaneously funny and frightening.

In a period article from the *New York World-Telegram*, Chaplin said, "I listened to Hitler on the radio. The mad, bitter voice. I listened only a few times. Then I had it, and we worked out some ordinary German words every American could understand. The rest was gibberish."[22] As if playing off of his comments on gibberish, the comedian later insightfully observed, "Mine made just as much sense as his do. It's not the words, it's the tone. Makes for complete mass hysteria. That voice bangs on your brain, and before you know it you're cheering."[23]

Hynkel's metamorphosis to a beast-like state during this time is punctuated by more traditional moments of visual Chaplin comedy, such as the microphone that recoils from his verbal attack or the beating of his chest like a gorilla. But even such physical comedy is not entirely divorced from Hitler. During the production of *Dictator* Chaplin was intrigued by some newsreel footage of Hitler where the dictator seemed to do a little dance after the signing of the French surrender. Chaplin told friend Tim Durant, "This guy is one of the greatest actors I've ever seen."[24]

At the end of Hynkel's gibberish tirade, the voiceover narrator/translator chillingly informs the viewer that the dictator has been discussing the Jewish race. Like everything else the narrator has told the viewer, this does not come as a surprise. But whereas earlier intrusions had been either comically unnecessary (translat-

ing "Libertad shtunk!") or a simple parody of "diplomatic" decoding
("Demokratien shtunk!" becoming "Democracy is fragrant")—obvi-
ousness here is the message of the movie—such racist slander was
the Hitler norm. Thus, even the use of the voiceover has changed
by scene's end, just as Chaplin has altered one's response to the
dictator from seeing a buffoon to viewing a monster. (A comically
lighter variation of this scene occurs in Woody Allen's black
comedy *Bananas*, 1971, with Castro as the target dictator.)

Although the shock value of Hynkel's mesmerizingly violent
speech is one way to demonstrate man as beast, the genre often
demonstrates how the mere thought of sex reduces man to the most
base and selfish of animal needs. Even in the more censorship-con-
scious days of *Dictator*, Chaplin manages to footnote this obsession.
For example, during the aforementioned Hynkel address, the over-
heated Hynkel stops to put a glass of drinking water down the front
of his pants—a slapstick commentary on the almost sexual nature
of this hateful, impassioned tirade. Along more directly sexual
lines, Chaplin later has the dictator snort at his pretty secretary like
a mating bull and take her in his arms (accompanied by another
snort of passion), only to be interrupted by the phone.

The second basic theme of black comedy is the absurdity of the
modern world, where the individual does not count. This victimization is realized in the Tramp-like Jewish barber (also played by
Chaplin) in *Dictator*. Suffering from a World War I injury, the barber
has been an amnesia victim until the eve of World War II. By this
time Hynkel/Hitler has already established his persecution of the
Jewish people. The barber's twenty-odd-years blank spot also acts
as an ironic metaphor for a real world that somehow missed the
ugly rise of Hitler during the same period. Regardless, the barber
is constantly endangered by a Hynkel-led racism that is patently
absurd. Indeed, it is the dark comedy absurdity upon which the
movie is founded. As Holocaust historian Ilan Avisar has stated,
with Chaplin playing both Hynkel and the barber, what better way
is there to demonstrate ludicrousness—"the great [aryan] dictator
looks so exactly like the small Jew that at the end of the movie the
closest colleagues and ardent admirers of the former cannot distin-
guish between the two."[25] (For additional information on World
War I and its unique relationship to this genre, as well as ties
between the Holocaust and dark humor, see Chapter 1.)

As a paradoxical aside, the little barber is even buffeted about in extra-filmic terms. At the close of the film, where mistaken identity allows the barber to speak in place of Hynkel, one quickly realizes that the antihero has really been displaced by Chaplin the impassioned filmmaker . . . calling for peace. Period critics protested this stepping out of character. The comedian replied, "The time had come when I simply had to stop kidding. They had their laughs. . . . But now I wanted to make them stop being so damned contented. This isn't just another war."[26]

In Chaplin's defense, several other contemporary major productions with political themes also included self-conscious conclusions. For example, William Dieterle's controversial film about the Spanish Civil War, *Blockade* (1938), ended with Henry Fonda dropping any pretense of story and making an impassioned plea to the film audience. John Ford's 1940 adaptation of *The Grapes of Wrath*, with Ma Joad's (Jane Darwell) uplifting final speech—tacked on by producer Darryl Zanuck to avoid a pessimistic ending, remains a controversial contradiction of John Steinbeck's original novel. And Alfred Hitchcock's stylish Nazi warning, *Foreign Correspondent* (1940), concludes with an emotional radio broadcast by a reporter (Joel McCrea) that quickly becomes a self-conscious message to America.

While period critics were less than enthralled by *Dictator*'s close, in the early 1940s Chaplin received requests to repeat the address, both at public rallies and over the radio. What has not been discussed, however, is the dark comedy implications of the speech. Whether it is aesthetically appropriate to step out of character is not the issue here. Despite the heartfelt feelings of Chaplin, the fact that he believed the little barber was not up to the situation makes the close pure wishful thinking . . . a fantasy exit. Ironically, later black comedies often purposely and mockingly embrace an impossible fantasy close, such as Yossarian's alleged escape at the close of *Catch-22*. It also helps explain why Chaplin's radio and rally performances of the speech, divorced from both the movie and the genre expectations of dark comedy, were popular.

Returning to the second theme of black humor, absurdity, this phenomenon is usually presented in two ways—through the chaos of an unordered universe and through the flaws of mortal man. Both are found in *Dictator*. The first and most fundamental simply has man being victimized for merely trying to exist. One has only to think of the World War I scenes that open the film, where the barber has the most frustratingly dangerous time playing soldier. An example would be his attempts to get away from the misfired cannon shell that anticipates his every move. Of course, the mere fact that he is reminiscent of the Tramp adds empathy and connects the viewer to an earlier body of work often grounded in comic chaos. In fact, this cannonshell which forever manages to point at the barber reminds one of *The Gold Rush* scene where Charlie is trying to get away from the rifle over which Big Jim McKay (Mack Swain) and Black Larsen (Tom Murray) are fighting. No matter where Charlie goes, this weapon only has eyes for him.

For all the comic frightfulness of an unordered universe, man has been a strong contributor to the absurdity of the dark comedy world. Manmade absurdity is the result of both general species incompetence and its perpetuation in human institutions. Hynkel the dictator is black comedy's most basic example of species incompetence—the crazed person in power playing God. Fittingly, celebrated Chaplin scholar Charles J. Maland reminds us that Hynkel is from Tomania, "A blend of the word for food poisoning and the suffix 'mania'—madness."[27]

Despite the physical resemblance between Hitler and Chaplin's Tramp, the filmmaker was not just playing one crazed leader. In a period publication Chaplin said, "I tried to make [Hynkel] a composite of all dictators. . . . Every actor has a yearning to play [the megalomaniac] Napoleon. I've got it out of my system. I've played Napoleon and Hitler and the mad Czar Paul all rolled into one."[28] Interestingly enough, during production the film was called *Dictators*, presumably because of Jack Oakie's inspired satirical performance as Benzino Napoloni, a scene-stealing caricature of Mussolini.

Dictator also displays the beginning stages of this craziness being institutionalized. For instance, witness the periodic interruptions by Field Marshal Herring (Billy Gilbert, a character patterned after fat Nazi leader Hermann Goering), to demonstrate new military inventions which always end with the casually dark-comic demise of each inventor. Institutionalized absurdity eventually means man's chaos-making abilities attain irrevocable steamroller proportions, which is the precise point reached by *Dictator* when Chaplin introduces his compromised controversial close.

In another 1940 article Chaplin revealed a provocatively personal view on the dangers of even the most modest example of institutionalization. He found himself acting arrogantly abusive by merely wearing the elaborate but regimental Nazi-like uniform called for by his Hynkel part. And this was off-camera, before any shooting was done. To Chaplin, the "uniform undoubtedly is a great deal to blame [for Nazi superiority]. The wearing of it often creates a false value of being better than one's fellow man, when in most instances the reverse is the case."[29]

Though a correlation between a uniform and threatening authority might be tied to several nationalities, it is especially pertinent to Germany, a country created by the battlefield "diplomacy" of "Iron Chancellor" Otto von Bismarck (1815–1898). Born in Prussia, a North German country noted for its warlike and militaristic spirit, Bismarck would unite through war what had previously been a loose confederation of German states. For Bismarck the military was the state, and what was good for the military (uniform) was more important than the individual citizen. Needless to say, this view was later greatly admired by Hitler.

Obviously, Chaplin skewers that perspective throughout the *Dictator*. And he constantly comes back to the movie's dark overtones, such as the late film observation of Hynkel's Minister of the Interior (Henry Daniell), "In the future each man will serve the interests of the state with absolute obedience. Let him who refuses beware." Chaplin's ongoing derailment of that view is best captured in naming the character Garbitsch, a punning put-down of Goebbels, Hitler's propaganda minister.

Appropriately, Chaplin manages to include uniform-directed humor throughout the movie. For instance, in Hynkel's opening speech he warns his nation, "We must sacrifice, tighten der belten." Immediately, the heavy Herring rises to do so, only to have his belt split when he sits down, sending its clanging attachments (such as his dress sword) to the ground. Later in the scene Herring accidently butts Hynkel down a flight of stairs, and the dictator comically strips the medals off the plump one's uniform.

In the Jewish ghetto, storm troopers paint "Jew" on the barber's window. The altercation that follows finds the Tramp-like barber whitewashing a trooper with the latter's own paint brush. The uniform-directed humor becomes broader during the next trooper invasion of the ghetto—the barber escapes after throwing a bucket of whitewash on a soldier.

There are numerous other uniform-directed scenes of comedy, such as Hynkel putting on a pompous cape that acts more like a straitjacket, a near foodfight with Oakie's Napoloni, and another Hynkel attack on fat Herring—including ripping off buttons and medals, tearing his gargantuan pants, snapping his suspenders. . . .

On another comedy level, the use of a uniform acts as the ultimate turning point for the film. On the eve of Tomania's invasion of Austerlich (Austria), Hynkel goes duck hunting and the barber escapes from a concentration camp. The dictator, amusingly dressed in what might be called "the basic Tyrolean short pants, suspenders, and feathered cap duck hunting ensemble" is promptly mistaken as the barber and arrested. And the fleeing Tomanian—uniformed barber is just as quickly accepted as Hynkel. Indeed, at this point the uniform has a rather Pied Piper effect, as armed troops methodically fall in around the barber as he walks toward the Tomania-Austerlich border. The uniform, or the absence thereof, has made all the difference.

The power of the uniform might even be used as a provocative explanation for the controversial conclusion, when filmmaker Chaplin seems to speak for the Jewish barber. It could be argued that the coat gave the Tramp-like figure the sudden assertiveness to speak out strongly for peace.

Regardless of one's perspective on this hypothesis, a final note about uniforms merits inclusion. Chaplin and Hitler were both great fans of the 1920s film movement German Expressionism. The most acclaimed movie of this school was *The Last Laugh* (1924), in which a doorman bases his self-respect and importance upon a military-like porter's uniform. Only this seems to impress his neighbors, because when he loses the position and uniform due to age, these same people turn on him.

The third theme of black comedy is the omnipresence of death. It permeates everything about the *Dictator*. This fact escalated further after World War II, when the extent of the Nazi crimes against humanity became known. Chaplin himself said that had he known of the actual concentration camp horrors he would not have made the film.[30] Consequently, when Garbitsch tells Hynkel that the Jewish prisoners are complaining about the quality of the sawdust in their bread, the dictator's indignant reply is that much darker today—"It's from the finest lumber our mills can supply."

The most entertaining *Dictator* examples of black humor death involve the nonchalant attitude toward loss of life in the Hynkel camp itself. Billy Gilbert's amusingly plump Herring often acts as a quasi-master of ceremonies in many of these scenes. For instance, Herring interrupts the dictator so that a bullet-proof suit can be demonstrated. The inventor steps forward and Hynkel tests it by shooting him. The man drops dead and the dictator nonchalantly remarks, "Far from perfect." On another occasion Herring brings in the inventor of a parachute hat. The patriotic fellow heils and jumps out the window. Hynkel and Herring momentarily lean out, and then the dictator observes, "Herring, *why* do you waste my time like this?"

Herring's most enthusiastic interruption, and consequently his most memorable dark comedy moment, occurs when he breathlessly enters Hynkel's chambers and happily announces the invention of a wonderful poison gas: "It will kill *everybody!*" Though intended for enemies of the Hynkel partly (and a macabre anticipation of the concentration camps), Herring's gung-ho eagerness to share this seemingly blanket endorsement of death is most appropriate for a dark comedy.

All great art works upon several levels. In *Dictator* there are two particular metaphorical death scenes that are especially striking. The first occurs early while the barber is part of a World War I attack. A fog rolls in and when it leaves the little fellow finds himself still advancing . . . but with the enemy! Though the barber has obviously lost his own unit in the fog, it also represents a comically chilling symbol of how his fellow Germans could one day see him as a fellow citizen and the next (as in a fog) be transfixed into his potential killers.

The second metaphorical scene involving death is *Dictator's* celebrated segment where Hynkel does his ballet of world conquest with a balloon-like world globe. Eventually he squeezes too tightly and the "world" blows up in his face. The standard text book interpretation is that his mad plans will not come to pass. But in terms of black comedy the symbolism should be taken further. This is a genre which often embraces the apocalypse, real or imagined. Consequently, win or lose, Hynkel's (or any other crazed leader's) dance of death is about the ongoing threat to civilation as we know it. Indeed, Hitler's final military orders, thankfully not carried out, were a scorched earth policy to his own defeated country. One has only to note the result of General Ripper's plan for world conquest in *Dr. Strangelove*—world destruction.

Fittingly, as if acting as a dark humor spokesperson, Chaplin stated at the 1940 release of *Dictator*, "There is a healthy thing in laughing at the grimmest things in life, laughter at death even. *Shoulder Arms* . . . had to do with men marching off to war. . . . Laughter is a tonic, the relief, the surcease from pain."[31]

Nothing gave more credence to Chaplin's commentary than the *Dictator*'s reception in Great Britain, a country at war with Germany since 1939. While controversy helped fuel the movie's box office success in the still-at-peace United States, Britain's reception was without reservation. The latter country was in need of comic bolstering. As a period footnote, the musical fantasy *The Wizard of Oz* (1939) had done only indifferent box office business in the United States. In Britain, however, it had a much more successful commercial run, because this country embraced the underdog story as a metaphor for their war with the terrible Hitler. Indeed, the country's air force often referred to military retaliation against Germany as being "off to see the Wizard."

Regardless, it seems more than fitting that dark comedy absurdist Franz Kafka's (1893–1924) favorite film comedian, Chaplin, had always represented to him a spokesman for people who "could no longer manage to do what they liked with their lives."[32] Moreover, a Kafka biographer would observe that the writer's perception of his responsibilities as a black humorist "uncannily anticipated the still-to-come films of Charlie Chaplin," such as *Dictator*[33] Kafka stories such as "The Penal Colony" foreshadow the future Nazi concentration camps . . . a place where the writer's three sisters would one day die.

The major difference between the works of Chaplin and Kafka is that the filmmaker was a mainstream artist in a much more high-visibility medium. But both men were dark comedy prophets sending out a warning about the precarious plight of modern man.

TO BE OR NOT TO BE

Unlike Charlie Chaplin and Groucho Marx, who experienced difficult early years, Ernst Lubitsch (1892–1947) was born into a stable and financially secure home. In contrast to Groucho's antiheroic tailor father, nicknamed "Misfit Sam" by customers,

Lubitsch's father was a tailor with a successful men's clothing store in Berlin. However, Lubitsch did share one trauma with the young Marx, having a parent consider him less than handsome. Moreover, Lubitsch's father attempted to use this fact to discourage Ernst's desire to be an actor: "Look at yourself. And you want to go on the stage? If you were at least handsome—but with *your* face? You'll join the business. With me, despite your homely face, you can always earn money." [34]

This admonition did not deter Lubitsch's desire to perform, but it possibly guided it in a particular direction. He decided to be a comedian. But not just any comedian. He became *the* German film comedian of the 1910s. His popularity rivaled that of America's John Bunny and France's Max Linder. While it is an overstatement to suggest, as movie historian Douglas Gomery does, that Lubitsch influenced Chaplin's Tramp, just the mere implication suggests the period significance of Ernst's comedian.[35]

Given the holocaust that was to come, the nature of Lubitsch's screen persona is shockingly ironic—he played an archetypal Jewish schlemiel named Meyer, the comic victim of goodnatured gags. Granted, this was an age of ethnic slapstick the world over. For instance, in American vaudeville at this time Groucho was using a German persona. Still, for Germany's favorite film clown to be a broadly Jewish figure in the decade before the rise of Hitler strongly embraces two givens in dark comedy—it is an absurd world, and people are undependable. One might also put a further provocative twist on this absurdity by suggesting that Lubitsch's stereotypical Jewish clown persona played into the future anti-semitic sentiment of the Nazis. Certainly, this is the position of author Scott Eyman's otherwise sympathetic biography of the director, *Ernst Lubitsch: Laughter in Paradise* (1993).

Regardless, during World War I (1914–1918) Lubitsch added directing to his film comedy resume. And after the conflict he helped bring international attention to German cinema by directing a series of historical costume pageants such as *Carmen* (1918, released in the United States as *Gypsy Blood*, 1921), *Madame Dubarry* (1919, released in the United States as *Passion*, 1920), and *Anne Boleyn* (1920, released in the United States as *Deception*, 1921). Though historical costume films might seem quite a departure from Germany's comedy answer to Chaplin's Tramp, it must be remembered these films became popular in "America for their comic 'humanizing' (i.e., sexualization) of history."[36]

Influential film theorist and psychological historian Siegfried Kracauer, though writing from a minority perspective, saw Lubitsch's costume epics in darker terms: "History, they seemed to say, is an arena reserved for blind and ferocious instincts, a product of devilish machinations forever frustrating our hopes for freedom and happiness."[37] I note this for two reasons. It is a statement equally applicable for dark comedy, and thus befitting *To Be or Not To Be* (1942), despite the film's upbeat close. Second, Lubitsch's historical costume pictures were part of what would be called German Expressionism. The pivotal dichotomy of this national cinema movement was a fate that offered only chaos or a frightening tyrant—common themes to black humor.

Regardless of one's perspective on linking Lubitsch's German film roots with his *To Be or Not To Be*, the director's often comically decadent slant on history in his 1920s productions was possibly an outgrowth of a decidedly dark-humor—oriented Berlin. At that time the city was Europe's own special Sodom and Gomorrah, the continent's cocaine center and S&M nightclub capital. Fittingly, people and products were not always what they seemed. For example, a characteristically macabre period joke in Lubitsch's native Berlin told of a

man left so bereft by the war that he decided to hang himself. He bought a rope, but since it was synthetic, it broke and he fell harmlessly to the floor. Taking this as a sign from heaven that he should live, he went into a cafe for some coffee. But since the coffee, too, was synthetic, it made him ill and he died.[38]

The acclaim accorded Lubitsch's German costume spectacles brought him to the attention of Hollywood's most celebrated couple, Douglas Fairbanks and Mary Pickford. They "imported" him to the United States to direct her, "America's sweetheart," in a more adult role. The film would be the historical costume production *Rosita* (1923). Critically well received, it helped establish Lubitsch in American film, where he would remain until his death in 1947. Pickford, however, would never escape the public's desire to see her in child-woman parts, and *Rosita* would be the most modest of commercial successes.

Less than a month after *Rosita*'s appearance, Chaplin released his ironic comedy of manners *A Woman of Paris* (1923). Lubitsch, already a Chaplin fan, was bowled over by the subtle style of the movie (sans the Tramp character), as was the world film community. It was a watershed work in understated sophisticated comedy. Chaplin gave witty style to sexual innuendo and the risque: "The Chaplin film seems to have given Lubitsch his cue."[39] Without merely imitating Chaplin, Lubitsch was able to put his own distinctive stamp on the comedy of manners. During the 1920s and 1930s this "Lubitsch Touch," probably at its apogee in *Trouble in Paradise* (1932), was required for all cinema afficionados.

Given Lubitsch's longtime interest in , and influence by Chaplin, one cannot help thinking, however, that 1942's *To Be or Not To Be* was, at least in part, an outgrowth of Chaplin's *The Great Dictator* (1940). Once again Chaplin had taken movie comedy into largely uncharted waters. But this time instead of a comedy of manners, it was comedy of the macabre. And period critics made the Chaplin-Lubitsch connection. For instance, the *Baltimore Sun* stated, "He [Lubitsch] dared to use a life-and-death intrigue with the Gestapo as a basis for fun and melodrama, and duplicate Chaplin's feat of counterfeiting Hitler."[40]

To Be is about a company of Polish actors about to stage an anti-Nazi play in Warsaw when the country falls to the Germans. The stars of the troupe are Maria (Carole Lombard) and Joseph Tura (Jack Benny). The latter is an egotistical ham with a propensity to play Hamlet (thus the film title), while Maria is a beautiful flirtatious actress who enjoys making her husband the most cuckolded of men. The company's fervent patriotism and Nazi play acting (complete with costumes and appropriate props) allow them to work for the Allied Polish underground movement.

To Be found neither the critical nor commercial success of *Dictator*. A number of factors contributed to this. An obvious explanation would be that Lubitsch's production appeared approximately eighteen months after Chaplin's at a time when it truly was a *world* war. While no doubt a factor, it should be noted that Poland's defeat had predated the release of *Dictator*, too. Lubitsch's greater sin for many period critics was using a real war-ravished setting (Warsaw) as a backdrop for his comedy. *New York Times* reviewer Bosley Crowther called it "callous and macabre."[41]

Chaplin, though obviously attacking Hitler and his allies, used neither real names nor real locations. Moreover, he avoided the stylized realism Lubitsch brought to a bombed-out Poland. Two weeks after panning *To Be*, Crowther further expanded upon his problems with the movie in the article "Against a Sea of Troubles."[42] Without mentioning Chaplin by name, the critic went on to observe, "Why, if he [Lubitsch] wants to make a picture with a story of such incredible proportions, should he not set it off in the realm of absolute make-believe?"[43] Crowther did not have a corner on these views, although he was the most verbose in his criticism. *New York Sun* reviewer Eileen Creelman was more succinct: "The tragedy of Poland is too close, too immediate, to lend itself to joking."[44]

Lubitsch also fell under attack for mixing genres. Creelman faulted the film for joining melodrama and comedy, while *New York Post* critic Archer Winston asked, "Is this a comedy with underground thriller asides, or is it an underground thriller with garnishings of the Lubitsch [comedy] touch?"[45] The *Dallas Morning News* seemed to mesh elements of both these reviews when it described the film as "in part like a tense, awesome melodrama in the hair-raising Hitchcock [thriller] manner."[46] And from the heartland of Indiana (Lombard's home state), the *Indianapolis Star* stated, "There are so many cross-currents of interest [genres] in the picture that you're likely to be quite mixed up in your feelings about it."[47] In his *New York Times* defense of the film, "Lubitsch Takes the Floor for Rebuttal," the director said, "One might call it a tragical farce or a farcical tragedy—I do not care and neither do the audiences."[48]

Unfortunately, many audiences did have problems with such genre juxtapositionings. Yet Lubitsch recognized that a pivotal element of dark comedy was this on-the-edge quality—life never limits itself to one emotion. He was also aware that a new genre was emerging: "I have tried to break away from the traditional . . . I was tired of two established . . . recipes: drama with comedy relief . . . [and vice versa]. I had made up my mind to make a picture with no attempt to relieve anybody from anything."[49] Lubitsch's last comments here are especially significant—"no attempt to relieve anybody from anything" is essentially a definition of black humor.

Now an accepted component of the genre is that the film's central artist or auteur purposely gives the viewer mixed messages.

An example is soundtrack music that does not match the visual, or graphic violence in the midst of a comic situation. Dark comedy is still not for everyone, nor does it try to be. But to the 1940s audience these juxtapositionings could be especially disturbing. Even the positive *To Be* review often second-guessed itself. The *Brooklyn Citizen's* Edgar Price wrote, "We laughed right out loud, to be sure, but when it was all over it didn't seem funny, at all."[50] Another critic's hesitancy even anticipated Susan Sontag's famous later essay "Against Interpretation" (1966), in which she suggests the modern world limits or "tames the work of art" by restricting its complexity to an assigned meaning.[51] Sontag prefers to trust the viewer over the critic. The similarly minded *To Be* reviewer states:

It may be that some spectators will find no conflict within themselves when they see *To Be or Not to Be*. If so, they can be assured of laughs, an exciting story, and some good performances. Others, like this reviewer, may find themselves enjoying the show but not entirely at ease over the transition from drama to comedy and back again. Still others would be justified in feeling the comedy out of place. Perhaps it would be better for you to see it for yourself.[52]

An excellent time-capsule comparison of the comedy mindset, then (1942) and now, can focus on the film's best line, which was used to open this chapter: "What he [Jack Benny's mediocre in-film actor] did to Shakespeare we're [Nazi Germany] now doing to Poland." The fact that nearly "every review in the American press, other than *Time* magazine, took exception to this line" was the catalyst for the aforementioned *New York Times* defense of the film by Lubitsch himself.[53] Yet, in screening today the line invariably gets the biggest laugh. The *Indianapolis Star* period reviewer casually captured this ambiguity when she said, "It's a picture we'd like to see again—about 20 years from now."[54]

A final possible reason for the film's not doing as well as Chaplin's *Dictator* (besides timing, added realism, and dark comedy's sometime compound genre nature) was the tragic death of *To Be* star Carole Lombard shortly after the movie's completion. In early 1942 the actress had returned to her home state to lead the country's first war bond rally. The rally was a huge success but Lombard was killed in a plane crash returning to Hollywood.

The nation mourned, and Lombard was posthumously awarded a medal from President Franklin D. Roosevelt. It read, "The first woman to be killed in action in the defense of her country in its war against the Axis powers."[55] The President also sent a cable to Lombard's husband, box office idol Clark Gable:

Mrs. Roosevelt and I are deeply distressed. Carole was our friend, our guest in happier days. She brought great joy to all who knew her and to millions who knew her only as a great artist. She gave unselfishly of her time and talent to serve her government in peace and in war . . . . She is and always will be a star, one we shall never forget nor cease to be grateful to. Deepest sympathy.[56]

I belabor this outpouring of grief to underline the national magnitude of Lombard's 1942 death. It precipitated the greatest demonstration of public mourning since the 1935 flying death of Will Rogers. Consequently, no *To Be* review neglected to make reference to this loss. And some critics, such as the *Brooklyn Citizen*'s Edgar Price, found the actress' death further dampened the desire to laugh.[57] Still, a more typical critical response was that of *Variety*: "Although there is a conscious feeling of her passing the first scene in which she appears, this is only momentary and quickly vanishes for the balance of the story."[58] Even her home state's *Indianapolis Star* reviewer stated, "There's no strangeness about Miss Lombard's being there, after the first few minutes," and the critic from her hometown paper, the *Fort Wayne News-Sentinel*, stated, "Carole Lombard's last motion picture . . . headlines theatre entertainment in the city this weekend."[59] Her performance, which still stands up today, was universally praised at the time. There was a sense that a talented comedienne had left her public with a final stellar performance. Thus, without minimizing the tragedy of Lombard's death, it probably did little to diminish the movie's box office. Indeed, to play the cynical critic, her passing might even have boosted *To Be*'s commercial reception, based upon some viewers' almost macabre fascination with a final role. Regardless, Lombard's death did delay the release of *To Be*. Lubitsch had to remove the now chilling line, "What can happen in a plane?"

It took the director a year to be able to discuss publicly the critical and commercial frustration he had suffered with the film. Once again he demonstrated the ongoing influence of Chaplin in his defense of *To Be*: "What is the only picture that is still remembered from the last war? It's not [director D.W.] Griffith's *Hearts of the*

World [1918], or any of those sad ones. It's Chaplin's *Shoulder Arms* [1918]."[60]

Not surprisingly, Lubitsch had even used Chaplin to defend his choice of title when the studio (United Artists) thought the Shakespearean *To Be or Not to Be* was too highbrow: "If for instance [serious actor] Paul Muni would appear in *The [Great] Dictator* audiences would enter the theatre with entirely different expectations as if Charlie Chaplin appears under the same title."[61] Lubitsch then applied this analogy to his film, effectively reasoning that linking Jack Benny to the title created a comic mindset not to be associated with *To Be* and a celebrated Shakespearean actor like John Gielgud.

Moving beyond the period controversy of the film, *To Be* remains an effective dark comedy today. Indeed, Mel Brooks underlined the fact when his 1983 remake followed Lubitsch's original nearly scene for scene. Critic Pauline Kael even complained that the new version "has nothing to take the place of that [original] anti-Nazi rambunctiousness."[62] While I have difficulty faulting a remake that manages to add a singing rendition of "Sweet Georgia Brown" . . . in Polish . . . one never loses sight of the original.

Lubitsch's *To Be* utilized, as do most black comedies, the interrelated themes of man as beast, the absurdity of the world, and the omnipresence of death. But the central motif for *To Be* is man as beast, keying upon his sexual weakness. The catalyst for this is the sensuality of Lombard's Maria. She initially appears in a skintight silk evening gown, which she feels will be a perfect costume for a concentration camp character she plans to play.

Her sexy in-film stage persona takes precedence over reality. (At its most basic, serious subjects in this genre are constantly displaced by sex.) Another example, besides Maria's inappropriate costume of choice, is her thoughts as the Nazis stand poised at Poland's border. She is planning an affair with the handsome young bomber pilot Lt. Stanislaws Sobinski (Robert Stack). Two bits of early dialogue leave no doubt as to the imminent cuckolding of husband Jack Benny's Josef Tura. Maria is very impressed that the lieutenant can drop three tons of dynamite in two minutes. For those missing the statement's sexual innuendo, Maria's maid Anna (Maude Eburne) puts it much more plainly: "What a husband doesn't know won't hurt his wife."

The "three tons of dynamite" comment does, moreover, represent another dark comedy example of the genre's propensity to connect sex and death—two phenomena that showcase a lack of control. Lombard's Maria futher accents this connection by the signal that activates each sexual rendezvous with the flyer. Whenever her husband goes on stage for his "To be or not to be" soliloquy from *Hamlet*, Robert Stack's character leaves the audience for Maria, with Shakespearean ponderings about suicide being the last thing on his mind.

Once the Nazis have taken over Poland, Maria's sexuality is used as a weapon against the enemy. Late in the film she will observe, "I started a [sexual] commotion with every Gestapo man I've met." Again there is the correlation with war and death. For instance, working for the Polish resistance she is recruited by one Nazi official who is quite taken with her sensuality. Lombard's character inspiringly observes that the "work" they might do together would be "an affair of state." He offers a romantic "blitzkrieg" (lightning war), but she prefers to call it "a slow encirclement." Thus, the business of deadly war maneuvers and sexuality are semantically linked. The comic topper to the scene has sexy Maria kissing him and immediately making the Nazi stiff-arm "Heil Hitler" salute. But for all Maria's play at being infatuated by German power players, such as the spying Professor Siletsky (Stanley Ridges) and Col. Ehrhardt (Sig Ruman), it is they whose work is disrupted by her.

Jack Benny's ham actor and the rest of his theater troupe are also working with the Polish resistance. But his antiheroic characters who might more normally surface in the screwball comedy genre, is constantly placed in dark comedy situations—for instance, when it seems that Maria will have to use her sexual gifts to assassinate a Nazi official. Benny's Josef Tura frustratingly interrupts, "*I'm* going to say who my wife kills." But he has no more success here than in limiting her lovers. Indeed, unlike the traditional antiheroic screwball male who is dominated yet ultimately made happy by the woman, the end of *To Be* finds Josef (after the troupe has escaped to England) being cuckolded again—but by someone other than Stack's character.

Even when Benny's Tura was pretending to be Nazi officer Colonel Ehrhardt earlier in the film, his entertainingly comic anger over the affairs of his wife put the resistance mission to kill Professor Siletsky in danger. But he was able to give the most memorable dark comedy line, after the one that opens the chapter. As Benny's Ehrhardt observes in a casual aside, "We [the Nazis] do the concentrating and the Poles do the camping." This came in for period criticism but today it seems entirely apropos.

The fact that the majority of the film's characters play actors pretending to be Nazis is an additional dark comedy touch, since the genre is constantly about things never being what they appear to be (see Chapter 1's reference to Melville's *The Confidence Man* and the analogy that life is like a costume party where all the disguised guests should be prepared to play the fool). Appropriately, Professor Siletsky is eventually shot and killed *on stage*.

Along the same lines, the periodic in-film productions of *Hamlet* are also fitting for this genre—most obviously, as one Lubitsch scholar noted, because it is "a play of murder and revenge which litters the stage with corpses."[63] *Hamlet* is also about a usurpation of power and a hesitancy of response to this crime, two items more than a little pertinent to the rise of Hitler. Moreover, the play speaks to the catatonic anxiety of the modern world. That is, *Hamlet* demonstrates how analysis (should he kill his murderous uncle?) is paralysis and that the ability to see every side of every issue prevents one from taking any side at all.

Lubitsch's use of two minor characters as extras in the play, Mr. Greenberg (Felix Bressart) and Mr. Bronski (Tom Dugan), also anticipates Tom Stoppard's later critically-acclaimed black comedy play *Rosencrantz and Guildenstern Are Dead* (1967), which is actually a play within a production of *Hamlet*. Rosencrantz and Guildenstern are minor *Hamlet* characters struggling to make sense of a complex world. Greenberg and Bronski are equally likable and vulnerable figures in *To Be's* in-film *Hamlet*, as well as surfacing periodically in the film as members of Tura's acting troupe. They too are struggling to understand a seemingly senseless world.

With each duo, death and dark humor are a given. For instance, Rosencrantz observes, "Eternity is a terrible thought. I mean, where's it going to end?"[64] Guildenstern soon adds, "Death followed by eternity . . . the worst of both worlds."[65] Though not always aware of their wisdom, these two wise fools reframe *Hamlet* in black comedy.

In Lubitsch's film, Greenberg and Bronski appear to be the only members of the troupe actively promoting dark humor, regardless of the consequences. Thus, at the beginning of *To Be* the company of actors is rehearsing an anti-Nazi play, with Bronski as Hitler. To spoof the Nazi party salute of "Heil Hitler," Bronski suggests saying "Heil myself." When the in-film director refuses the change, Bronski pleads, "But it'll get a laugh." Greenberg then adds, "A laugh is nothing to be sneezed at."

Indeed, variations of these comments, à la anything for a laugh, are pivotal to both characters. For instance, when Lombard's Maria models the sexy dress for the concentration camp scene, the director and her co-star find the idea in poor taste and veto it. Maria is vain, like Benny's Tura; her reasoning for wearing the dress was merely as a star turn. Only Bronski and Greenberg see the costume in dark comedy terms. Consequently, Greenberg says of the contrast between the camp and the provocative costume, "That's a terrific laugh!"

Stoppard's Rosencrantz and Guildenstern and Lubitsch's Greenberg and Bronski are not limited, however, to the comic aside. They are all capable of the poignant insight that juxtaposes the real world with that of the stage. For example, there is the letter that dictates the death of Rosencrantz and Guildenstern instead of Hamlet, and which prompts Guildenstern's shocked but articulate observation, "Dying is not romantic [as in a play] and death is not a game [as on stage] which will soon be over. . . . Death is not anything . . . death is not . . . It's the absence of presence, nothing more."[66]

A comparably moving *To Be* scene finds Greenberg and Bronski discussing the threat of Hitler backstage during a production of *Hamlet*. Shortly before going on, Greenberg recites the famous Shylock passage from Shakespeare's *The Merchant of Venice* (1595-96) which includes the lines, "If you prick us [Jews], do we not bleed? If you tickle us, do we not laugh? If you poison us, do we not die?"

In this case, the juxtaposing of *Merchant* and the then-contemporary world (Nazi-occupied Europe) had a great deal in common— the liquidation of the Jews. The late nineteenth-century Jew was hunted and tortured only just less systematically than by the Hitler Germans. Indeed, shortly before the first staging of *Merchant*, a huge approving London audience had witnessed a prominent Jew being hanged, drawn, and quartered. This earlier period also found Jews forced to wear yellow badges, anticipating Nazi Europe. Most chillingly, during Shakespeare's time Jews so recently had to buy themselves off from mutilation that in the market place an object was said to be "worth a Jew's eye."

By having Greenberg quote Shylock, Lubitsch has found the perfect timeless commentary for this 1942 film. In fact, he has Greenberg repeat Shylock's words twice in the film. As an ironic final footnote to this material, Greenberg delivers it in a sympathetically compassionate manner. But the student of Shakespeare knows this passage in *Merchant* is delivered by Shylock with blisteringly revengefulness, because sadly enough Shylock quickly becomes the villain of the play.

The key difference between Lubitsch's and Stoppard's comedy teams is that one dies, or as the latter artist has titled his 1967 play, *Rosencrantz and Guildenstern Are Dead*. But that difference is based on the fact that pioneering 1940s black comedy was more likely to provide some hope, while the 1960s watershed decade for the genre tended to accent the "dark" of dark comedy.

By using minor characters, both productions have accented the plight, even tragedy, of the common man in a modern, terrifying world. And while no blueprint for survival has been formulated, just the recognition by these individuals provides a degree of comfort. Certainly, the purpose of art for many is to address the horrors of reality and allow people to rise above the disorder of his or her creation, however briefly.

Lubitsch, like his film comedy director contemporary Preston Sturges, frequently gave the best lines to his supporting players. After Felix Bressart's Greenberg and Tom Dugan's Bronski, Sig Ruman's Colonel Ehrhardt was especially gifted by Lubitsch. Besides the once controversial quote which opens this chapter, Ehrhardt is the "target" of the film's funniest suicide attempt. As noted earlier, bumping one's self off is a given for dark comedy. In this case, Ruman's character is the last in a long line of *To Be* characters attempting to bed Lombard's sexy Maria. Bronski, dressed as Hitler, enters Ehrhardt's quarters to retrieve Maria for the escape flight to England. When Ehrhardt sees what appears to be der Führer, he comically self-destructs, assuming he will be executed for dallying with Hitler's mistress. Behind closed doors one hears the sound of a shot. There is a pause, and then Ehrhardt yells for Schultz, his assistant. Thus, the attempted suicide gets two laughs, first the comic misunderstanding and then the incompetence of somehow missing one's head.

A black humor variation on suicide also occurs on the flight to England. To get rid of the two German pilots (Robert Stack's flyer is on board), Bronski's Hitler tells the men to jump . . . without parachutes. It is a brilliant gag on the mesmerizing evil that was Adolf Hitler. Both pilots are quickly earthbound with only a loyal Nazi "Heil Hitler" before exiting.

To Be was Lubitsch's most controversial film. Like the equally pioneering dark comedy *Duck Soup*, the film is now considered a classic. And with similar subject matter, *To Be* is now more fairly compared to *The Great Dictator*. These three films are a pivotal foundation for much of what would follow in this genre.

In the most positive manner, these movies all have a comic-strip nature to them. The broadness of several characters merely heightens the dark comedy traits, from Groucho's Firefly leading Freedonia off to war, to Chaplin's Hynkel playing Hitler. It might be remembered that Nathanael West's now celebrated black comedy novel *Miss Lonelyhearts* (1933, the same year as *Duck Soup*) was originally conceived as a comic strip.

Each of the three films addressed in this chapter is dramatically focused on a brief sequence of events, not unlike the series of frames in a comic strip . . . a sinister comic strip. And the characters are comically pared down to the outline of a few traits. Modern black humor movies are often more darkly sophisticated, but the fundamental themes of the genre are all here. One might liken them to Rosencrantz's capsulization of *Hamlet*: "Let me get this straight. Your father was king. You were his only son. Your father dies. You are of age. Your uncle becomes king. . . . Unorthodox."[67] This chapter's three films also keep things tight, but they entertainingly give you everything you need to enjoy the genre . . . while remaining ever so unorthodox.

NOTES

1. Harpo Marx (with Rowland Barber), *Harpo Speaks!* (1961; repr. New York: Freeway Press, 1974), p. 27.

2. Ibid., p. 38.

3. Groucho Marx, *Groucho and Me* (1959; repr. New York: Manor Books, 1974), p. 22.

4. Frederick R. Karl, *FRANZ KAFKA: Representative Man* (New York: Ticknor and Fields, 1991), p. 9.

5. Deborah Crawford, *Franz Kafka: Man Out of Step* (New York: Crown Publishers, 1973), p. 99.

6. Andrew Bergman, "Some Anarcho-Nihilist: Laff Riots," in Bergman's *We're in the Money: Depression America and Its Films* (New York: Harper and Row, 1972), p. 37.

7. John S. Cohen, Jr., *"Duck Soup*, a Marxian (Brothers) Burlesque That Is Below Their Standard," *New York Sun*, November 24, 1933. In the *Duck Soup* file, Billy Rose Theatre Colllection, New York Public Library at Lincoln Center.

8. Raymond Durgnat, "Four Against Alienation," in Durgnat's *The Crazy Mirror: Hollywood Comedy and the American Image* (1969; repr. New York: Dell, 1972), p. 158.

9. Ibid.

10. Martin A. Gardner, "The Marx Brothers: An Investigation of Their Films as Special Criticism" (Ph.D. diss., New York University, 1970). Richard Hofstader, *The Paranoid Style in American Politics* (New York: Alfred A. Knopf, 1965).

11. Teet Carl, "'Fun' Working with the Marx Brothers? Horsefeathers!" *Los Angeles Magazine*, October 1978, p. 145.

12. Allen Eyles, *The Marx Brothers: Their World of Comedy* (New York: Paperback Library, 1971), p. 109.

13. Gerald Weales, "Duck Soup," in Weales's *Canned Goods as Caviar: American Film Comedy of the 1930s* (Chicago: University of Chicago Press, 1985), p. 80.

14. Neil Schmitz, *Of Huck and Alice: Humorous Writing in American Literature* (Minneapolis: University of Minnesota Press, 1983), p. 20.

15. Louis Chavance, "The Marx Brothers as Seen by a Frenchman," *The Canadian Forum*, February 1933, p. 175.

16. Charlie Chaplin, *My Autobiography* (1964; repr. New York: Pocket Books, 1966), p. 22.

17. Charles Chaplin, Jr. (with N. Rau and M. Rau), *My Father, Charlie Chaplin* (New York: Random House, 1960), p. 93.

18. Ibid., p. 196.

19. Ibid., p. 88.

20. Michael Chaplin, *I couldn't smoke the grass on my father's lawn* (New York: G.P. Putnam, 1966), p. 47.

21. Chaplin, *Autobiography*, p. 327.

22. "Chaplin Says He Just Had to Make That Speech," *New York World-Telegram*, October 19, 1940, p. 7.

23. Ibid.

24. David Robinson, *Chaplin: His Life and Art* (New York: McGraw-Hill, 1985), p. 493.

25. Ilan Avisar, *Screening the Holocaust: Cinema's Images of the Unimaginable* (Bloomington: Indiana University Press, 1988), p. 135.

26. "Chaplin Says He Just Had to Make That Speech," p. 7.

27. Charles J. Maland, *Chaplin and American Culture* (Princeton, N.J.: Princeton University Press, 1989), p. 171.

28. "The Great Dictator," *Sidney Morning Herald*, November 5, 1940, Women's Supplement section, p. 7.

29. Reginald Gardiner, "*The Great Dictator*: Charlie Chaplin's Gift of Humor and Satire to the Totalitarian State," *New York Herald Tribune*, September 16, 1940. In *The Great Dictator* file, Billy Rose Theatre Collection, New York Public Library at Lincoln Ceter.

30. John McCabe, *Charlie Chaplin* (Garden City, N.Y.: Doubleday, 1978), p. 197.

31. "Mr. Chaplin Answers His Critics," *New York Times*, October 27, 1940, Section 9, p. 5.

32. Crawford, p. 99.

33. Ibid., pp. 72–73.

34. Herman G. Weinberg, *The Lubitsch Touch: A Critical Study* (New York: E. P. Dutton, 1971), pp. 4–5.

35. Douglas Gomery, *Movie History: A Survey* (Belmont, Calif.: Wadsworth Publishing, 1991), p. 128.

36. Gerald Mast, revised by Bruce F. Kawin, *A Short History of the Movies*, 5th Ed. 1971 repr. New York: Macmillan, 1992), p. 120.

37. Siegfried Kracauer, *From Caligari to Hitler* (1947; repr. Princeton, N.J.: Princeton University Press, 1971), pp. 52–53.

38. Weinberg, p. 18.

39. Arthur Knight, *The Liveliest Art: A Panoramic History of the Movies*, revised (New York: Macmillan, 1978), p. 110.

40. Donald Kirkley, *To Be or Not to Be* review, *Baltimore Sun*, March 12, 1942. In the *To Be or Not to Be* file, Billy Rose Theatre Collection, New York Public Library at Lincoln Center.

41. Bosley Crawther, *To Be or Not to Be* review, *New York Times*, March 7, 1942, p. 13.

42. Bosley Crowther, "Against a Sea of Troubles," *New York Times*, March 22, 1942, Section 8, p. 3.

43. Ibid.

44. Eileen Creelman, "Carole Lombard's Last Picture, the Somber 'To Be or Not to Be,'" *New York Sun*, March 7, 1942. In the *To Be or Not to Be* file, Billy Rose Theatre Collection, New York Public Library at Lincoln Center.

45. Archer Winsten, *To Be or Not to Be* review, *New York Post*, March 7, 1942. In the *To Be or Not to Be* file, Billy Rose Theatre Collection.

46. John Rosenfield, "Nazis Can Be Had Even by Jack Benny," *Dallas Morning News*, March 21, 1942. In the *To Be or Not to Be* file, Billy Rose Theatre Collection, New York Public Library at Lincoln Center.

47. Corbin Patrick, "Comedy Is Serious: Lubitsch Film Seen with Mixed Emotions," *Indianapolis Star*, March 12, 1942, p. 13.

48. Ernst Lubitsch, "Mr. Lubitsch Takes the Floor for Rebuttal," *New York Times*, March 29, 1942, Section 8, p. 3.

49. Ibid.

50. Edgar Price, *To Be or Not to Be* review, *Brooklyn Citizen*, March 7, 1942. In the *To Be or Not to Be* file, Billy Rose Theatre Collection, New York Public Library at Lincoln Center.

51. Susan Sontag, *Against Interpretation: And Other Essays* (1986; repr. New York: Achor Books, 1990), p. 8.

52. Winsten, n.p.

53. Weinberg, p. 225.

54. Patrick, p. 13.

55. Joe Morella and Edward Z. Epstein, *Gable & Lombard and Powell & Harlow* (New York: Dell, 1975), p. 238.

56. Ibid., pp. 237–38.

57. Price, n.p.

58. *To Be or Not to Be* review, *Variety*, February 18, 1942. In the *To Be or Not to Be* file, Billy Rose Theatre Collection.

59. Patrick, p. 13. "Carole's Last Picture," *Fort Wayne [IN] News-Sentinel*, March 7, 1942, p. 11.

60. Scott Eyman, *Ernst Lubitsch: Laughter in Paradise* (New York: Simon and Schuster, 1993), p. 303.

61. Ibid., p. 298.

62. Pauline Kael, *State of the Art* (New York: E. P. Dutton, 1985), p. 111.

63. Leland A. Poague, *The Cinema of Ernst Lubitsch* (Cransbury, N.J.: A. S. Barnes, 1978), p. 92.

64. Tom Stoppard, *Rosencrantz and Guildenstern Are Dead* (New York: Grove Weidenfeld, 1967), p. 71.

65. Ibid., p. 72.

66. Ibid, p. 124.

67. Ibid, p. 49.

4

Coming of Age . . . With a Vengeance

The extreme always seems to make an impression.
— J. D. (Christian Slater) in *Heathers* (1989)

It's best not to be too moral. You cheat yourself out of too much life. Aim above morality. If you apply that to life then you're bound to live it fully.
— Maude (Ruth Gordon) in *Harold and Maude* (1971)

There is a tendency to link the cynicism of black comedy with age, such as the provocative words of acclaimed author Paul Fussell: "To survive and prosper in this world you have to do so at someone else's expense or do and undergo things it's not pleasant to face."[1]

While one would be foolish to deny the ties between age and dark humor, there is also a propensity for youthful comic nihilism. This was first brought to my attention through correspondence with celebrated actor Alec Guinness. I had long admired his film work, especially the early acclaimed dark comedies for Britain's Ealing Studios, such as *Kind Hearts and Coronets* (1949) (see illustration 10) and *The Ladykillers* (1955). In the former, Guinness plays eight different royal victims, all in the same family. In the latter role, instead of being an army of victims, he is a comically sinister, fang-toothed leader of a crime gang.

In the summer of 1989 I was doing research in London for a book, and Guinness was appearing on stage in Lee Blessing's cold-war dark comedy, *A Walk in the Woods* (1986). Two diplomats, one from America and the other from the Soviet Union, are attempting to hammer out a nuclear arms-control agreement. Not surprisingly, Guinness's character, the Soviet, has the lion's share of the strong lines, such as "They [governments] are too irrational. All of them. *And* all of them are getting nuclear weapons. Once we only had to be rational in English and Russian. Now we must do it in Hebrew, Hindi, Afrikaans.[2]"

After seeing the performance I could not resist contacting him about his thoughts on dark comedy. At its most basic, he felt, "It is a way of expressing our built-in cruelty while joking about it."[3] Later, implying that with age comes restraint, the actor observed, "Perhaps . . . it [black humor] is adolescent. Now at the age of 75 I'm beginning to grow up, I hope, and it doesn't have the same appeal as 50 years ago."[4]

Guinness's thoughts on an adolescent slant to black comedy are particularly pertinent to this chapter. With dark humor taking off in the 1970s, I have selected a pivotal coming-of-age example of the genre for each of the three final decades of the century: *Harold and Maude* (1971), *Heathers* (1989), and *Natural Born Killers* (1994).

It has never been easy bridging the gap from adolescence to adulthood. But since the birth of the affluent 1950s baby-boomer generation there has often been a greater degree of hostility showcased between parent and child in the popular arts. And often, it has been the adults who have been found most wanting. For instance, J. D. Salinger's watershed novel *Catcher in the Rye* (1951) launched this "me-generation" of alienated young people . . . forever victimized by adult "phonies." In 1955 James Dean's film character became a cult legend fighting that same phoniness, particularly his screen parents, in the celebrated movie *Rebel Without a Cause*. Fittingly, one of the key figures in *Heathers*, played by second-billed Christian Slater, uses the initials "J. D." as his name. Slater's character sees Salinger phoniness everywhere, as well as Dean's need to rebel, whether a case exists or not. Some critics used *Catcher in the Rye* as a dark-humor measuring device. For instance, when *The New Yorker*'s Pauline Kael (probably America's most influential film critic ever) reviewed *M.A.S.H.* (1970) she said *Catcher* hero "Holden Caulfield would, I think, approve."[5]

10. Alec Guinness in *Kind Hearts and Coronets*.

One might bring any number of additional causes, beyond derailing phoniness and youthful rebelliousness, for the increased adolescent violence to be found in the post-1950s trilogy that is the focus of this chapter. But the most engrossing would come from André Bishop's "Preface" to the black comedy play *Assassins* (1991). This production brings together a fraternity of presidential assassins and would-be assassins over a hundred-plus years, from infamous successes like John Wilkes Booth to funny-sad failures like Lynette "Squeaky" Fromme. Bishop's hypothesis behind America's propensity for violence is that we live in a country "whose most cherished national myths, at least as currently propagated, encourage us to believe that in America our dreams not only *can* come true, but *should* come true, and that if they don't someone or something is to blame."[6]

Bishop's perspective on black humor could be applied to any character, regardless of age. But it seems especially relevant to the young figure, both because of youth's impatience to change things (especially revenge against in-crowd peers and/or unsympathetic parents), and the love/hate relationship with a charismatic figure. This is best exemplified in *Assassins* by dialogue from "Squeaky" Fromme: "Then I met Charlie [Manson]. . . . I was sitting on the beach in Venice. I'd just had a big fight with my daddy about, I don't know, my eye make-up or the bombing of Cambodia. He said I was a drug addict and a whore and I should get out of his house forever—"[7] The parents which are soon to surface in this chapter's trilogy are perhaps like Squeaky's, experts dealing with the dysfunctional family.

Something to note, however, before examining the trilogy in detail, is that unlike many modern dark comedies, this coming-of-age variety tends to close with a happy ending. Of course, happy is a relative term. For instance, in *Harold and Maude* the title male character (Bud Cort) seems finally ready at the end to lead a productive normal life, despite Maude's (Ruth Gordon) suicide. In contrast, the young murderous couple of *Natural Born Killers* (Woody Harrelson and Juliette Lewis) eventually end up with children and a big recreational vehicle, but seem just as prepared to kill if the situation calls for it . . . or even if it does not. Theirs is not unlike the violent "I'm back" look of Malcolm McDowell's coming-of-age character at the close of *A Clockwork Orange* (1971). Finally, the finish of *Heathers* finds one member (Winona Ryder) of a violent duo prepared to be a good person again, despite her partner-in-crime (Christian Slater) blowing himself up in front of her.

So why the qualified happy endings? The preponderance of upbeat closes for other black comedies of this nature suggests that in America the darkest of genres can attempt to provide a modicum of hope. Even in the Quentin Tarantino–scripted *True Romance* (1994), where everything points toward the death of the violent young couple, they escape to Mexico, though the young man (Christian Slater) loses an eye in their final gun battle.

Ours is a very violent age for young people, and when art hits so close to home, as coming-of-age dark comedy does, then this art unmistakably resonates with life. Combine that with the hope society normally links to the young and one has a possible explanation for why this particular variety of black humor is more likely to have a relatively upbeat close.

HAROLD AND MAUDE

One ad campaign for the movie said: "Harold's 20 and in love with death. . . . Maude's 80 and in love with life." [8] But this is more than a strange love story of Bud Cort's Harold and Ruth Gordon's Maude. It is also a hodgepodge dark-comedy look at parenting, the military, the church, psychiatry, the police, and computer dating.

The film is most infamous for the many fake suicides Harold futilely stages in trying to receive some attention from his busy high-society mother, Mrs. Chasen (Vivian Pickles). The simulated suicides include the hanging with which the movie opens, slashed wrists and throat while in the tub, drowning in the pool, immolation, and a gunshot to the head (see illustration 11). There are also acts of apparent self-mutilation, such as seeming to chop off his hand. As grizzly as these sound, the film's comic genius is its ability to incorporate Harold's choreographed violence into an offbeat romance and make it work.

No small part of this success is due to the boy's mother: "Vivian Pickles is an actress who is particularly gifted at exaggerating understatements; many of Mrs. Chasen's reactions [actually, little or no reaction] to Harold's bleak pranks are as funny as they are meant to be."[9] Pickles's actions range from her nonresponse to Harold's apparently drowned body as she does pool laps, to her

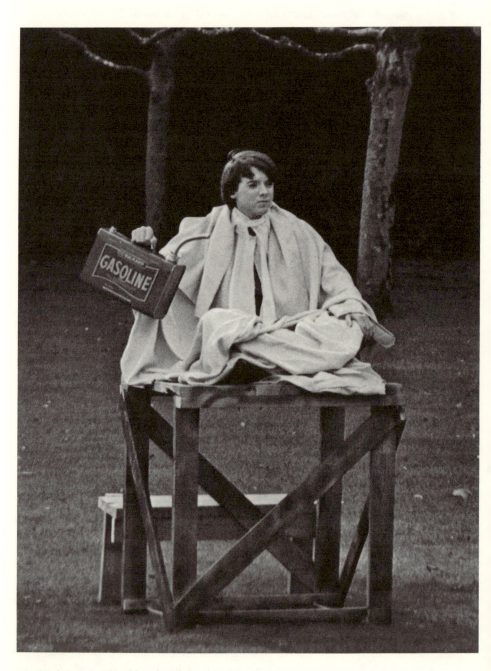

11. Bud Cort in *Harold and Maude*.

mildly bothered "Harold, please!" as he seems to shoot himself in the forehead. Fittingly, her character is given no first name, just "Mrs. Chasen." This suggests her formal, self-centered nature to her son and everyone else, despite all his attempts to get her attention. In contrast, the sympathetic title characters are known by their first names, Harold and Maude.

Despite the movie's celebrated status today, period critics often found the work wanting . . . a common occurrence for this genre. Indeed, some reviewers even took their own black comedy jabs at the film. For example, *Variety*'s critic said it "has all the fun and gaiety of a burning orphanage." [10] Others, like the *New York Times*'s Vincent Canby, more baldly panned the picture: "You might well want to miss . . . a comedy that pretends to be as thoroughly in favor of life as [Frank Capra's populist] *You Can't Take It With You*, whereas it's quite as much about death as it appears to be."[11] Canby's comments echo those 1940s complaints about *To Be Or Not To Be* (1942) mixing genres (see Chapter 3). Some mainstream publications, like *Time* and *Newsweek*, did not even bother to review the film, which opened shortly before Christmas. Maybe the release date was one more shock effect.

Harold and Maude was not, however, without period support. But when the movie received rare high praise, as was the case with prominent critic Judith Crist's *New York* magazine review, the parent studio (Paramount) could not resist building an ad campaign around it: "IT IS A JOY! An enchanting excursion into the joy of living. Wonderfully perceptive."[12]

In the months following its release, *Harold and Maude* found critical praise in a number of intellectual film journals. For instance, *Film Quarterly* described it as "one of the best movies to come out of Hollywood in years. It is a love story, a sentimental black comedy, a ludicrous tear-jerker, a grisly social satire."[13] This critique is especially important because it represents early recognition that dark humor is about mixing genres. In the years following its 1971 release, a cult following grew around the picture. By late in the decade this success had become official: Paramount struck new prints of the movie for a limited re-release.

At its most basic the film is a rescue mission of Harold by Maude. The boy's life has become a theater of death. He is constantly faking suicides. Though initially done to get some attention from his mother, he soon finds the attempts are also quite effective in scaring off the computer dates she keeps forcing upon him. In addition, Harold's dark lifestyle involves driving a hearse and attending funerals . . . anyone's. His clothing is often black, and he has the pasty complexion of a fresh corpse.

Maude is not without a dark side, either. She too enjoys taking in funerals; this is how she first gets to know Harold. Gordon's character can also plan a suicide. But unlike Cort's figure, Maude actually goes through with hers. She feels being eighty is an age ceiling one does not go beyond, and she executes this belief at the film's close. With all that said, however, Maude is still a life force that gets Harold to examine all the possibilities of his world.

This awakening is begun by her getting him to use all his senses, or as one critic described it, treating "him to a sensual smorgasbord." [14] Among these treats, he eats ginger pie, strokes a tactile sculpture, learns to play a banjo, inhales from her "adorifies" (drug water pipe), is introduced to yoga breathing, gets stoned, and re-examines the world around him. In addition, Maude is constantly philosophizing about the desirability of nonconformity, embracing life, and rebellion. The film's writing and Ruth Gordon's performance are such that this Maude-as-teacher component never comes across as didactic. For instance, at one point Harold tells Maude that her tendency to steal cars upsets people. She responds, "I'm merely acting as a gentle reminder: here today gone tomorrow, so don't get attached to things."

The forever-active Maude does not limit herself to abstract philosophy. Her individualism and spontaneity has Gordon's character instructing Harold in everything from two real escapes from the police to avoiding induction into the army. In the latter case, she is acting upon the special request of Harold. Vivian Pickles's Mrs. Chasen has finally realized her computer dating scenarios for Harold are not going to work. Consequently, she calls in his Uncle Victor (Charles Tyner) to expedite the boy's induction. If marriage is not going to settle him down, maybe the army can. Maude concocts a plan where Harold acts like a potential gung ho recruit who attacks an anti-war activist (Maude) and seems to drown her. This is enough for Uncle Victor; his nephew is too psychotic for the army. Thus, Harold does not have to serve—a pivotal period statement since America was still in Vietnam.

Most modern love stories are, however, unconventional, and they do not get much more unconventional than Harold and

Maude's; eventually the couple is shown in bed. But this inevitable scene for Gordons and Cort's characters would prove controversial. Director Hal Ashby had shot footage of the couple kissing passionately and then lying back on the bed. But the studio (Paramount) said it would be distasteful for the audience, an odd reading for a dark-shock-comedy film. The compromise is a morning after scene, with both in bed. Maude is sleeping and Harold is sitting up, blowing soap bubbles. Even this less provocative rendition is still disconcerting today to many of my college students.

Though I am opposed to censorship, given the ongoing reactions of my contemporary classes, Paramount's 1971 fears were probably warranted. Regardless, the morning-after approach with Maude asleep is a more effective showcasing of the scene's most moving detail—the fleeting view of the concentration camp number tattooed on Maude's arm. If one's own affection had not already gone out to this octogenarian free spirit, her ability to still embrace life after such a nightmare experience makes her the most poignant of characters.

Ironically, what Harold takes to be a new beginning (the consumation of their relationship and a forthcoming wedding) is an ending for Maude, since she still plans to commit suicide on her birthday. But before this latter event, there is Harold's shock-effect fun of informing his mother just who he is going to marry . . . complete with a picture of Maude. One might liken the situation to Harold's earlier fake suicide attempts to get her attention.

This is the catalyst for Mrs. Chasen to send her son for another round of counseling with her favorite establishment figures: army representative Uncle Victor, Erick Christmas's priest, and G. Wood's psychiatrist. Their collective bafflement at Harold's forthcoming marriage represents just one more example of undercutting the alleged insight of the establishment. But through the several visits to these three in which the viewer has joined Harold, Wood's psychiatrist has been the least offensive. And his attempt to hold onto a rational worldview has been the most successful of the three. Yet Harold's romantic plan finally derails the psychiatrist's hold on a rational approach to life: "A very common neurosis, particularly in this society, whereby the male child subconsciously wants to sleep with his mother. Of course what puzzles me, Harold, is you want to sleep with your grandmother."

Naturally, the prognosis is unfavorable for Harold's relationship with Maude. But Harold has never listened to these counselors. Shockingly for him, it is Maude who ends the relationship. She swallows a lethal dose of unspecified pills, and though he rushes her to the hospital, it is in vain. But even before the viewer can be certain of Maude's passing, the film shot selection and editing seem to be preparing for another suicide. As is sometimes the case in dark comedy, the editing skewers the linear progression of time. Thus, the movie footage cuts back and forth between Harold waiting at the hospital and his racing along at extreme speeds in the sports car he has converted into a miniature hearse. Late in the sequence the viewer shares the death news with him, and shortly thereafter he appears to drive the automobile off a cliff. (The film's director, Hal Ashby, had won a 1967 Oscar for editing *In the Heat of the Night*.)

Does Harold die? For once he would seem to have a good reason for suicide. Plus, it would be consistent with the genre's traditional dark close. Moreover, by holding the camera shot on the wrecked car for an unusually long time, the filmmaker makes the viewer think a dead Harold is a given. But then the camera tilts slowly upward and Harold is found on the cliff overlooking the crash site. He has evidently jumped from the vehicle like James Dean's character in *Rebel Without a Cause*. But unlike that figure, and despite Maude's passing, Harold is ready to start living. In fact, the close finds him playing the banjo she has given him. And as Steve Martin would always suggest in his 1970s period stand-up act, it is impossible to be sad when banjo music is played. Consequently, Maude lives on in the awakened Harold. Or, as the film's screenwriter, Colin Higgins, observed: "We're all Harold, and we all want to be Maude. We're all repressed and trying to be free, to be ourselves, to be vitally interested in living, to be everything we want."[15]

As a longtime student of the picture, from its release during my early college days to my current use of it in a university film class I teach, what I find most interesting is its employment of a screwball comedy structure. Earlier in the chapter *Harold and Maude* was credited with mixing several genres, including love story, tear-jerker, and social satire. But its screwball comedy tendencies seem somehow to have been missed, despite its obvious traits. In writing extensively on this genre, it seems pivotal to briefly expand upon the film's creative use of screwball comedy.[16]

The importance comes from how screwball comedy is utilized in *Harold and Maude*. The normal reason black humor has a mixture of genres is for the shock comedy effect of their juxtaposing. But screwball comedy in this film is parodied so darkly and ambitiously that it demonstrates how black humor can also trash a target genre just as easily as it can trash an institution like the church or the military. (See Chapter 2.)

Variations of most screwball comedy components inundate *Harold and Maude*. The antiheroic male is characterized by five key elements: abundant leisure time (frequently because of wealth), childlike naivety, urban setting, apolitical nature, and ongoing frustration. All five apply to Bud Cort's character. Indeed, he is not so much childlike as child. And with no attention from his wealthy mother, he is frustrated in his elaborate shock-effect attempts (staged suicides) to get her back into his life. Harold's wide-open schedule allows plenty of time for attending countless funerals, choreographing suicides, and automotive body work in converting his sports car into a hearse. Politics is beyond him.

In the traditional screwball comedy the antihero is threatened with a marriage that will either cause him "comic rigidity," or make permanent this state where the "character is so tightly jammed into the rigid frames of his functions that he has no room to move or to be moved like other men."[17] This rigidity is nicely showcased by Cary Grant's professor in *Bringing Up Baby* (1938). His fiancée informs him that their "child" will be the brontosaurus skeleton he is reconstructing. Katherine Hepburn's figure brings life into his dead world. Fittingly, when she accidentally sends this skeleton crashing down, it also acts as symbol of what she has done to the last vestiges of his academic rigidity.

When *Bringing Up Baby* was loosely remade as *What's Up, Doc?* (1972), the same antiheroic rigidity applied, only now the professor was trying to get music out of rocks. Cary Grant and director Howard Hawks even made a sequel of sorts to *Bringing Up Baby* entitled *Monkey Business* (1952). But one need not be a professor to suffer from comic rigidity. John Cleese's married, uptight British barrister in *A Fish Called Wanda* (1988) is an excellent example of a fossilized screwball comedy male in need of some life . . . which is provided by Jamie Lee Curtis's con woman. Interestingly enough, the name of Cleese's character is Archie Leach—Cary Grant's real name.

The other type of screwball male has not yet become metaphorically rigid, but it is a distinct danger. Probably the best example of this is Dudley Moore's title figure in *Arthur* (1981). His free-spirited life is based on being ever so rich. This is how Peter Pan would live if he had the money. But neither Peter nor Arthur has any thoughts of growing up. Therein lies their charm and their attractiveness. With Arthur any rare adult trait still has a childlike twist to it. For instance, the martinis delivered to his toy-strewn bedroom come by way of an elevated electric train. Unfortunately, this fantasy life is threatened by a work-oriented fiancée and her fascist businessman father and soon-to-be boss. Then Liza Minnelli's blue collar love interest comes into Arthur's life and helps him avoid such an ugly, grown-up plight.

Ruth Gordon's Maude is the romantic screwball rescuer of man-child Harold. Instead of a smothering mother-like fiancée or wife, the rigidity-oriented threat in Harold's life is his mother. Early in the movie Mrs. Chasen tells him: "It is time you settled down and stopped flitting away your talents on these amateur theatrics [fake suicides] . . . Go have a talk with [career army officer] Uncle Victor." It is obvious that this uncle is Chasen's brother. Besides looking and sounding alike, what could be more appropriate for Ms. Rigidity than the stereotypical stiffness of a military brother. Victor adds to that image both by his first name and the mechanical saluting sleeve that has replaced the arm lost in combat. This talk has no discernible impact on Harold, so his mother takes another slant:

You have led a very carefree, idle, happy life up to the present, the—the life of a child—but it is time to put away childish things and take on adult responsibilities. Oh, we would all like to sail through life with no thought of tomorrow. But that cannot be. We have our duties, our obligations, our principles. In short, Harold, I think it's time for you to get married.

Director Ashby then cuts to a church interior with the camera tilted high above the altar. Uplifting organ music fills the sanctuary, and one assumes that Mrs. Chasen is in the process of putting her marriage decree into effect. But like any good dark-comedy filmmaker, Ashby has been toying with the viewer. Harold is simply attending another funeral. It could be argued, however, that a metaphorical marriage begins that day, since Harold first meets fellow funeral hobbyist Maude at this ceremony. As if in honor of this event, as well as the genre's tendency to juxtapose conflicting music and visuals, the coffin is put into the hearse just as a marching band goes merrily past the church. (As an aside on the genre's use of oppositional music, this film is especially good and varied in the technique, from the often-clashing rock songs written and performed by Cat Stevens to the simple instrumental of "What Child is This" as Harold peacefully dangles from his noose at the film's beginning.)

Without rehashing the movie scene for scene, Maude's influence gives Harold the strength to continue standing up to the rigidity of his mother. The impoverished Maude leads a much richer life than Mrs. Chasen and her circle of society friends. She shares everything with Harold, from the reviewing of the five senses to replanting a sickly stolen tree in a cathedral-like forest. Maude is a walking endorsement of the free spirit, always aware of "how the world still dearly loves to cage." Despite being nearly eighty, in most every other way she is a standard eccentric screwball heroine, from living in a former train car to teaching Harold the Johnny Weissmuller Tarzan yell. She still models in the nude and regularly goes home from each funeral with a new "hot" car.

Maude's influence on Harold is apparent soon after his initial visit to her train-car residence. He returns home to meet the first of the computerized dates his mother has arranged. Harold then "treats" them to an apparent immolation suicide just outside the window. The date cannot exit the mansion quickly enough, leaving Mrs. Chasen and Harold standing together. But while the mother seems mystified by what has taken place, her son is slowly turning his eyes for a direct address stare at the camera (the viewer). The accompanying nodding of his head implies *anything* is possible. Mrs. Chasen is oblivious to all of this, as well as to its apparent source in Maude.

This direct-address rapport between Harold and the viewer makes one much more sympathetic to the dark comedy antihero. Moreover, the audience member is further drawn to Harold because he is the only character with this power. Direct address also provides both the viewer perk of being an insider and the added humor effect of Harold's awareness that he is a character in a fiction. Direct address undercuts the complete fictional story situation—a one-person spoofing of the film itself. Nothing could be more consistent with dark comedy's open season on everything.

While Maude rescues Harold from the rigidity symbolized by his mother and the establishment (especially Uncle Victor), this octogenarian has also loosened Harold from a lurking stiffness of his own. Maude loves a stranger's funeral as much as the next person—just look for her yellow umbrella among all the black ones. And as it turns out, she is very serious about suicide, embracing it as a kind of personal euthanasia. Still, Maude gives Harold a free-spirited tutorial on life and outrageousness. One critic affectionately described Ruth Gordon's character as a "warm, weird concentration camp survivor."[18]

Consequently, there should be no expectation that Harold will be anything less than "weird." His first response to Maude's death is typical Harold driving his car off a cliff for another fake suicide. But his next appearance, playing the banjo Maude has given him, speaks volumes about his now broader outlook on life. The establishment is a straitjacket that hinders human dignity, even if that only means the freedom to be outrageous, and Harold will not be contained.

Such rhetoric is not the dark humor norm. But as noted at the beginning of this chapter, coming-of-age black comedies often have more upbeat closings than the genre standard. It is as if youth must be given a future. Of course, if one plays devil's advocate, Harold's survival should be balanced with Maude's suicide. The story's healthiest and happiest character picks an arbitrary date and kills herself. Seen in this manner, even Harold's happiness has a deathly cost. Ironically, what has proven to be catharsis for Harold (Maude's suicide) is something he has never followed through on.

The often screwball comedy substructure of *Harold and Maude* works on several levels. Consistent with dark comedy, the film skewers this or any other genre. Second, screwball's normal romantic triangle herein puts Harold in a sexually perverse situation—pairing up with his mother, or someone the age of his grandmother . . . plus a few years. Third, screwball comedy's propensity to feature eccentric relatives both enlivens *Harold and Maude* and better showcases dark comedy's tendency to key upon the dysfunctional family. Fourth, screwball comedy's frequent merging of a romantic duo from diverse economic stations when applied to *Harold and Maude* creates a controversial situation, so fitting for dark comedy. While Harold and Maude get along, his mother tries to stop the relationship. In screwball comedy, class differences are overcome both by the couple and pivotal family members, such as Dudley Moore's cinema grandmother in *Arthur*.

As a final commentary on dark comedy, *Harold and Maude* and its use of screwball comedy, one must keep in mind that the latter genre is about "implosion"—drawing people together. Black humor embraces just the opposite—explosion . . . maximizing differences for comic effect, as well as getting one's way, such as Harold's fake suicides to drive computer dates away.

I once wrote a book on screwball comedy subtitled the "Genre of Madcap Romance." With dark humor, one need only focus on the single syllable "Mad."

HEATHERS

Unlike *Harold and Maude*, *Heathers* was uniformly praised when it was released in 1989. There was no need for the slow, cult following build-up of the former film. *Newsweek* said of *Heathers*, "As black as pitch, this twisted comedy of high-school horrors is a work of genuine audacity."[19] *Variety* stated, "Daniel Waters' enormously clever screenplay blazes a trail of originality through the dead wood of the teen comedy genre."[20] The *Nation* said: "The film lets you fulfill one of the core fantasies of adolescence: seeing all the popular kids in their graves."[21] The *Chicago Tribune* likened the high-school Bonnie and Clyde (Winona Ryder and Christian Slater) to "haunted characters—in a surprisingly bland Midwestern setting, where the hottest entertainment in town is cow-tipping."[22]

Fittingly, the "bland Midwestern setting" is Sherwood, Ohio, a literary reference that cannot go unexamined. In 1919, Sherwood Anderson wrote *Winesburg, Ohio*, a unified collection of short stories that laid bare small town mid-America. Anderson wrote of "grotesques," repressed villagers who so narrowly grasped some truth that it became a falsehood. And with it came increased human isolation and the inability to communicate one's feelings.

Anderson's work was part of what literature terms "the revolt from the village," a movement of the late 1910s and the 1920s that focused on small-town hypocrisy and emptiness but "was in actuality an over-all attack on middle-class American civilization."[23] The new wave was precipitated by Edgar Lee Master's *Spoon River*

Anthology (1915), "Though it required five years for the influence of that book to pass thoroughly over from poetry to prose."[24]

Winesburg, Ohio would be one of those pivotal prose works. It is sometimes argued that dark comedy novelist Nathanael West's *The Day of the Locust* was influenced by this Sherwood Anderson work. Carl Van Doven's watershed essay "the Revolt from the Village" (1921) begins with a brief overview on how "For nearly half a century native literature has been faithful to the cult of the village, celebrating its delicate merits with sentimental affections."[25] And Anthony Channell Hilfer's overview volume of the movement, *The Revolt from the Village: 1915–1930*, examines even more deeply the roots of America's affection for the village and how this affection soured.[26] Understandably, this reinterpretation of a basic American institution created a storm of controversy. *Winesburg, Ohio* has always been a pivotal book in the movement, after *Spoon River Anthology*. Consequently, setting *Heathers* in Sherwood, Ohio, is immediately sending out a message: beware of adults who are narrow-minded "grotesques."

Heathers is saturated with adult "grotesques," but the dysfunctional families of Veronica and J. D. lead the parade. The viewer is given access to several interactions between Veronica and her unperceptive mother and father (Jennifer Rhodes and Bill Cort). These conversations have a pathetic pattern that is repeated throughout the film with only slight variation. For instance, the first example finds Veronica's dad, Mr. Sawyer, observing: "God damn, will someone tell me why I read these spy novels?" Winona Ryder's character constantly replies to such questions with, "Because you're an idiot." And then her father comes back with the self-deprecating line, "Oh yeah, that's it." The darkly comic topper to these father-daughter conversations is the cloying final line by Veronica's mother: "You two," as if there were some sort of meaningful, warm dialogue going on. And if there is any danger of hurt feelings, Mrs. Sawyer is always quick to offer pâté as a peace offering. As in Anderson's book, *Heathers* has very little communication going on among the characters.

While Veronica's parents are not fully attuned to their child, or to life in general, they are not dangerous. The same cannot be said of J. D.'s father. He is a contractor who frequently blows up old buildings anonymously if they threaten his new project. Though few details are given, it appears that J. D.'s mother was so unhappy in the relationship that she secretly entered one of these buildings shortly before it exploded—another example of suicide for the genre. J. D.'s mother was the only adult he had ever loved, and her surreal wave to him from the about-to-detonate structure obsessed him. (Fittingly, the most celebrated story in *Winesburg, Ohio*, "Mother," is about a loving mother and son who cannot communicate.)

When J. D. and his father converse there is a disturbing reversal of roles. For instance, their first talk has J. D. say, "Hey, son, I didn't hear you come in."

"Hey Dad, how was work today? Gosh, I almost forgot to introduce my girlfriend," J. D.'s dad replies.

"Veronica this is my Dad; Dad, Veronica. Son, why don't you ask your little friend to stay for dinner?," says J. D.

The only time this father from hell seems remotely happy is when the viewer sees him show a videotape of his latest building detonation to Veronica and J. D. Again, it is implied that the father acted before he had total clearance to dynamite the structure. But this vigilante blast exhilarates him. Eventually Christian Slater's character fully embraces all his father's values, from attempting to blow up the school to observations like, "Chaos is great."

One does not meet J. D. immediately. This film begins with three attractive high school girls playing croquet (see illustration 12). All named Heather, they are "the most popular clique in school." Veronica is there, too. The scene takes place in her backyard, and this is her initiation into the "Heathers." Ryder's character is buried in the ground up to her head, with the clique allegedly welcome to smack her up side of the head with a croquet ball.

Appropriately for dark comedy, the sentimental song "Que Sera, Sera" is heard on the soundtrack as this potentially lethal approach to croquet is played. One could argue this is the most inspired use of a contrasting song in the genre. "Que Sera, Sera," made popular by Doris Day in Alfred Hitchcock's 1956 version of *The Man Who Knew Too Much*, is about a little girl asking her mother how she will grow up. That image is a wonderfully ironic clash with the nasty Heathers.

Los Angeles Times film critic Sheila Benson took this alleged initiation scene, where Veronica Sawyer is buried in the ground up to her neck as a croquet target, quite literally.[27] But most other reviewers avoided critiquing this segment. Obviously there is no

12. Left to right, Winona Ryder, Kim Walker, Lisanne Falk, and Shannen Doherty in *Heathers*.

single correct "reading" of the scene. But it would seem more appropriate to link this episode with Veronica's later comic nightmare about Heather Duke's (Shannen Doherty) suicide/murder and the bizarre funeral that follows.

The initiation sequence is not as flamboyantly shot as the nightmare, but it is still establishing the nasty tendencies of these three bitch goddesses. Moreover, it is only in this opening scene that Veronica, buried up to her neck, provides any direct-address comments to the viewer. She seems to imply that if such initiation were possible, the Heathers would do it, because there are no cooler cliques to try for. Moreover, as was noted earlier in the chapter, the use of direct address creates a special bond between a character and the viewer.

The film really starts with the three Heathers and Veronica conducting their regular lunchtime poll at school. This question asks what you would do if, after inheriting a fortune, you discovered the world would soon end? While this provides a comic opportunity for some offbeat answers (a satire of the young), the most significant thing that occurs over lunch is the cruel prank played on overweight student Martha Dunnstock (Carrie Lynn). A fake romantic note is written to Martha allegedly from the high school quarterback Kurt Kelly (Lance Fenton). Naturally, the girl ends up being humiliated by Kurt and his linebacker best friend Ram (Patrick Labyorteaux).

The scene reveals three additional significant points of interest. First, Ryder's character has the talent to quickly and easily reproduce anyone's handwriting. Second, Heather Chandler (Kim Walker) is not only the leader of the Heathers, she is the cruelest and most biting with her wit: "Fuck me gently with a chainsaw." Third, Slater's J. D., effectively playing a teen version of Jack Nicholson, is both introduced in this segment and revealed to have a romantic power over Veronica. Indeed, Heather McNamara (Lisanne Falk) is moved to ask Veronica if she drools much.

The next time Veronica meets J. D., she apologies for the Heathers, adding, "They're, like, people I work with, and our job is being popular and shit." Ryder's character feels she has deserted her old friends to join a clique with which she is no longer happy. J. D., with his moody good looks and motorcycle, seems to be someone with whom she can better relate.

Veronica Sawyer's break with the Heathers is a result of Heather Chandler taking her to a college kegger party, where she is sexually harassed and becomes physically ill. Yet Heather No. 1 blames everything on Veronica and threatens to ruin her social reputation.

A pivotal scene follows later that night. Sawyer is in her second-story bedroom furiously writing away in her diary: "I want to kill. And you have to believe it's more than just selfish reasons. More than for just a spoke in my menstrual cycle." After adding she must stop this Heather, Veronica observes: "killing Heather [Kim Walker] would be like offing [killing] the wicked witch of the west, wait, east, west, God I sound like a fucking psycho."

Suddenly J. D. magically appears in the window and Veronica nearly loses it. Yet Slater's character can be seen as an answer to her diary wish for death to Heather No. 1. Indeed, *Newsweek* compared J. D.'s figure to Goethe's Mephistopheles, a devil to whom Faust sold his soul for riches and power.28 *The New Yorker* added: "This cocksure demon [J. D.] may have materialized out of what Veronica has written: he goads her to become his accomplice in making her dream come true."29 *New York* magazine suggested he was an "avenging angel" or "the Devil."30 Of course, the normal domain of demons and the like is the horror genre, where if some sort of pact is made with the devil there is generally no breaking it. Yet, by film's end and several murders later, Veronica can return to being the most thoughtful of students with absolutely no psychological baggage to carry around. As one critic observed, the walk away from several killings without guilt "is the most profound cynicism of *Heathers*."31 One is reminded of the old Flip Wilson routine where his Geraldine character would alibi about any misdeed, "The devil made me do it!"

Regardless, the earlier reference to the old world figure of Mephistopheles might explain why Veronica wears a monocle (something much more common to Goethe's period than hers) whenever she writes. Ryder's character also scribbles away with such a dramatic flourish it neatly satirizes the perception of the nineteenth-century romantic artist.

Whether one believes Slater's character is the devil of the week, or that J. D. simply stands for "juvenile delinquent," he is the catalyst behind making Veronica's deathly dreams come true. And as is a given for this genre, where sex and death often feed on each other, this young couple quickly seal their relationship with a game of strip croquet. How appropriate that the film should open in the same setting—but then it is violent croquet, while now it is sexual.

Veronica and J. D. are two teenagers with more than time to kill. If they had a working moral it might be the derailing of the old popular maxim, "You can't make an omelet without jeopardizing the lives of a few innocent people." Except there is nothing innocent about Heather No. 1, their initial target. As with the many wives Charlie Chaplin's title character knocks off in *A Monsieur Verdoux* (1947), the *Heathers* viewer feels no remorse over her exit. The viewer assumes this Heather is the architect of a nasty yet entertaining high school language. Britain's *Sight and Sound* went so far as to call it "as inventive and ribald as anything in *A Clockwork Orange*" (1971).[32] For example, "what's your damage" is a sign of impatience, while "how very" is a term of contempt. This "teen-speak," as *Films in Review* labeled it, is important for several reasons.[33] Besides its refreshingly comic slant, it gives the audience member a reason to tolerate for a time the self-styled "bitches" who each refers to herself as Heather. Also, it allows the viewer to not become as emotionally close to the Heathers mob, what with their otherworldly lingo.

Of all the killings, the demise of Heather No.1 seemingly starts off innocently. Veronica and J. D. go to Heather Chandler's home for mild revenge . . . or at least Ryder's character does. With Heather No.1 sleeping and her family gone, the wannabe Bonnie and Clyde enter the house and decide they will prepare a memorably gross wake-up drink. Veronica feels a mixture of milk and orange juice topped off with a phlegm gob would be perfect. Unfortunately, neither she nor J. D. can produce phlegm on command so they go with J. D.'s mix—a cup of the macabre Liquid Drano, in a lovely shade of blue. Veronica nixes this idea but then accidently picks up the cup with the lethal contents and heads for Heather's room. J. D. starts to tell Veronica but then thinks a murder would be so much more entertaining. And it is. The late but not so great Heather downs the drink and has one of cinema's great death scenes, particularly when she falls forward onto and shatters a large glass coffee table. But Veronica and J. D. do not need any exhilaration; they adjust very quickly and painlessly to murder.

Initially, this means protecting themselves with a fake suicide note, and Veronica is very impressed with J. D.'s ability to come up with great lines. Kiddingly she asks if he has done this before.

Immediately one's thoughts turn to the earlier metaphorical suggestion that he is the devil or some demon, especially in the ease with which he has Ryder's character accepting murder.

This killing also brings up a subject addressed in Chapter 1, Darwin and the historical ties to dark comedy. A Darwinian slant, the survival of the fittest, is often ready fodder for this genre. Sometimes it can be hidden in a passing reference, such as Nathanael West naming a character in his black humor novel *The Dream Life of Balso Snell* (1931), Beagle Darwin, combining the evolutionist's name and the ship from which he made so many of his discoveries. Or, as with *Films in Review* critic Charles Epstein, it can be applied much more broadly, defining *Heathers* as a "Darwinian battleground" in the midwestern high school.[34]

Most teens feel this "battleground" at some time, especially with groups like the Heathers setting the standards, or bullying jocks creating the fear factor. The ultimate Darwinian survivors in the movie are J. D. and Veronica. Slater's character has survived seven moves, with in-your-face clique groups at seven schools. He has also witnessed his mother's unofficial suicide when she knowingly walked into a building set to explode soon. And when he has been harassed, people tend to die, such as the two obnoxious athletes previously mentioned. J. D., too, eventually dies, but it is on his own terms. Like his mother, he decides to blow himself up.

Veronica goes J. D. one better. She survived being an egghead in a school that did not appreciate them (few do). She then managed to both join the elite school group and later get out of it. (It helps if you kill the leader of the offending clique.) But her most accomplished success in this "Darwinian battleground" is her victory over J. D., from faking a suicide by hanging (throwing him off her track), to beating him in a gun battle near the film's close. Her temporary fascination with the revengeful J. D. could be likened to genre critic Robert Warshow's insight on why the public is so often taken (in a guilty-pleasure sort of way) with the movie gangster figure. Warshow suggested the gangster "is what we want to be and what we are afraid we may become."[35] In many ways that same logic can be applied to fans of dark comedy. Even as adults most persons could come up with a list of expendable people. Naturally, very few would ever act upon this. But by merely having a list, one is implicated in J. D.'s actions, as well as in the real-life murder cases, that have for years secretly captured the public's fascination.

After the demise of Heather No.1, the duo become more ambitious. Veronica and J. D. kill the two detestable football players. The jocks have spread a rumor that she performed oral sex with them simultaneously. Despite her legitimate reason for some sort of revenge—dark comedy's man as beast—she does not believe J. D.'s plans for murder . . . or does she? He has told Veronica they will be using "Ick luge" German bullets, which at worst will only give their victims superficial wounds. But before describing the bullets he asks her if she has ever taken German. With Veronica's no he spins his "Ick luge" tale, the German words meaning "I lie." Slater's J. D. also has Ryder's character prepare some more suicide notes, hardly standard procedure for victims about to merely suffer modest flesh wounds. Veronica is said to be a gifted student, but she either wants these events to happen and/or J. D. can deaden the thinking process as well as people.

When Ryder's figure claims to be upset with the jock murders, Slater's character responds that football season is over and all these pituitary cases had to offer the school is date rape and AIDS jokes. J. D.'s comments are reminiscent of the 1910's and 1920's "Futurist" movement which believed that civilizations could progress only if periodically purged of the lower class rabble. (See Chapter 1.) Later in the movie Heather No. 2 (Shannen Doherty) makes an even more damning comment on the lower classes as cannon fodder. An obese, unpopular girl, Martha Dunnstock, attempts to kill herself by walking into traffic with her suicide note pinned on her blouse. After this comically pitiful act, Doherty's Heather states what a better place this world would be if "every nimrod followed her [Martha's] cue."

In Chapters 1 and 2 much is written about black comedy ties to war settings, such as *M.A.S.H.* (1970) or *Catch-22* (1970). But even when the genre does not openly embrace combat, dark humor is metaphorically about war. Examples stretch from the inevitable execution of Chaplin's title character in *Monsieur Verdoux* (because he could not kill on a scale comparable to a nation at war), to the casual observation made by Jessica Lange's character in *Crimes of the Heart* (1986), "There are plenty of good sane reasons to shoot another person." An excellent romantic comedy gone dark that fully embraces this battleground mentality has the inspired title

The War of the Roses (1989), punning both the actual war of that name and a battle between former lovers. *Heathers* quickly escalates into a warlike situation. After the killing of the jocks, Kurt and Ram, Veronica even writes in her diary that her teen angst has a "body count."

Dark comedy's man-as-beast theme (especially vulnerable to sex) is especially apparent when guerrilla warriors J. D. and Veronica kill the jocks, who are promised sexual favors if they appear behind the school at dawn. With this kind of incentive, they are incapable of considering any trickery. Like a resistance operation, J. D. has mapped everything out and is in hiding when they appear. The jocks are soon history, but nearby police who have discovered the bodies cause a temporary problem for J. D. and Veronica. Instead of trying to drive off, the couple partially disrobe and pretend to be making out. The investigating officer, unable to think beyond sex, does not suspect them for a second, though he enjoys watching them. And when he reports to his partner by walkie-talkie (still watching), his sidekick's only pressing question is whether the couple is nude.

Before their escape J. D. and Veronica plant Kurt and Ram's alleged suicide note, which paints them as tortured gay lovers. J. D. also leaves some stereotypical comic gay items, like a picture of Joan Crawford. All of this makes for the ultimate black comedy funeral. Unlike the frequent examples of this ritual in *Harold and Maude*, where the black comedy is in someone going to a normal funeral just for the fun of it, this particular *Heathers* funeral is a genre classic because the ritual itself is in such poor comedy taste (just like making light of teen suicide). The funeral includes everything from the boys being laid out in their caskets in full football regalia (including helmets), to one father making a big production of forgiving his dead gay son. Indeed, to top this scene, the film's next funeral is a surrealistic fantasy which turns out to be a Veronica nightmare.

While J. D. is becoming more and more enamored of chaos via violence, Veronica is concerned about her lack of control over him. She wonders whether her next stop is prom or hell. She attempts a break from J. D., and he begins to implement his most destructive plan—a scheme to blow up the school with the student body and make it appear to be a giant suicide pact. Such an apocalyptic close fits the nickname sometimes applied to the film, the *"Dr. Strangelove* of teen movies." Fittingly, *Heathers*'s young, first-time screenwriter, Daniel Waters, had dreamed, "I was going to write the greatest teen film and Stanley Kubrick [director of *Dr. Strangelove*] was gonna direct it."[36]

If Veronica's movement from murder accomplice back to good girl seems rather sudden (and it does), part of that shakiness comes from Waters's original draft of the script where Veronica was "almost like a 'female Travis Bickle' [the violent lead character in *Taxi Driver*, 1976], blowing herself up at the end of the movie."[37] Of course, in the final cut of *Heathers* these characteristics have been transferred to Slater's figure.

If an explanation is needed for Veronica retiring from her Bonnie and Clyde union with J. D., however, it would be the realization that the popular and yet cruel students she and J. D. killed all ended up being praised into martyrdom. Absurdly, they were even more present and powerful in death. So, for Veronica, what was the point? One is reminded of Luis Buñuel's and Salvador Dali's controversial film *Andalusian Dog* (1929, see Chapter 1). Their nonsense takeoff on the art house film was constantly being interpreted as if there was a story by critics and filmmakers the world over. Though the director initially found this to be a great joke, it eventually became old. Here was a truly unintended slant on dark comedy's longterm ties with absurdity.

Though Veronica never becomes Travis Bickle, she reaches a point where she knows a confrontation with J. D. is necessary for two reasons. Their split makes her a witness who must be eliminated. Second, she cannot allow J. D. to keep killing, especially on the epic scale he plans. Fittingly, suicide plays a part in Veronica's accomplishment of both tasks. But she is rushed into the first situation, since Slater's character has told her parents that she is suicidal . . . setting up an explanation for J. D. killing her and making it look like yet another suicide. He has also hung a Barbie doll up in her room, as well as leaving the written message "Prepare the handwriting" —translation: your suicide is next.

Her defense is a scene that borrows directly from *Harold and Maude*. Veronica pretends to hang herself from a beam in her bedroom, fooling J. D. when he comes by. But before Veronica ends her "death scene," her mother enters the room. The older woman's casual response, both visually and verbally, to what should be a horrific spectacle immediately conjures up images of Harold's mother coming in to find him hanging from a beam.

Veronica's trick buys her time to stop J. D. the next day. His character plans to make the explosion of Westerburg High and its allegedly willing student body an indictment of shallow contemporary life in these United States . . . coming back full circle to the literary symbolism of the story taking place in Sherwood, Ohio.

In an earlier portion of the film, dead Heather No. 1 resurfaces in a Veronica nightmare, complaining that the afterlife is so boring and griping about how much they have to sing "Kum Ba Yah." This is the inspired sort of scene one wishes for the conclusion. Instead it is Veronica the good stalking J. D. the bad in the high-school basement, where he is setting up the explosives.

The direct confrontation is not, however, without interest, given the aforementioned speculation about J. D.'s other-worldly power, or what the *New York Times* described as a "demonic sitcom."[38] In an interview added to the original video release of *Heathers*, Veronica's Winona Ryder observes, "It's God versus my boyfriend [J. D.] and God's losing." Luckily for the school, Ryder's character seems to have more luck, since she stymies J. D.'s attempt to destroy both the school and the student body.

Veronica also gets to pay Slater's figure back for a celebrated earlier dark comedy act. After the killing of the two football players, Ryder's character begins to feel guilt. As if to atone for this through self-mutilation, she burns her hand with an automobile cigarette lighter. Immediately, her lover J. D. grabs the hand and puts his face close to the wound, as if to check its severity, comfort her, cradle the hand. . . . Instead, he sticks his unlit cigarette in the still hot wound and manages to get a light. Having shown *Heathers* to numerous university classes, that scene invariably receives the biggest gasp/comedy laugh of any movie I have projected.

Veronica's cigarette revenge comes near the close. J. D. has wired himself to blow up in front of the school. She stands several yards away on the high-school steps. Just before the explosion Veronica slips a cigarette into her mouth. The heat of J. D.'s exit blast lights her cigarette. She has won—with a vengeance.

Sooty and bloody from her ordeal, she enters the school and meets the overdressed Heather No. 2 (Shannen Doherty) and takes the symbolic hair tie that represents leadership of the elite Heathers. Veronica puts the cloth tie in her hair and tells Doherty's character there is a new sheriff in town. Veronica then runs into the fat unpopular Martha, who has failed earlier at suicide, and invites her over for prom night in order to have a girls' night party. Veronica has returned to the good. Indeed, her reference to the western, via the new sheriff comment, is quite the contrast with dark comedy. That is, the traditional western, especially where the focus character takes metaphorical credit for being the sheriff, is very much a genre about law and order, hardly the stuff of dark comedy. This apparent genre flaw, however, is not without a defense. As noted earlier in the chapter, black humor tends to end on a somber note. Yet coming-of-age examples of the genre frequently break this rule, whether it is Veronica walking away from her crimes or Harold deciding not to include himself in the sports car going off the cliff.

There is a sort of perverse logic, moreover, in allowing this type of dark comedy to happen, because in both *Heathers* and *Harold and Maude*, while the leading characters survive, their partners in love commit suicide. Consequently, one can dispute the conclusion of these and many other examples of the genre as dark or light as one might want. And in several classroom discussions through the years many of my students have argued that the conclusion of *Heathers* is so "nice" for Ryder's character that they have merely "read" the finale as a satire of a happy ending that would be unlikely. One could apply this argument to such other seemingly upbeat dark comedy conclusions as *Catch-22* (1970) and *The Player* (1992). Regardless of how one defines the black humor conclusion, its provocative nature is fitting for a genre based in controversy.

As an interesting extension of the youth-oriented dark comedy, both the screenwriter (Daniel Waters) and director (Michael Lehmann) of *Heathers* were in their twenties when they made this watershed work which was also the first major screen credit for both men. Waters's material literally drew, in part, from his midwestern high school writing. Consequently, the freshness of the movie makes one believe "These two may be settling a few old [high-school] scores."[39]

Like any real work of art, however, one need not be locked into a single interpretation. The coming-of-age slant is dominant in *Heathers*. But it also addresses the misused power of the media, a phenomenon which will be examined later in this chapter with *Natural Born Killers* (1994). *Heathers* can also be seen as an unconventional attack on the war film, from its frequent references to "body counts" and mad bomber J. D., to British critic Alan Stanbrook's observation that the film "is about an organization [the Heathers] that runs the world behind its back."[40] But when one Heather (dictator) dies, another just takes over, which is the message of Woody Allen's dark comedy *Bananas* (1971). And J. D.'s total embrace of chaos becomes a bigger threat than the Heathers.

One is tempted to close with the old German proverb, "In times of war the devil makes more room in hell." Only in this book, the proverb could have "black humor" substituted for the word "war." In this genre the condition is always "war," regardless of apparent setting.

NATURAL BORN KILLERS

Harold and Maude (1970) was initially a critical and commercial failure. *Heathers* (1989) won rave reviews but did not find a theatrical audience. It was reborn by word of mouth on the video store circuit, just as *Harold and Maude* was kept alive as a cult event in the art house movement.

Contrarily, *Natural Born Killers* (1994) opened to mixed reviews but huge box office returns. Those critics that approved of the film raved. *Entertainment*'s Owen Gleiberman said *"Natural Born Killers* is brilliant—the most haunting experience I've had at the movies this year."[41] Syndicated critic Roger Ebert wrote, "Seeing this movie once is not enough. The first time is for the visceral experience, the second time is for the meaning. . . . *Natural Born Killers* is like a slap in the face, waking us up to what's happening."[42]

Ebert's reference to the "visceral experience" should be addressed first, since it is the most striking aspect of this extremely dark comedy, which involves the violent road odyssey of a '90s-style Bonnie and Clyde (see illustration 13). But instead of the signature line of the Depression duo, "We rob banks," Mickey and Mallory (Woody Harrelson and Juliette Lewis) could have observed, "We kill people."

Director Oliver Stone presents this psychedelic death "march" in the most formalistic manner (where the viewer is aware of the artist's mark on the film). Thus, different types of movie stock are used: shots cut back and forth between color and black and white; animated footage periodically surfaces; regular film speed alter-

13. Woody Harrelson and Juliette Lewis in *Natural Born Killers*.

nates with slow motion and fast editing. And Stone uses unrealistic rear projection. Outside Mickey and Mallory's 1970 Dodge Challenger, or through their sleazy motel window, blown-up montages of everything from newspaper headlines to actual footage of history's frightening figures appear. The movie is shot at extremely tilted (even berserk) camera angles, many more than one might expect in film noir, the genre to which it is most associated. On the soundtrack, music moves from opera to rock. Through the use of slide projection words are projected on Mickey and Mallory. Many of these techniques are also used to incorporate footage from earlier movies. The most significant with relationship to *Natural Born Killers* is *The Wild Bunch* (1969), director Sam Peckinpah's masterpiece to a lyrical sense of violence via editing and slow motion.

For Stone to embrace these methods so ambitiously is relatively rare in a mainstream Hollywood movie. Fittingly, the film has been compared to the surrealistic avant-garde classic *Andalusian Dog* (1929, see Chapter 1).[43] And, *Newsweek* observed, "the film's multifarious formats are as precisely placed as the planes in a cubist Picasso."[44]

There are five reasons for this formalistic, self-conscious incorporation of technology and technique. First, as is often the case with dark comedy, this approach can disorient the viewer. Difficulty in following the story apes the plotless nature of life. If some people are bothered by this, so be it. The genre takes creative risks, including the possible alienation of viewers. Second, *Natural Born Killers* uses such devices to shock the viewer, like the bloody, decapitated body sitting upright that appears more than once. But it need not be such a grizzly shock. There is also a scene where bullets suddenly become cartoon figures searching out their prey. The idea, as always, is to keep the viewer off balance. Appropriately, Stone's own description of his directing style perfectly matches his use of the media: "I take you out of your comfort zone."[45] Third, it should not be forgotten that such images are also meant to showcase the thoughts going on inside the minds of Mickey and Mallory. Sometimes access to the mind explains why a character acts in a certain manner before a specific incident occurs. For instance, Mallory's lethal nature towards sexually aggressive males becomes more explainable when one is made privy to incidents of molestation by her father (Rodney Dangerfield). These short segments from the past are often in black and white, such as Mickey's boyhood witnessing of his father's suicide. There is a tendency to think of black and white being more real and representative of the past; witness its effective use in *Schindler's List*.

A fourth way in which Stone uses formalistic methods for a premeditated purpose is to underline that *Natural Born Killers* is a dark comedy. Too much realism can undercut a genre of this type. For instance, Stone commissioned animator Mike Smith, of MTV's *Liquid Television*, to create a cartoon sequence where Mickey and Mallory are hypermuscled heroes. As critic Roger Ebert observed, "He [Stone] lets you know he's making a comedy."[46] Though few reviewers made the special effects/comedy connection, some critics seemed to inadvertently recognize the phenomenon. *The New Yorker* reviewer Terrence Rafferty had just such a comment, actually very comedic in and of itself: "it's one of the least disturbing films about mass murder you'll ever see."[47]

A final way Stone uses his *Natural Born Killer* formalist style, or what one critic calls the ability to "grab your lapels and scream in your face,"[48] is as an indictment of both the media and society. The timing could not have been better for such an attack. The O. J. Simpson case was still unfolding. And by the time Simpson went to trial for murder the phrase "media circus" took on otherwise unheard-of dimensions. Additional bizarre, high-profile cases surfaced near the film's opening. These include the grown Menendez brothers, who claimed they had been molested years before by their rich parents and thus felt justified in killing them; Lorena Bobbitt's trial for cutting off her husband's penis; and David Koresh and his Waco, Texas, religious cult going up in smoke. Brief clips of these events and numerous other major media stories which involve violence not noted here are included at the film's close. Director Stone described *Natural Born Killers* in the following manner: "I'm making the point that the killers have been so idealized and so glorified by that media that the media has become worse than the killers."[49]

Complementing this is a scene near the movie's close where Mickey is about to execute tabloid/TV star Wayne Gayle (Robert Downey, Jr.). Gayle has been with the duo throughout their escape and feels like one of them. When he begs for his life he suggests a bond has grown between them. Mickey/Stone says, "No, not really. You're scum, Wayne. You did it for the ratings. You don't give a shit about us or anybody, except yourself. That's why nobody gives a shit about you." Mickey and Mallory then shoot Gayle. And though this is just one of over fifty murders they commit, the film is as much about how people respond to violence as it is about violence itself. For instance, when Mickey and Mallory are on trial for murder, one of their many fans outside the court building holds up a poster proclaiming "Murder Me, Mickey." There are many other fans who hoist up signs that simply showcase Mickey and Mallory on the cover page of numerous magazines. Fittingly, the start of the Simpson case, which paralleled the release of *Natural Born Killers*, also created an army of fans for an accused murderer. Like it or not, it certainly gives more credence to controversial Stone's position about violence and the media.

These have been the five reasons for this director to embrace such a formalistic helter-skelter approach: disorient the viewer's narrative expectations; shock the audience into new perspectives; reveal the thoughts (past and present) of the superstar psychopaths Mickey and Mallory; accent the fact that it is a comedy; and emphasize the film's ongoing assault upon our violence–driven media and society.

To highlight the all-important violence in *Natural Born Killers* means keying upon the couple (Mickey and Mallory) as they combine elements from *Bonnie and Clyde* (1967) and *A Clockwork Orange* (1971). The former has been an ongoing model for young outlaw couples on the road/on the run. *A Clockwork Orange* features a young violent character (Malcolm McDowell) who thrives on violence and death, as do Mickey and Mallory.

The viewer is given more information about Mallory (as opposed to Mickey), which marks a departure from Stone's standard focus on the male. Early in the movie, via flashbacks, one witnesses what Mallory had to contend with in the most dysfunctional of families. She is constantly sexually mauled by her father, while the whole family (including Mallory's mother and brother) are verbally abused and physically threatened. But this is softened by the most inspired casting of recent years; Rodney Dangerfield plays the father. Dangerfield's stand-up comedy persona is an antihero forever spouting "I don't get no respect" as the opening for his jokes. Though he is playing against type, one is more likely to stay with a controversial character if you liked him/her in something else. Dangerfield comes across as on aging Ralph Kramden giving Alice that "Boom Zoom to the Moon" threat. And as is consistent with dark humor, Dangerfield's casting in the part is a shock.

If the viewer is still not buying into this as black humor, Stone turns all of Mallory's family flashbacks into the darkest of television parodies—the *I Love Mallory* show. The program has very phony sets, canned laughter, the most garish make-up, and performances not unlike what you might expect of a local community theater cast on acid. Some critics came up with their own titles for the program. For instance, *Time* offered *Father Knows Worst*, and *Rolling Stone* referred to it as *Incest with a Laugh Track*.[50] Regardless of titles, *Natural Born Killers* offers both background on Mallory's past and a metaphor of what she will become—a television star . . . only this time as a killer.

In contrast, the viewer does not see as much of Mickey's past. He has, however, also been abused, as well as having been on the scene when his father committed suicide with a shotgun.

Mickey and Mallory meet when he delivers a fifty-pound, blood-stained sack of very red meat to her house. This is not your typical home delivery, unless you are raising tigers in the basement. Once again Stone is saying, "read" this as dark comedy.[51] But there are other variations of the same violent symbolism, from Woody Harrelson's character's bloody clothes, representing all the murders to come, or more specifically, his murder of her parents on the next visit. Juliette Lewis's Mallory is most enthusiastic in helping Mickey with this nasty task. Here is the ultimate in dysfunctional families.

While these killer lovebirds go on their three-week odyssey of death, the momentary flashbacks imply that they are merely products of their environment, making one question the film's title; *Natural Born Killers* suggests a genetic situation. But there are much more controversial topics for a director of such provocative films as *JFK* (1991) and *Born on the Fourth of July* (1989). Besides the media as villain, which will soon be addressed further, some critics asked if Stone was not criticizing violence and yet exploiting it at the same time.

He has commented in various ways. There is the peevish response, "Was I supposed to make an dull movie?"[52] But a more somber Stone "believes the movie is ultimately anti-violent, because the killers escape their demons in the end."[53] (The close of the film finds Mickey and Mallory several years in the future still cruising the highways . . . but now they are driving the recreational vehicle with two small children, another on the way, and not a weapon in sight.) Is this a happy ending? Or, will there be a new comic nightmare version of *I Love Mallory*, with Mickey molesting their kids? A punster might label this question as being about a "heart of Stone." But the director has sincere feelings about felons found to have had abused childhoods. After all, this is the same director who had the word "demon" projected onto his '90s Bonnie and Clyde.

If the talented but hardly subtle Stone had wanted to put another closing message across, be it more projected words or the hail of bullets that closes *Bonnie and Clyde*, he would have done it. This is merely another example of a more upbeat conclusion in the coming-of-age variety of dark comedy. Moreover, in addition to the media, Stone had never thought of Mickey or Mallory as the film's real villain. That honor is reserved for Downey's Wayne Gayle, the Australian host of television's *American Maniacs*, which features interviews with serial killers. And when the nasty ones are not available, the show-within-the-movie re-creates an actual "dramatization." Gayle personifies that "new breed of reportage the Spanish have so beautifully nicknamed *telebasura* (telegarbage)"[54]. By blaming a violent society on the media, instead of on the perpetrator, one could say Stone is merely "killing the messenger." Interestingly, the film's near close finds messenger Gayle killed.

Though I suggest this only with tongue firmly in cheek, Stone might also have received a great deal of pleasure from slamming the fourth estate, given his often rocky relationship with critics. This same type of affectionately provocative stance occurred privately with Charlie Chaplin's *Monsieur Verdoux* (1947). The often woman-plagued Chaplin becomes a "Lady Killer" (the working title of the script, much of which was written during his messy paternity scandal with Joan Barry).

Whatever the motivation for the media-as-monster theme, it takes off in the second part of *Natural Born Killers*, after Mickey and Mallory have been in prison for a year. Just as Rodney Dangerfield was perfect casting for Mallory's dad, Robert Downey's Wayne Gayle is an inspired match. This is most advantageous for the picture, since Downey's Wayne carries the second part of the film. There are other strong characters, too. For example, Tommy Lee Jones's cartoon-creepy warden, Dwight McClusky, and the equally bored characterization by Tony Sizemore of the sadistic cop/author Jack Scagnetti. Naturally, Mickey and Mallory cannot be slighted, either. But it is Gayle's deadly push to interview Mickey on live television after the Super Bowl that creates a penal holocaust.

Gayle uses his gift of stroking egos to get by Jones's Warden McClusky. At first Gayle must eradicate the warden's opposition to letting in the media. But as Downey's smooth television personality makes clear, Andy Warhol's fifteen minutes of fame theory certainly works on the warden. McClusky immediately succumbs to the temptation of fame. When Scagnetti later questions McClusky on this "fall," the warden sheepishly answers, "You can't say no to the media"—a statement that might be used as the subtitle for *Natural Born Killers*. We are mesmerized by television—either what appears on it or by the chance to appear on it ourselves.

Out of this power base comes Downey's Gayle as the central player. Like Scagnetti and McClusky, Gayle is also cartoonish. But Downey adds an almost likable comic touch to his performance, despite the self-centeredness of his character. When he pitches the allegedly historic nature of his show he sounds like legendary nineteenth-century huckster P. T. Barnum. Gayle boasts this is "the first in-depth interview with the most charismatic serial killer ever!" Even his homework for the show is funny. For instance, he interviews a psychiatric specialist to air during the show. This expert observes, "They [Mickey and Mallory] know the difference between right and wrong. They just don't give a damn." But just as American humor's wise fool can provide insight into his or her comic comments, the specialist has provided a similar service. The many fans of Mickey and Mallory are fascinated that their duo "just doesn't give a damn." Add this perspective to a media that plays to the lowest common denominator and one ends up with many possible Mickeys and Mallorys. Anything for ratings. This is reminiscent of *Network* (1976), in which Peter Finch's character is killed because his ratings have dropped.

Downey's Gayle could also be linked to P. T. Barnum in an additional manner. The nineteenth-century huckster's basic philosophy was that people did not mind being fooled if they were entertained. For example, one might liken a Barnum attraction, such as his famous exhibition of an alleged mermaid, to an elaborate practical joke, something his autobiography frequently notes the showman had also long enjoyed staging in private.

Both Gayle and Barnum, however, have entertainment masquerading as hard news. But a fake mermaid is hardly as dangerous, barring a rash of drownings by wannabe mermaids, as the media lionizing of killers. Still, the bottom line for both showmen, Barnum's practical joke positioning notwithstanding, is the belief that the public is dumber than a post. In fact Barnum's most quoted axiom is, "There's a sucker born every moment." Coincidentally, Gayle says something very similar to Mickey after the conclusion of the live prison television interview: "Thanks [while embracing Mickey]. Every fucking moron in the world just saw that, mate."

The scenes with Gayle also tend to be the most consistently funny. For example, during the interview Mickey says that only the love of Mallory could destroy his demon. Gayle jumps on this and in direct address to the camera (the viewer) sarcastically observes as the segment goes to commercial break, "Only love can kill the demon? Hold that thought." Again, direct address enables the viewer to better relate to a character, especially one (Gayle) who recognizes some of the craziness going on despite the fact that he is also hypocritically profiting from—and possibly contributing to—just that craziness.

It only gets stranger for Downey's character when the couple forces him to accompany them and document the media-conscious Mickey and Mallory as they escape from prison. As Gayle's reporter becomes immersed in the violent breakout, he eventually is caught up in the killing and actually exchanges gunfire with the authorities. Thus, he becomes a study of how the media's glorifying of criminals can create copycat violence.

This conclusion teaches Gayle the ultimate life lesson: a Darwinian state provides both total freedom and total danger. Mickey and Mallory execute Gayle, the only surviving person in their prison escape group. Naturally, Downey's character pleads for his life but with no luck. Yet, his death does project several slants on "reading" the movie.

First, the killing duo normally allow one victim to survive to document their crimes. However, in the case of Gayle, the "lone survivor" is to be the videotape recordings of the dramatic prison escape. How darkly comic that the mechanical device which has made Gayle's career will now chronicle its conclusion.

Second, though unlike Hal, the evil computer of *2001* (1968), where he is in charge, the past success of Gayle's television program *American Maniacs* suggests one more example of mankind's ability to create a unique mechanical device but inability to control its use.

Third, before the prison interview of Mickey, both he and Gayle had talked at length about *American Maniacs'* past ratings of other infamous "maniacs." The episode devoted to Mickey and Mallory had finished second only to the Charles Manson program. Mickey was unbothered by this, explaining that Manson was "the king." How ironic, with Gayle's eventual execution, that this TV host will presumably be both star/victim of not only the last edition of *American Maniacs* but probably its highest rated program. After all the on-air murder of Peter Finch's character in *Network* (1976) also resulted in top ratings. Only in that case *Network* was warning about the near future, whereas *Natural Born Killers* is today, and director Stone closes the movie with newsreel footage of media-made, criminal-related superstars. With today's world one does not have to travel an acceptable path to fame. The young couple of *Natural Born Killers* just murdered people. Lots of people. The media took care of the rest.

Fourth, the prison interview and ongoing live coverage of the escape are broadcast after America's most watched sporting event—football's Super Bowl. As noted in Chapter 2's examination of the football conclusion of *M.A.S.H.* (1970), the sport represents an excellent contemporary microcosm of this violent, darkly comic world. War/football is the perfect chaotic symbol of every person's ongoing battle for day-to-day survival. Thus, director Stone could have had no better lead-in to this black humor interview than the celebrated Super Bowl.

Fifth, when Gayle attempts to demand a logical reason for his impending murder, Mickey provides a fitting answer for a genre based in the absurd: "This is not about you, you egomaniac. I kind of like you. But if we let you go we'd be just like everybody else . . . killing you . . . is a statement. I'm not 100 percent sure of what it's saying." Again, the message of dark comedy is—there is no message. Forced for a statement, however, one might hypothesize that Gayle symbolizes all sensationalistic media and that by killing him the problem was gone. And this would be the last killing . . . done by Mickey and Mallory. As if to augment this suggestion of Gayle's significance, his last action before his execution manages to side-swipe religion, too—a popular target for dark comedy. Gayle puts his arms out in a Christ-like crucifixion pose. The camera adds bigger-than-life physical stature to Gayle by shooting from a low-angle placement. The scene is largely shot in black and white, seemingly to minimize period differences in use of color and the knee-jerk response most viewers have to black and white representing something old. Add Gayle's beard and his mysterious quasi-religious chanting (which some unseen chorus briefly supports), and the Christ-like connection is hard to avoid. The scene could be called another example of director Stone's overselling a position. But this genre has produced several more blatant examples of Christ comedy, from the full-length film version of Britain's *Life of Brian* (1979) to Robert Altman's take-off scene on the Last Supper in *M.A.S.H.*.

Sixth, whether one buys Stone's position that the media has become the new, all-powerful religion of today, Gayle's Christ-like actions during his execution could be interpreted with yet a different slant. As Mickey so aptly described Gayle—an "ego Maniac"—the host's actions might merely represent Gayle's own overblown view of himself. And, as with Barnum, the bottom line is putting on a good show, regardless of the circumstances or costs. For example, in the prison escape Mallory prepares to shoot someone and Downey's character reaches over, not to stop her but rather to adjust his camera. People be damned; the camera reigns.

Regardless of which characters most fascinate, *Natural Born Killers* resonates with a cast that seems frighteningly contemporary, especially as accented by Stone's documentary footage close of today's real Mickeys and Mallorys. Indeed, at the end "Mallory suggests that perhaps the whole episode was staged for television . . . [with] none of it actually taking place."[55]

This hint of manipulation fits nicely into Stone's film résumé, best represented by his conspiracy-packed *JFK*, based on the murder of President John F. Kennedy. As critic David Ansen negatively suggests, director Stone and "Wayne Gayle are two sides of the same coin."[56] This fits the analogy that the modern American artist often indulges in his or her own variety of entertaining hoaxes. The viewer places confidence in what the storyteller relates, forming a kind of contract. Thus, Stone is an artist in suckering the too-accepting viewer into truths he or she otherwise might not have examined.

Whether or not one accepts the Stone-Gayle connection, it provides several provocative slants on the film. It introduces yet another possible reason for Gayle's domination of the second half of the movie—Stone consciously or subconsciously is casting himself in the film. It also addresses a comment Stone frequently made on the television promotion circuit (*The Tonight Show, Late Night with David Letterman* . . .) when the film was just being released. He would defend his use of movie violence to help curb real violence. But when pressed further he often added, "What did you want to have me make, a boring picture?" (see note 52). Once again Barnum and Stone's Gayle come to mind. And as long as O. J. Simpson stories keep surfacing, Stone and other artists have an ongoing publicity campaign for movies of this nature.

The three films examined in this chapter—*Harold and Maude, Heathers,* and *Natural Born Killers*—are watershed examples of coming-of-age dark comedies during the final three decades of the twentieth century. We have moved from black comedy dictators to dark humor teenagers bent on the same shock comedy. Yet, each variation under this dark-comedy umbrella embraces the genre's three interrelated themes: people as beasts, the absurdity of the world, and death's omnipresence. Indeed, one might further condense the three to the misuse of power by high authorities. But whereas the examples of this type in Chapter 3 keyed on traditional national areas such as the government and military complex, the teenage version focuses more on the home front—parent and peer pressure . . . with media's ever-growing influence.

The dysfunctional family is alive and well in many dark comedies. Each of this chapter's three films demonstrates a different variation on the phenomenon. In *Harold and Maude* the teenager suffers from neglect and periods of verbal abuse. *Heathers* demonstrates both psychological abuse (J. D.'s father) and the general neglect of Veronica's forever sedentary parents. Mallory's father (Rodney Dangerfield) is physically, sexually, and verbally abusive. In contrast to the populist films of a Frank Capra, much as *It's a Wonderful Life* (1946), where the family and related traditions are everything to the genre, parents—when present—in dark comedy are a major cause of the violence.

J. D. gets his demented sense of black humor and "dynamite solves all" philosophy from an equally demented construction-company–owning father in *Heathers*. The abuse Mallory receives from her father in *Natural Born Killers* is the catalyst for killing her parents (the girl's mother did not protect her) and scores of others. *Harold and Maude*, the earliest of the three, demonstrates two variations on dark parental influences. The most obvious is the neglectful, military-like mother. But one should not miss the surrogate father, the mother's military officer brother. The latter represents the age-old fear of "Big Brother" government/military replacing the family unit—be it George Orwell's novel *1984* (1949) or the early moments of *To Be or Not To Be*, when the play-within-the-film has Jack Benny's Nazi character turn a child against his father with a gift from the loving Führer.

Any parental void increases the dangerous power of the media, which turns the nasty Heather No. 1 angelic, or the murdering Mickey and Mallory into media idols. And the most shocking factor in the process is how these fifteen minutes of Andy Warhol fame characters are eaten-up by a public wanting their own fifteen minutes in front of the camera.

NOTES

1. Paul Fussell, *Thank God for the Atomic Bomb and Other Essays* (New York: Summit Books, 1988), p. 104.

2. Lee Blessing, *A Walk in the Woods* (New York: New American Library, 1986), p. 43.

3. Alec Guinness, letter to the author, May 23, 1989.

4. Ibid.

5. Pauline Kael, *Deeper Into Movies* (Boston: Little, Brown, 1973), p. 93.

6. André Bishop, "Preface," in Stephen Sondheim and John Weidman, *Assassins* (New York: Theatre Communications Group, 1991), p. xi.

7. Stephen Sondheim and John Weidman, *Assassins* (New York: Theatre Communication groups, 1991) p. 42.

8. Joseph M. Boggs, *The Art of Watching Films* (Mountain View, Calif.: Mayfield Publishing, 1991), p. 58.

9. Vincent Canby, "Hal Ashby's Comedy Opens at Coronet," *New York Times*, December 21, 1971, p. 51.

10. *Harold and Maude* review, *Variety*, December 15, 1971.

11. Canby, p. 51.

12. *Harold and Maude* advertisement, *Village Voice*, December 23, 1971, p. 66.

13. Michael Shedlin, *Harold and Maude* review, *Film Quarterly*, Fall 1972, p. 51.

14. Ibid.

15. Ibid., p. 53.

16. See my book *Screwball Comedy: A Genre of Madcap Romance* (Westport, Conn.: Greenwood Press, 1986); monograph, *Screwball Comedy: Defining a Film Genre* (Muncie, Indiana: Ball State University Press, 1983); article, "Screwball Comedy An Overview," *Journal of Popular Film and Television*, Winter 1986; chapter, "Screwball Comedy," in *Handbook of American Film Genres* (Westport, Conn.: Greenwood Press, 1988).

17. Henri Bergson, "Laughter," in *Comedy*, ed. Wylie Sypher (Garden City, N.Y.: Doubleday Anchor Books, 1956), p. 175.

18. Richard McGuinness, "Creatures Nosing for Crumbs," *Village Voice*, December 23, 1971, p. 66.

19. *Heathers* review, *Newsweek*, April 3, 1989, p. 67.

20. *Heathers* review, *Variety*, January 25, 1989, p. 15.

21. Stuart Klawans, *Heathers* review, *Nation*, April 17, 1989, p. 530.

22. Dave Kehr, "*Heathers* a Corrosive Satire with a Weird Energy," *Chicago Tribune*, March 31, 1989, Section 7, p. 34.

23. Anthony Channell Hilfer, *The Revolt from the Village: 1915–1930* (Chapel Hill: University of North Carolina Press, 1969), p. 5.

24. Carl Van Doren, "The Revolt from the Village," *Nation*, October 12, 1921, p. 407.

25. Ibid.

26. Hilfer, pp. 3–136.

27. Sheila Benson, "*Heathers* Gets Lost in a Moral Thicket," *Los Angeles Times*, March 31, 1989, section 6, p. 15.

28. *Newsweek*, p. 67.

29. Pauline Kael, *Heathers* review, *The New Yorker*, April 17, 1989, p. 115.

30. David Denby, "The Satirical *Heathers* Might Be Called Apocalyptic Sick Comedy," *New York* magazine, April 3, 1989, p. 68.

31. Benson, p. 15.

32. Alan Stanbrook, "Invasion of the Purple People Eaters," *Sight and Sound*, Winter 1990, p. 49.

33. Charles Epstein, *Heathers* review, *Films in Review*, September 1989, p. 424.

34. Ibid., p. 423.

35. John Raeburn, "The Gangster Film," in Wes D. Gehring, ed., *Handbook of American Film Genres* (Westport, Conn.: Greenwood Press, 1988), p. 58.

36. Steve Pond, "Student Body Count," *Rolling Stone*, April 20, 1989, p. 38.

37. Ibid.

38. Janet Maslin, "Getting Even," *New York Times*, March 31, 1989, Section C, p. 8.

39. Denby, p. 68.

40. Stanbrook, p. 50.

41. Owen Gleiberman, "American Psychos," *Entertainment*, August 24/September 2, 1994, p. 90.

42. Roger Ebert, "Killers a Biting Indictment of Society," syndicated by Universal Press, *Cedar Rapids Gazette*, August 26, 1994, p. W–7.

43. Stanley Kauffmann, "Apocalypse Now [Natural Born Killers]," *New Republic*, October 3, 1994, p. 26.

44. David Ansen, "Raw Carnage or Revelation?" *Newsweek*, August 29, 1994, p. 55.

45. Stephen Schiff, "The Last Wild Man," *The New Yorker*, August 8, 1994, p. 52.

46. Ebert, p. W–7.

47. Terrence Rafferty, "Helter Skelter," *The New Yorker*, September 5, 1995, p. 106.

48. Schiff, p. 42.

49. Ibid., p. 49.

50. Richard Corliss, "Stone Crazy," *Time*, August 29, 1994, p. 67.

51. Peter Travers, "Movie's Blood from a Stone," *Rolling Stone*, September 8, 1994, p. 84.

52. Jerry Carroll, "Oliver Stone on His 'Natural Born' Overkill," *San Francisco Chronicle*, syndicated, in the *Muncie Star*, August 28, 1994, p. B-10.

53. Susan Spillman, "Taking Aim at the Mayhem and the Media," *USA Today*, August 26, 1994, p. D-1.

54. Chris Change, "Feed the Reaper," *Film Comment*, July/August 1994, p. 38.

55. Richard A. Blake, "Stoned Again," *America*, September 17, 1994, p. 23.

56. Ansen, p. 55.

5

When Film Noir Becomes Dark Comedy

You're gettin' ready to blow? I'm a mushroom-cloud-layin' mother fucker! Every time my fingers touch brain [cleaning up after an accidental shooting] I'm *SUPERFLY, TNT*, I'm the *GUNS of NAVARONE.*

—Jules (Samuel L. Jackson) to hitman partner
Vincent Vega (John Travolta) in Quentin Tarantino's
Oscar-winning script for *Pulp Fiction* (1994)

Many genres utilize black humor, from the horror film *An American Werewolf in London* (1981), with a comically recurring dead character; to the Clint Eastwood European westerns (nicknamed the "spaghetti westerns") made with Italian director Sergio Leone, where Eastwood's laconic character, the "Man with No Name," brought a whole new dimension to the then-current phrase "body count." (In the Vietnam war, body counts were a regular part of American television's nightly news.) Movies such as these can be called a "compound genre," where elements of several movie types come together. If forced to limit a particular film to one label, the viewer must decide the movie's dominant genre traits. Consequently, the aforementioned horror film or Eastwood's westerns still are best pigeonholed into those categories.

Outside the classroom, where a professor can screen a quintessential genre example, such as John Ford's 1939 western classic *Stagecoach*, most mainstream American films add elements of other genres. It is then up to each viewer to ascertain which type best defines the work from his or her perspective. The preceding chapter examined three movies that can be filed, in the post-James Dean (1931–1955) world, as rebellious coming-of-age films. However, they are so immersed in black humor that this would seem to supersede the other genre.

This is not to suggest that since the volatile 1960s (in society and the arts) most genres have not produced some movies with strong dark comedy overtones, even in the most unlikely places. Two such examples are director Bob Fosse's Oscar-winning musicals *Cabaret* (1972) and *All That Jazz* (1979). But some genres are more predisposed to be overwhelmed by black humor, such as the coming-of-age trilogy examined in the previous chapter. Still, the closest genre fit for black comedy is *film noir*.

Film noir (black film) is an American genre first noted by French critics in the 1940s. As the title suggests, this movie is dark both in story and setting. As Robert Towne, the Oscar-winning screenwriter for *Chinatown* (1974, a later pivotal example of the genre) observed, "The noir hero is essentially someone who is born under a black cloud, who has character deficiency and is drawn to a dark fate, who is deeply self-destructive.[1]

Several period events contributed to noir birth. Despite America and her allies winning World War II, a great deal of disillusionment followed in the post-war 1940s. A hot war had merely been exchanged for a cold one, with atomic bombs as an option. Our Soviet Union ally had quickly become an enemy, attempting to dominate the world with communism.

The war's close also revealed the abyss of man's imhumanity to man—the Holocaust. How could such a event have occurred? Could it be so terrible that, as one critic observed, "Most people just do their job . . . [even if] it's shove Jews in ovens"[2] (See Chapters 1 and 2 for black humor ties to the Holocaust).

Sexuality and death are prominent in both noir and dark comedy. Noir titles often imply as much, such as *Murder My Sweet* (1944) or *Kiss of Death* (1947). A potentially threatening woman was an outgrowth of World War II's close. Women had successfully replaced men in the marketplace as the latter went off to war. When veterans returned, the so-called "Rosie the Riveter" frequently had mixed feelings about quitting. If "Rosie" threatened the 1940s male at one extreme, tough-guy fiction by such authors as Raymond Chandler and Dashiell Hammett are peopled with the most provocatively dangerous of women. These characters are a male sexual fantasy, but a fantasy synonymous with death.

Another period influence on noir is the Existentialism of Europeans Jean-Paul Sartre and Martin Heidegger, where man is alone in a godless, irrational world. (See Chapter 1 for more dark comedy ties.) Another European connection were those Jewish German filmmakers who found themselves in Hollywood after escaping Nazi Europe. If this experience was not enough to draw them to noir, or dark comedy, the film foundation for most of these artists was 1920s German Expressionism. This national cinema movement is seeped in fatalistic darkness, forever teetering between tyranny and chaos.

A central theme of film noir is quite at home in dark comedy— exposing the botched American success story. That is, both genres suggest that the American dream cannot be obtained by earnest and honest efforts. Those figures who do find themselves in positions of authority and societal esteem did not get there fairly. As John Huston's evil power player in *Chinatown* chillingly observes, "Most people never have to face that at the right time and right place, they're capable of anything."

The noir protagonist is often a tough-guy detective, such as Chandler's Phillip Marlowe or Hammett's Sam Spade. But unlike pioneering detective Sherlock Holmes, who can look at a footprint and tell how much change the imprint maker had in his pocket, noir figures are more antiheroic: "They cannot easily discern the truth. . . . They have the desire to be faithful and good, but they make mistakes, they misread events, and they always, always are forced into unpleasant compromises."[3] This portrayal might just as well be applied to the dark comedy character. In fact, the black comedy novels of Nathanael West are sometimes described metaphorically in this manner, as a moral detective story. West scholar Robert Emmet Long describes the writer's *Miss Lonelyhearts* (1933): like [Dashiell] "Hammett's fiction, the quester figure is alone in . . . an irrational world; and curiously, in the early draft . . . Miss Lonelyhearts [a male] is even compared to a detective."[4] And the characterization of this *moral detective* and *quester* figure matches the work of many dark humor writers, especially that of Franz Kafka, such as in his posthumously-published novel *The Castle* (1926).

Just what is the difference, then, between black comedy and film noir? As with any similar genres, it is a question of degree. In this case, the deciding factor is which element, dark comedy or thriller suspense, takes precedence over the other. For instance, the film noir classic *The Big Sleep* (1946), with Humphrey Bogart as Chandler's Phillip Marlowe, gives this lone operator numerous wise-crackingly suggestive lines. However, to use a sports analogy, at no time does the dark-humor straw stir this film-noir drink. Such is not the case in *The Player* (1993) or *Pulp Fiction* (1994), which are examined late in this chapter.

An additional difference between the two genres is that the major film-noir character is seldom as antiheroically vulnerable as the pivotal figure in dark comedy. For instance, Bogart's persona (he played both Marlowe and Spade) can be victimized only so far. In contrast, the black humor figure is often no more than a pawn of fate, a leaf on the wind, such as the central characters of *Little Big Man* (1970), *Chinatown* (1974), *The World According to Garp* (1982), and *After Hours* (1985).

Before examining two definite crossover (from noir to dark comedy) movies, *The Player* and *Pulp Fiction*, it would be helpful to critique a film on the black comedy bubble, *Chinatown*, especially because it is considered such a classic noir, a "black retooling of *The Big Sleep* for the Watergate [disillusioning] era."[5] Despite that noir status, even here there is a strong argument for labeling it a dark comedy.

The central character in *Chinatown* is private eye J. J. (Jake) Gittes (Jack Nicholson). He is fooled into slandering Hollis Mulwray (Darrel Zwerling), an important water engineer for Los Angeles. Being duped is not good for the business, so Gittes opens his own investigation. Things become all the more interesting when Mulwray turns up dead. At first the death is considered a suicide, but Jake soon has reason to believe it was murder.

These are two other key characters, Mulwray's wife Evelyn (Faye Dunaway) and his father-in-law, Noah Cross (Jack Huston). Gittes's attempt to put the story together involves close interaction with both of these characters. In fact, each of them puts him on retainer for different reasons related to the death. Evelyn wants to know if her husband was murdered, while Noah is interested in finding the last person with whom Mulwray was seen alive, a beautiful young woman. The latter character is the one Gittes had wrongly placed Mulwray with in an alleged love triangle at the story's beginning.

The story is, as the *New York Times* observed, "A labyrinth of successive revelation."[6] Gittes, playing one of the more vulnerable noir detectives (one critic labeled him an "intellectual under-achiever"[7]), struggles with the clues as much as does the viewer.

Beyond a more vulnerable hero, what has been described is standard noir territory. As the scenario expands, however, dark comedy elements proliferate. Water commissioner Mulwray is killed—by drowning—during a drought. The person responsible for ordering the murder—and for the out to control drought-stricken Los Angeles's water supply—is named . . . Noah. Huston's evil character, who has had a child with his daughter, carries the surname Cross.

During Gittes's nosing-around investigation, said nose is slit by a pint-sized Cross gangster, a cameo played by director Polanski. Besides being such a darkly comic wound for a detective, it serves as an ongoing source of more such humor for the remainder of the film. For instance, when a cop who dislikes Nicholson observes, "what happened to your nose, Gittes? Somebody slam a bedroom window on it, Gittes?" Gittes replies, "Nope. Your wife got excited. She crossed her legs a little too quick. You understand what I mean, pal?" When the replacement water commissioner asks him if it still hurts, Gittes says, "Only when I breathe." And the ugly bandaged nose comically invalidates all the romantic scenes between Gittes and Mrs. Mulwray, as well as acting as a general high-visibility metaphor for life being less than positive.

Critic Pauline Kael adds that Polanski "must have known that many of us would recognize him [in the cameo] and that the association with the Los Angeles knifing of his wife [actress Sharon Tate, a victim of Charles Manson's "family"] would provide an extra dimension of perversity."[8] One might apply the same Tate perspective to the film's close, where Mrs. Mulwray is killed. *Chinatown*'s Oscar-winning screenwriter Robert Towne observed, "Roman's argument was: 'That's life; beautiful blondes die in Los Angeles. Sharon had.' He didn't say that, but that's what he felt."[9]

Many of the movie's other scenes, short and long, have a pronounced dark comedy edge. An example of the former would be Gittes's visit to the Los Angeles morgue. His friend the coroner has a terrible hacking cough but when asked how he feels responds, "Never better!" A longer scene could be showcased by the visit of Gittes and Evelyn to a Noah Cross–operated nursing home for clues. Using the excuse that they wanted to place their semi-crazed father in the institution, Nicholson's character asks the supervisor if the home takes people of the "Jewish persuasion." When the institutional representative apologetically says no, Gittes tells him not to apologize, because Dad would appreciate that. While Nicholson's figure is clearly not racist, his darkly comic set-up for the line further demonstrates the breadth of society's hypocrisy. Plus, it is a crack that is not necessary to advance the storyline. The lie about their father needing to be institutionalized has already gotten them in the door. Polanski and Towne seem anxious to embellish their movie with black comedy at every opportunity. Even the violent fight that closes the retirement home scene has a black humor bent to it; Gittes finally wins a fray against a man you love to hate, and Nicholson does so by using methods that a traditional good guy would not. For instance, Jake pulls henchman Mulvihill's (Roy Jenson) coat over the heavy's head and then rams Mulvihill's head into some iron grating . . . several times.

The funniest sustained dark comedy scene is Jake's initial meeting with Evelyn. She has come to his office first, and when Gittes arrives he is so anxious to tell a story about a Caucasian using the intercourse habits of the Chinese that he waves off the attempted interruptions of his staff. This very amusing story is made all the more entertaining because Evelyn is standing behind him all the time. Their physical positions here are also a visual metaphor for the rest of the movie—Evelyn generally knowing more than Jake, and he often playing the fool.

Essentially this noir and/or dark-comedy film is about the futility of good intentions. This brings one to *Chinatown*'s close. Gittes's compassion for Mrs. Mulwray has him risking his career getting Evelyn and her daughter/sister Katherine (Belinda Palmer) out of town, safe from the evil Noah Cross. But what transpires is the worst possible scenario. Evelyn is killed and Katherine falls into the hands of her father/grandfather Noah. Gittes's intervention has only made things worse.

Towne's script originally had Evelyn getting away at the end. Polanski was responsible for the dark conclusion. The director has said of this finish: "When people leave the theater, they shouldn't be allowed to think that everything is all right with the world. It isn't. And very little in life has a happy ending."[10]

Appropriately, critic Kael has likened *Chinatown* to *The Day of the Locust* (1939), the last novel by pioneering dark humorist Nathanael West.[11] I would focus the comparison further by keying on each work's close. In each case an innocent character is killed, and sexual perversity plays a part in both deaths. *Locust* has an individual being wrongly accused of molesting a child and being torn apart by a Hollywod mob originally gathered for a film premiere. *Chinatown* has Katherine falling into the incestuous hands of Noah, while a crowd looks on. West scholar Long has described the violent close to *Locust* as "rebellion that is merely chaos."[12] This pocket definition of dark comedy very much applies to *Chinatown*—Jake has orchestrated an escape, a "rebellion" if you will, from the ogre father/grandfather so effectively played by John Huston. But it all comes to such a sorry conclusion. Ironically, the story implies that a similar incident had occured to Jake years before, also in Los Angeles's Chinatown. Here is the sense of fatalism mentioned earlier in this chapter. In fact, at the close one of Gittes's assistants helps the devastated man from the site by saying, "Forget it Jake, it's Chinatown."

The Day of the Locust is set in Hollywood, a perfect backdrop for dark comedy since things are never what they seem—from false storefronts to millionaire actors masquerading as tramps and truck drivers. In *Chinatown* Hollywood plays a more peripheral, yet important, role. At the film's opening, one of the first things you see are the autographed pictures of movie stars on the wall behind Jake's desk. When Gittes thinks he has closed a big case his barber tells him he is getting to be "a regular movie star." Later Jake discovers he has been tricked by Ida Sessions (Diane Ladd) into thinking she was Evelyn Mulwray. When he next meets Ida she has just been murdered and her pocketbook produces a Screen Actors' Guild card. Evil Noah Cross, who hired her, makes the most of his Hollywood backdrop.

Chinatown even boasts a sex scene spoofing the old censorship days of Hollywood. That is, Jake and Evelyn find themselves in a passionate kiss that ultimately leads to bed. But the viewer sees nothing of the sexual act. Instead, the first bedroom shot finds them lying in bed well after the act, with Jake's limp arm hanging off the bed, cigarette in hand. One need not be Freud to grasp the limp arm symbolism. Here was a scene that could have been very explicit, given the 1960s elimination of the censorship office. The director toying with the audience is a hallmark of dark comedy. One can be certain of nothing in life . . . or the movies.

The only pivotal *Chinatown* sex scene occurs before the movie opens—the incest of Cross and Mulwray. It is a metaphor for everything that follows, the moral and political/business incestuousness that infects the city and, presumably, all "civilized" society. When Nathanael West biographer Jay Martin terms the close for *Day of the Locust* "apocalyptic,"[13] he might just as well be speaking of *Chinatown.* And "apocalyptic" is a given in dark comedy, be it literal (the mushroom cloud conclusion of *Dr. Strangelove,* 1964) or the threat of letting Malcolm McDowell's character loose at the close of *A Clockwork Orange* (1971).

There is no "correct reading" of *Chinatown.* To borrow an observation originally applied to a novel: "Each new generation of . . . [viewers] will bring its own needs to the . . . [work] and find there something of its own image."[14] If re-released today, this film noir picture would no doubt generate an equal amount of dark comedy discussion. My position here has merely been to examine a celebrated film very much associated with one genre and demonstrate the abundance of dark comedy present. To quote Jack Nicholson, "All art [and criticism] is one thing—a stimulating point of departure."[15]

The two movies that are critiqued next in this chapter, *The Player* and *Pulp Fiction,* also have some film noir characteristics. But two decades after *Chinatown,* both movies are discussed more as black comedies. And as with most dark humor, their central characters attempt to offset the apparent chaos that surrounds them. It is a situation familiar to more than one of us.

THE PLAYER

This film has many noir characteristics, from an individual who must play detective to a murder mystery set in the dark, contrasting lighting which has become a signature for the genre. Yet most critics from the heartland to Hollywood have placed the movie in the category of black humor. For instance, *Indianapolis Star* critic Bonnie Britton entertainingly observed, "Robert Altman's [director] highly entertaining new black comedy . . . dices, slices and skewers Hollywood with more flourish, style and wry precision than a knife-wielding chef at Benihana of Tokyo."[16] Celebrated film historian and critic Leonard Maltin wrote, "Sharp black comedy . . . a biting examination of Hollywood greed and power, with eternal renegade Altman near the top of his form."[17] But *GQ* critic Diana Rico had probably the best capsule review: "a droll black comedy in which reptilian studio executives will do anything—even commit murder—to get ahead."[18]

Rico was also on the money in the title for her essay — "S.M.A.S.H." It reflects both the success of *The Player* and its many ties with Altman's first major critical and commercial success, *M.A.S.H.* (1970), a dark comedy that still dwarfs much of the remainder of his career (see Chapter 2).

Altman himself is very open about the connection, especially the conclusions. In *M.A.S.H.*, "We come to a point and then suddenly the loud speaker says, 'Tonight's movie has been *M.A.S.H.* . . .' At the end of *The Player* what we are saying is that the movie you saw is the movie you are about to see."[19]

The latter part of the previous quote, "The movie you saw. . . ," might seem vague but it is pivotal Altman. *Film Comment* even used the complete quote for its cover-story article on the director (May–June 1992). Altman's films frequently bring themselves full circle from their beginnings. Thus, throughout *M.A.S.H.* the loudspeaker has been announcing different movies off-duty soldiers might see. At the end of *M.A.S.H.* the loudspeaker formalistically (self-consciously) spouts out *M.A.S.H.* and goes through the real cast. In *The Player* a paranoid vice-president of production (Tim Robbins) is being stalked by an upset screenwriter. Robbins's character, Griffin Mill, thinks he has killed the writer. But near the picture's close he receives a story pitch (a brief description of a possible film) over his car phone, from the same person who had threatened him before. And what this writer offers as a story is exactly the film the audience has seen. Mill accepts, if the still-anonymous scripter can guarantee a happy ending—meaning no whistleblowing.

The Player then proceeds to close with a traditional rendition of a Hollywood upbeat movie ending. Griffin pulls up to a stereotypical white house, picket fence, flowers everywhere, and the beautiful wife rushing to meet him. But this exaggeration is dark comedy. Altman observed, "We're saying that happy endings are absolutely ludicrous . . . bullshit. Three weeks later he's beating her up and she's suing for divorce and he's got cancer."[20]

This comment indirectly addresses a commercial danger mentioned earlier. The dark comedy genre, by its very nature, often repels the general public. Altman has even stated, "If they're [the audience] interested in me, that's great, I'd love to have them, but I'm not going to serve them anything on a platter."[21] These are the feelings of many dark comedy artists, because the genre is about shock and/or painfully cerebral subjects.

Fittingly *The Player* and *M.A.S.H.* take on authoritarian institutions—the movie business and the military. While this has often been Altman's intention in other films, these are his two most effective examples. Appropriately, the director likens himself to documentary filmmaker Frederick Wiseman, who is famous for his antiauthoritarian works, such as *High School* (1968) and *Basic Training* (1971), which baldly state their targets through the titles. But while Altman has chosen a given prey, he always suggests that his dark comedy barbs apply to most other organizations. Critic David Sterritt observed of *The Player*, "its ingenuity in using the illusions of cinema as a metaphor for the illusions—and delusions—of modern life is a perfect match."[22] It is a situation that fits the aforementioned signature line of cartoonist Walt Kelly: "We have met the enemy and he is us."

Altman's earlier critiquing of the happy ending as "bullshit" also applies to the cinema techniques that can distance the viewer beyond Kelly's comment. For instance, in *The Player* and most of his other films, especially *M.A.S.H.*, Altman utilizes overlapping dialogue. People in the movies normally take turns talking. That is hardly the case in life, where people interrupt, shout over, compete with rival nearby conversations. Consequently, in the Altman dark comedy, chaos can emerge from reality. Unfortunately, however, audiences often are bothered by this cinematically unusual device.

Altman further accents the dark comedy chaos by having overlapping storylines and/or sketchy narratives, plus large ensemble casts. The old definition of art as "where you get it right [clear]" does not apply to Altman's *The Player* and *M.A.S.H.*, where one is often hard pressed to follow a certain conversation or plot point.

No one's life has a plotline, but most viewers want it in their movies. Altman takes a genre known for its chaos and manages to enhance that characteristic by borrowing from reality.

The large ensemble cast can be a further audience distraction, especially in *The Player*, which is filled with dozens of major stars in the briefest of cameos as themselves—glitzy background decorations. Although a typical Altman dark comedy device, it is appropriate for a production about Hollywood to have a producer, Griffin Mill, run into Burt Reynolds and Cher, or attend a party where Jack Lemmon plays the piano in the background, while stars like Jeff Goldblum and Rod Steiger schmooze in every direction.

Though this horde of celebrities is not out of place, it works as a further dark comedy slant. The gimmick "underscores one of *The Player*'s major points, which is the shallowness of an environment where the famous function as little more than markers in a shoddy game of power and position."[23] A further dark comedy item from the real world merits noting. This scathing look at Hollywood was the toast of the town months before its commercial release. As a stand-up comic once observed in an otherwise unrelated monologue, "Do these people have a forgiving nature . . . or are they just stupid?"

The milling stars of *The Player* also act as a distraction from a rather haphazard plotline that dovetails back and forth between murder mystery and studio politics. But then, haphazard narrative describes many dark comedies. As literary critic Michael Reynolds has observed, "In a work depicting the loss of standards [certainly applicable for dark comedy], it seems perfectly appropriate for time to be skewed."[24]

The New Yorker critic Terrence Rafferty has likened the film to a combination of Nathanael West and the British dark comedy troupe Monty Python,[25] both of which attack the milling masses. One could read *The Player*'s movie crowd, whatever the star quality, as metaphorical murderers of Hollywood's past. Even the sequences where the industry dedicates some past movies to the Los Angeles County Museum of Art comes off as a joke. The film crowd spends more time eating and talking then listening to the speakers. And the biggest dark joke is that film philistine Tim Robbins's Griffin Mill was pivotal in organizing and speaking at the gathering. This living a lie and the easy compartmentalization of emotions is a chilling depiction of dark humor.

Griffin Mill knows a good classic film but does not make them today. Rafferty's review is fittingly entitled "killer," by which he means the demise of American filmmaking. Robbins's character meets the writer he will ultimately murder at a screening of the Italian neo-realism masterpiece *The Bicycle Thief* (1949). Griffin Mill has gone there specifically to meet the writer he thinks is sending him threatening postcards. When Mill attempts small talk, he offhandedly says maybe they could remake *The Bicycle Thief*. The quick comeback by the writer suggests Mill would probably give it a happy ending, the complete antithesis of new-realism's slice-of-life, nonprofessional-cast approach. While the scripter's crack was dead on, there is a historical precedent for using *The Bicycle Thief*, a precedent of which Altman was undoubtedly aware. When the director of *Thief* was first doing his own "pitch" for production costs, a Hollywood studio offered to back him . . . if he used Cary Grant in the lead!

Altman does not, however, exempt himself from his Hollywood targets, despite being a long-time maverick, outside the system for most of his career. In the Altman interview that follows the first video release of *The Player*, the director confesses his own self-centered, anything-for-a-pitch past. In a separate interview Michael Tolkin, who wrote the novel and the screenplay, observed, "We just looked into our own corrupted hearts."[26]

The Player represents a great deal more than a vehicle for confession—there is a rich assortment of black comedy material. The threatening postcards to Mills are often darkly comic, such as, "In the Name of All Writers I'm Going to Kill You." From something as seemingly innocuous as postcards, one could address the murder itself as black humor. Griffin and the writer struggle. The producer falls backward into a coal bin entrance. When the scripter goes down to see if he is O.K., Mill springs up and proceeds to knock the writer down, repeatedly smashing his head on the pavement, finally drowning him in a pool of rain water which has gathered at the bottom of the entrance.

It is funny in the sense that Mill's well-tailored, yawningly orchestrated life had yet to suggest he was capable of anything so Darwinianly spontaneous, let alone murder. And once Mill finds he can live with being a killer, like Martin Landau's character in *Crimes and Misdemeanors* (1989) or John Huston's Noah Cross in *Chinatown* (1974), the humor becomes all the more chilling.

Though Robbins's character is normally less than sympathetic, the murder can be dissected in this untroubled manner because the victim is akin to the typical playground bully. He unceasingly taunts Mill at a time when the producer is actually attempting to be sincere. Thus, there is also a degree of voyeuristic pleasure in seeing the bully killed. The dark comedy continues at the burial site. Passages of the writer's work are read aloud. The speaker treats the words as if they are from the King James version of the Bible whereas they are actually quite abysmal. The bully was also a crummy writer, so his significance sinks ever lower. As a footnote to the burial, the victim's girlfriend comes dressed in white, a sharp contrast to the other mourners' dark clothing and a clear reference to the bright cemetery clothing of Ruth Gordon's character in *Harold and Maude* (1971). Ironically, this writer's girlfriend, June (Greta Scacchi), later states, "I like words and letters but I'm not crazy about complete sentences." Not surprisingly, June's capsule review of her dead lover was that he was "uniquely untalented."

The day after the murder Mill arrives late at a meeting. His colleagues, more specifically rival producer Larry Levy (Peter Gallagher), have been suggesting that screenwriters should be eliminated, but in the more traditional sense of being fired. Levy feels every genre could easily be drawn from the newspapers. And he might be correct in at least one case—Mill suddenly notes an article about a murder . . . the murder he has committed.

Robbins's character suffers through dark comedy situations even more intense than this. When he is brought downtown by the police for questioning, the scene slides into a comic nightmare befitting the surrealism of Luis Buñuel. The otherworldly looks of Lyle Lovett as Detective DeLongpre seem fitting for the film he mentions, *Freaks* (1932), a traveling sideshow of real-life freaks. Lovett's character keeps repeating a macabre chorus from the movie, "One of us, one of us . . . " Whoopie Goldberg as Detective Avery is initially more concerned with finding her jumbo box of tampons than questioning anyone. A very nervous Mill also becomes the target of humor literally based on these surreal surroundings. As the producer's anxiety increases the camera goes into an ever-increasing closeup of his face. Eventually the closeup is so tight that the shot is reduced to a protesting mouth and terrorized eyes. On the sound track Altman has added the laughter heard earlier, only distorted, plus the repetition by Lovett's character, "One of us, one of us . . . "

Detective DeLongpre has periodically appeared earlier in the film following Mill. Is he the disgruntled writer, a stalker, a cop. . . ? But what makes him so chillingly funny are his piercing eyes and an appearance that labels him the eternal outsider. Though one might place Lovett's character back in *Freaks*, his eyes are reminiscent of a scene from Alfred Hitchcock's *Strangers on a Train* (1951). Farley Granger is a professional tennis player being stalked by Robert Walker's psychopath. At one such encounter Walker's figure sits in the stands while the lead character plays a match. The eyes of all the spectators follow the ball back and forth over the net . . . all the spectators except for the psychopath, who stares directly at Granger's character throughout each game.

There are no redeeming qualities to any of Mill's colleagues, with the exception of his first girlfriend, Bonnie Sherow (Cynthia Stevenson). Altman pulls constant dark comedy from the group, including the outlandish pitches Robbins's character has to wade through each day. The most inspired is writer/actor Buck Henry's pitch for a sequel to *The Graduate* (1967). But if the story was not darkly comic enough, Ben and Elaine still are together *plus* . . . Mrs. Robinson is living upstairs, a victim of a stroke or a disease to be determined at a later date. But the topper to this is the fact that Buck Henry wrote the script for the original *The Graduate*. Yet Altman suggests we're all "players."

Mill's new girlfriend, the former lover of the man Mill has murdered, comes across as the most ostentatious of artists, whose vacuous exterior covers the most opportunistic of black comedy leading ladies. *Chicago Tribune* critic David Kehr felt Altman "has chosen to make a snide joke of her ridiculing the character for her pretentious and amateurish paintings while suggesting that her motives may be venal after all."[27] In several television interviews the director described her as a male fantasy with darkly comic tendencies.

The circus these and other characters put on is a "nightmarish slapstick" reminiscent of the Marx Brothers' comedy chaos in *Duck Soup*.[28] (For more on this film and the comedy team see Chapter 3.) But while we laugh *with* the Marxes because they prick pretention, one laughs *at* most characters in *The Player*, since they are not aware of the pretention, from Mill ordering a different type of expensive mineral water at each opportunity, to his glad-handing every movie "somebody" that goes by or is even in the vicinity.

With all this negativity coming from the screen, Whoopi Goldberg's Avery provides comic relief of a lighter nature. This is not to say she cannot provide the comical shock effect. When Mill is brought to her police office, everything is very casual at the beginning, right down to discussing films. But out of nowhere she suddenly asks Mill, "Did you fuck her?" This is a reference to the murder victim's girlfriend June. When Mill becomes more than a little startled and feigns confusion, Avery tells him it is quite simple. She then repeats her question to the letter, with pronounced pauses between each word.

Despite a scene like this, she provides a more likeable personality to identify with. For example, early in the investigation she visits Griffin Mill's office. He is late in arriving and this allows her to pick up one of his Oscars and start to recite a mock thank-you speech for "this great honor." It is the kind of thing most people would be tempted to do in a situation like that. Later she mentions the Universal film tour she always takes visiting relatives to each year. Ironically, this is the only other studio she has ever visited. She represents an authentic person.

Whoopi's character knows Mill committed the murder, but she cannot prove it. When he is cleared for lack of evidence, once again dark comedy allows the other side to win; her likable presence, however, makes his freedom more bothersome for the viewer.

Of course, the last act of dark comedy between the police and Mill is at the hands of the bungling authorities, as is often the case with law enforcement people in Hitchcock films. Regardless, a witness has been found from the night of the murder. But her eyesight is poor and she observed the night-time act from a distance. The police put Lovett's bizarre-looking character in the identification line with Mill and several additional people. Naturally, the witness picks Lovett's detective DeLongpre. The chances are he would have been picked out of every police line this side of *Freaks*. *Rolling Stone* called him "crazily unforgettable."[29]

Just having a Hollywood focus ups *The Player*'s dark comedy potential. Whereas the movies are sometimes a component of the genre, *The Player* keys upon the industry, whether it is death threats on movie postcards or film posters on which Altman's moving camera (*Time* described this technique as "prowling like a house dick on roller skates"[30]) briefly lingers on to suggest forthcoming danger. And as is always the case in movieland, things are never what they seem to be—the apparent poison pen writer turns out to be innocent . . . and dead, while his obvious killer walks free as an innocent man. And *The Player*'s most realistic scene is the movie being shot within the film, *The Lonely Room*, with Lily Tomlin and Scott Glenn.

Even the movie's most promising possibility for aesthetic purity, the script hilariously pitched by Andy Civella (Dean Stockwell) and Tom Oakley (Richard E. Grant), is comically betrayed by Hollywood's dark sense of creativity. It is a grim tale, with no stars, and a close where the innocent heroine dies in the gas chamber. Grant's character says it must end this way because, "It's reality, and that's what happens." This is not to be a film with Bruce Willis rescuing Julia Roberts at the end. But naturally that is exactly what occurs. And to make it more ironic, script writer Oakley, who had been so adamant earlier about the project remaining true to reality, has also been converted to Hollywood's mutilation of his script and the industry's pretty-picture style. One is reminded of George Orwell's novel *1984* (1949), where central character Winston Smith is not only defeated by the evil government, à la "Big Brother," but he must come around to support the system before he is liquidated.

This is a world "that canonizes greed, the deal, the sure thing, condones irresponsible wealth and power, shows contempt for originality and builds gilded altars to self-interest. The bottom line is the only line."[31] Again one must remember that although the surface target is Hollywood, the implication is that it applies to most industries and people . . . a metaphor for everyone's world.

So much ongoing self-interest (such as Gallagher's Larry Levy going to an A.A. meeting, not because he is alcoholic but rather because that is where the deals are being made) has the viewer second-guessing every situation. For instance, when someone corners Griffin Mill for a story pitch, his standard line is keep it to twenty-five words or less. The obvious explanation is so many people are throwing story ideas at him he must limit the time spent with each writer. But after watching Altman's leveling of everything Hollywood, one begins to wonder if Mill just has trouble processing more than twenty-five words.

While this installment of dark comedy would have been impossible a few years ago, many today hail *The Player* as savior. For instance, "There's a widespread feeling among critics and in the industry that the quality of American movies is in free fall."[32] As noted earlier, black comedy has always been there, but today it is at center stage.

Probably the most darkly comic aspect of *The Player* is not that nasty people can win but rather that Altman finds that possibility less than surprising. At one point in the film Mill tells new love June that she is a "pragmatic anarchist," a description which more aptly fits Altman. That is, at some point in his career he has played all the Hollywood games. Yet, he is still capable of exposing all in *The Player* . . . and then being celebrated in the film capital for doing it!

In the past Altman has frequently attacked American myths as showcased in genre films, be it the military of *M.A.S.H.* or the west of *McCabe and Mrs. Miller* (1971). Generally this means pushing the envelope into dark comedy. The unique aspect about *The Player*, however, is its "reflexivity"—a film which turns back on itself, be it "genre genre" (movies about movies) or the relationship between the audiences and cinema. *The Player* gives the viewer both of these qualities. The "genre genre" slant is a given (the viewer is behind the scenes at a studio). But at a more cerebral level is Altman's ingenuity "in using the illusions of cinema as a metaphor for the illusions—and delusions—of modern life."[33] Like all art, it is layered for the different demands of different "readers." At its most basic it is a Hollywood murder mystery with occasional movie posters acting as an unofficial story guide, just as the intercom system does in *M.A.S.H.* But the dark laughter comes from the viewer's possible temptation to embrace the values of profit, power, and ego—given that opportunity, regardless of the business and setting.

One is reminded of Mark Twain's short story, "The Man that Corrupted Hadleyburg" (1899), written in his disillusioned later years. The tale is about a hypocritical town that is given an opportunity to prove its worthiness but instead only reveals its smug self-centeredness. The citizens of Hadleyburg are good . . . as long as there is no temptation. But introduce that element and everything is different. The town only finds a semblance of respectability when it changes its motto from "Lead us not into temptation" to "Lead us into temptation" . . . allowing them to face such things directly.

Mill's ability to live with his crime and prosper, like John Huston's Noah Cross in *Chinatown*, is also reminiscent of Twain's short story "The Facts Concerning the Recent Carnival of Crime in Connecticut" (1876). The title's crimes are the result of a man meeting and killing his conscience. The individual is never particularly good in the first place, which is reflected in his conscience's appearance—a two-foot dwarf with every feature misshapen. Still, by killing this conscience the unnamed narrator observes, "You behold before you a man whose life-conflict is done, whose soul is at peace; a man whose heart is dead to sorrow, dead to suffering, dead to remorse; *a man without a conscience!*"[34]

When one first meets Griffin Mill, his conscience might be no more than two feet tall, too. But Tim Robbins somehow succeeds, as *Variety* suggests, in "making the morally loathsome character palatable."[35] Who has not dreamed about knocking off his/her conscience, at least as it relates to guilt, big or small? But Altman's *The Player* manages to improve upon Twain's "Carnival of Crime" because Mill is much more likable than the central character of the short story. Now while Twain has wisely given his central figure no name—all the better to make him an everyman figure—Mill seems to have retained more human qualities. That way the audience is more likely to identify with him. Thus, when immoral acts are committed the viewer is affected more directly.

For those not sucked into identification, relief must be tempered with horror that the conscienceless remain and seem to be forever on the rise. As with Edvard Munch's *The Shriek* (see frontispiece), sometimes it seems that all the survivor has left is a death-rattling scream. Just as all lines of Munch's lithograph appear to lead toward the work's focus—the yelling head—all roads of dark comedy seem to lead toward the same destination—a cry from a head resembling a death skull. In art schools, Munch's lithograph is sometimes seen as all the more disquieting because the viewer never knows what the cry meant. But this ambiguity is more than fitting for dark comedy. No specific reason underlines the universality of the humor condition's horror.

Do these screams test civilization? Is there a choice involved in hearing them? Can one help? With dark comedy going beyond satire, it presupposes that there is nothing to do but squeeze out a laugh whenever possible. Laugh or go crazy. With such little hope, maybe the most entertaining critique of *The Player* takes time out for its own stab of black humor. For instance, *Rolling Stone*'s review recycled a revised version of a nineteenth-century school yard ditty about the infamous Lizzie Borden. In an 1890s trial that rivaled another generation's O. J. Simpson case, Borden was found not guilty of the mutilation murders of her father and stepmother, both apparently the victims of numerous blows from an axe. For years playgrounds echoed with the dark comedy rhyme of "Lizzie Borden took an axe and gave her mother forty whacks. And when she saw what she had done, she gave her father forty-one." It was a case that fascinated many dark comedy humorists, such as the occasional black humor of Robert Benchley.

In an inspired opening to his *Rolling Stone* review, appropriately entitled "Setting Up Hollywood for the Kill," critic Peter Travers wrote, "Robert Altman took an axe and gave his business forty whacks. And when he saw what he had done, gave his audience forty-one." Travers nicely balances Altman's undercutting of Hollywood and his sometimes manipulating of a voyeuristic audience. While Lizzie Borden inadvertently provided an impetus for dark humor, Altman artistically showcases the phenomenon at center stage. Times have changed, yet as Travers' Lizzie–inspired ditty suggests, are things really that different?

PULP FICTION

Quentin Tarantino begins his film with two definitions of pulp: "A soft, moist, shapeless mass of matter," and "A magazine or book containing lurid subject matter and being characteristically printed on rough, unfinished [i.e., pulp] paper." In terms of *Pulp Fiction* (1994), which was written and directed by Tarantino, one might have added, "A rough mass of a comically skewed narrative on the life and hard times of a hit man." (See illustration 14).

Before examining this inspired film (Oscar-winning best original screenplay)—with even the staid *Nation* observing, "If the usual Hollywood product is checkers, then this is chess,"[36]—it would be helpful to briefly break down the narrative. Tarantino has frequently referred to it as "three stories . . . about one story." Because of the nonlinear nature of the work, however, it is easier to think in terms of six segments. First, in a brief pre-credits scene, a husband and wife stick-up team begin a restaurant robbery. Second, two hit men finish an assignment. Third, the crime lord has a hit man chaperon his sexy wife. Fourth, a boxer paid to take a dive does not follow directions. Fifth, the viewer returns to the hit

14. Publicity poster for *Pulp Fiction*.

men and a snag in their mission. Sixth, the story comes back full circle to the pre-credits restaurant robbery.

Tarantino has said of his unconventional organization, "It's not like I'm on this major crusade against linear narrative. What I am against is saying it's the only game in town."[37] Translation: another example of dark comedy keeping one off-balance.

For all the film's pluses, its greatest strength is tough guys discussing less than likely topics. Tarantino showcased this skill earlier with the critically acclaimed *Reservoir Dogs* (1992), where gangsters consider everything from the merits of tipping to the meaning of Madonna's song "Like a Virgin." The best *Pulp Fiction* dialogue exchange is between hit men Vincent Vega (John Travolta) and Jules (Samuel L. Jackson) on the fact that Jules does not like to eat pork because it's a filthy animal. Vincent suggests dogs are also less than clean:

Vincent: How about dogs? Dogs eat their own feces.

Jules: I don't eat dog, either.

Vincent: Yes, but do you consider a dog to be a filthy animal?

Jules: I wouldn't go so far as to call a dog filthy, but they're definitely dirty. But a dog's got personality. And personality goes a long way.

Vincent: So by that rationale, if a pig had a better personality, he'd cease to be a filthy animal?

Jules: We'd have to be talkin' 'bout one charmin' motherfuckin' pig. I mean he'd have to be ten times more charmin' than that Arnold on *Green Acres*.

Critic Owen Gleiberman has perfectly captured the Tarantino blend of the profane and the comic: "We're caught up in dialogue of such fiendishly elaborate wit it suggests a Martin Scorsese film written by Preston Sturges."[38] That is, it has the grittiness of Scorsese's *Mean Streets* (1973) coupled with the screwball comedy world of Sturges's *Palm Beach Story* (1942; for more on this genre, see my *Screwball Comedy: A Genre of Madcap Romance*, 1986). Gleiberman might have been looking over Tarantino's shoulder as the artist wrote his script, because the directions for the first scene note, "The boy and girl sit in a booth. Their dialogue is to be said in a rapid-pace *His Girl Friday* fashion."[39] (*Friday* is a classic screwball comedy laced with black humor; see Chapter 2 of the text in hand.)

Not surprisingly, there are parallels with the other directors focused on in this chapter, Oliver Stone and Robert Altman. Fittingly, Tarantino wrote the original script for *Natural Born Killers* (1994). But he and Stone differed on how the material was to be presented, so Tarantino had his name taken off the credits, though he did retain story acknowledgment. Both directors use black comedy, but Tarantino likes "things unexplained."[40] In *Natural Born Killers* Stone wants to link the violence to the media and an "entertainment product of unintended dark comedy. He desires that points be made and underlined. Stone has noted another difference: "Quentin, you're in your 20s. You're making movies about movies. I'm [Stone] making movies about the life that I've lived to my 40s."[41] Tarantino is more interested is making the smaller picture, versus the Stone epic. Moreover, Tarantino enjoys the leisurely presentation of characters through pop culture dialogue, like the aforementioned references to Madonna and the television sitcom *Green Acres*.

As a point of reference, it should be added that Tarantino is a huge fan of television memorabilia, especially of the 1950s and 1960s. He collects items like television-related board games and lunchboxes. Indeed, when possible he enjoys playing board games with stars of the original series. Thus, during *Pulp Fiction* he played the *Welcome Back, Kotter* game with John Travolta, whose Vinnie Barbarino character brought the actor his first recognition. Tarantino even records the score on the box, with an autograph from the star. (These are hardly the type of "groupie" things the very egotistical Stone would consider.) It is possible that Travolta's name in *Pulp Fiction*, Vincent, was purposefully made close to Vinnie. As it happens, some television performers actually note parallels with their work and Tarantino films. For example, Jerry Seinfeld has said, "I thought *Pulp Fiction* was very much in the tone of a lot of things we do. Some of that coffee-shop stuff between John Travolta and Sam Jackson—I thought, that's like a me-and-George scene [his television co-star]."[42] (The lengthy *Pulp Fiction* dialogue excerpt occurs in a coffee shop.) Interestingly enough, Tarantino has often admitted to being a big fan of *Seinfeld* and that he often quotes lines from the show.

Regardless of how one feels about an influence here, the Seinfeld connection is important for another reason. The television program is often referred to as using the "nothing premise"—basing the

whole show on such mundane subjects as buying a suit or borrowing a tennis racket. The "nothing" reference does not have anything
to do with quality but rather the casual manner in which most
people slide through life. Besides being a protective device to ignore
the larger and more frightening elements of life, it also records the
simple fact that whether you are Jerry and George, or two hit men
for the mob, existence comes with a lot of small talk, though maybe
not quite so amusing.

Tarantino has, however, gone out on a limb to defend the
small-talk realism of his hoods. In an otherwise excellent *Film
Comment* interview, the questioner pushes for Tarantino to admit
this is not typical gangster speech. The writer/director responds,
"To me, they [the actors playing hit men] don't necessarily break
the reality. You hear stories about gangbangers doing routines from
movies before they do a drive-by shooting."[43] Other sources back
up Tarantino's position. The most amusing is a 1970s Richard Pryor
routine based entirely upon the everyday side of gangsters, which
he drew from his early nightclub days.

Moving to another type of television, Stone's *Natural Born Killers*
suggests the media lies about its purpose; Tarantino acknowledges
all of society's lies and moves on to a day-to-day "nothing premise"
that occupies much of everyone's time. The young director says
"The Vietman War and Watergate were a one-two punch that
basically destroyed Americans' faith in their own country. The
attitude I grew up with was that everything you've heard is lies."[44]
Consequently, he is more decentralized than Stone is in pointing a
black humor finger.

Tarantino has more links with the dark comedy of Robert
Altman. As critic Owen Gleiberman has observed, "Tarantino's
characters are overlapped in the ingenious lapidary style of Altman."[45] That is, the little stories within the big picture use the same
characters effectively. Gleiberman insightfully adds that Tarantino
is capable of overlapping the time frame. For instance, the restaurant robbery opening that briefly starts the film is not completed
until the movie's final segment. Also several characters appear in
more than one part of the film.

The day-to-day "nothing premise" is also showcased in Altman's
work. For instance, his *M.A.S.H.* (1970, see Chapter 2) is peppered
with such segments, like the near-the-front discussion of what
constitutes a good martini, which is topped off with Elliott Gould's

character pulling a jar of olives out of his large coat, á la the magic pockets of Harpo Marx.

Both Altman and Tarantino are major movie fans. Altman's *The Player* is even set at a film studio. It takes a dark look at the people currently running the industry and celebrates earlier classic Hollywood moments, from constant use of 1930s and 1940s film posters as clues, to a pervasive homage with less obvious twists. For example, it keys upon past genres (such as the noir movie being made within the film) and populates the film with dozens of stars, past and present. The latter touch is especially effective because, though cameos by famous people frequently derail a storyline (such as Stone's *JFK*, 1991), what could be more appropriate, if you were a Hollywood insider, than seeing lots of stars. Moreover, since the film is a dark comedy look at the present industry, having all these Hollywood cameos adds a comically perverse slant. It is as if mainstream Hollywood is only too happy to put itself down. In *Nashville* (1975), Altman is more sympathetic with the characters, but he still throws another dark barb at the entertainment industry, except this time it is country music.

With Altman's longer career one can also see his tendency to more lightly spoof the movies or the arts in general. The most appropriate examples to note here, given this chapter's key upon dark comedy and film noir, would be Altman's *M.A.S.H.* and *The Long Goodbye* (1973). The latter movie, starring Elliott Gould, boasts a feature-length parody of film noir. In *M.A.S.H.* there is a scene where Hawkeye (Donald Sutherland) and McIntyre (Elliott Gould) are put under temporary house arrest and they immediately slip into noir/tough fiction dialogue:

McIntyre: They finally caught up with us, huh?

Hawkeye: Where'd we fail?

McIntyre: I don't know. I think it was the woman. Something tells me I've seen her some place before.

Hawkeye: She was the one in Tangiers.

McIntyre: We don't blame you [the guard].

Hawkeye: You're [the guard] only doing your duty.

The two genres, noir and dark comedy, have ties to each other, even if they are not always recognized.

Tarantino's homage is a less obvious weave, from addressing past genres like film noir (see also his *Reservoir Dogs*, 1992) and the more recently recognized black humor. For example, the basic plot segments of *Pulp Fiction* are stereotypical givens in the film industry: hit men doing their job, a boxer double-crossing the mob and not taking a fall, a restaurant robbery. . . . These are all nicely chronicled in earlier film noir/crime genres. But in *Pulp Fiction* Tarantino so infuses them with dark comedy that this genre becomes dominant, such as Travolta and Jackson's characters discussing the menu differences between a McDonald's in the United States and Amsterdam, or the ethics of massaging a married woman's feet—and whether the jealous husband has the right to drop-kick the man out a two-story window. There is a darkly comic discussion about how upset one should get if one accidentally blows off the head of a colleague in the back seat of a car in which one is riding.

As incongruous as the last juxtapositioning of humor and mayhem may seem to many (see Chapter 1), it is a way of coping. Critic Richard Blake observed, "While gangsters fret about the disposition of the inconvenient remains of . . . [a man] in the car, they discuss the quality of the coffee. Perhaps theirs is the sanest way of dealing with such a world."[46]

Though it initially would seem unlikely, one could also defend Tarantino's values in *Pulp Fiction* as not without a religious quality. Like the late dark comedy work of Mark Twain, though generally questioning God, it frequently wrestles with theological questions. Tarantino's film has an ongoing argument about whether Vincent and Jules "witness a miracle, and one of them undergoes something of a religious conversion at the end of the film and tries to save, in a spiritual sense, the others."[47] The case in question has Jules defusing the restaurant robbery: "Normally both of your asses would be dead as fuckin' fried chicken. But you happened to pull this shit while I'm in a transitional period."

An additional twist to *Pulp Fiction* and religion is how Jules recites the Bible's *Ezekiel* 25:17 before he executes someone. The memorized passage ends with: "You will know my name is the Lord when I lay my vengeance upon you." Originally Jules did this for dramatic effect (dark anti-religious comedy?). But after the "miracle," when someone surprises Vincent and Jules at pointblank range and starts shooting . . . only to miss them completely, Jules begins rethinking the *Ezekiel* passage. Now he keys upon the section which asks individuals to be "shepherds" of the weak. He has even told Vincent, with obvious Biblical implications, "I'm gonna walk the earth." Did a conversion come out of this moral vacuum? There is no "correct" reading. But the film ends with the implication that Jules is quitting the violent life. In dark comedy one might merely chalk the whole thing up to the genre's embracing of absurdity—hit man finds God. And because of the nonlinear storyline, the viewer already knows that Vincent, who does not believe in miracles, continues with the mob and is killed.

Another institution, besides religion, with which the genre often toys is the military. There is only one such short, hilarious scene in *Pulp Fiction*, but it is memorable. There is a flashback to the childhood of boxer Butch (Bruce Willis). Christopher Walken's military character, Koons, visits Butch and gives him his father's gold watch. It seems that three generations of the family had worn it to war. Butch's father had not survived Vietnam. He and Koons had spent years in a prisoner of war camp. And the only safe place his father had to hide the watch was up his rear for five years. Then he died—of dysentery. Walken's character performs the same service for the boy and is now returning that all-important watch.

Walken's Koons is shot at a low camera level, a child's point of view, and seems disproportionately funny, as if a uniformed God Almighty had dropped in for a chat. And to have such a figure then relate stories about hiding a watch up his rear very much undercuts the speaker and his occupation. It is as if this is the biggest accomplishment to come out of Vietnam (and maybe it was). I am not labeling this scene as being serious social commentary, but rather as a modest ridiculing of all things military. It must be remembered, too, that Tarantino finds dark humor in the most unusual places. For instance, *Pulp Fiction* and *Forrest Gump* came out the same year and represent opposite ends of the comedy spectrum: dark comedy versus populism.[48] Yet the director saw *Gump* "as a subversive black comedy, so they're [*Pulp Fiction* and *Gump*] not that different."[49] Whether one accepts this unusual perspective or not, Tarantino's linkage should make it easier to accept the closeness of film noir and dark humor.

Tarantino's tendency to use an ensemble cast, as with Altman, sometimes necessitates that the critic, if possible, focus on the most central of figures. In *Pulp Fiction* Travolta's Vincent Vega would be that figure. Top-billed and Oscar-nominated, Travolta redefined cinema's idea of a hit man. *Entertainment Weekly* might have defined Travolta's performance best with the phrase "goofy charisma."[50] There is not one degree of the cocky, posing, *Saturday Night Fever* (1977) Travolta. Here his character, Vincent, is a stoned but often philosophically amusing hit man who is just interested in surviving day by day. *The New Yorker* likened the title *Pulp Fiction* to his face, "luscious but squashy, easily bruised, the look of a former pretty boy who can still inspire tall tales."[51] Like Tarantino, Vincent has heard all the lies. Like Holden Caulfield he has met all the phonies. (Tarantino had likened his *Pulp Fiction* saga of "three stories . . . about one story" to the work of J. D. Salinger.[52]) Vincent would feel comfortable with Raymond Chandler's view of life's cheapness, "It is not funny that a man should be killed, but it is sometimes funny that he should be killed for so little. "[53]

Travolta's character appears in more episodes than any other, and the episode action fluctuates greatly. But in each case that "goofy charisma" says even a hit man can be an antihero. Thus, the viewer first meets him on an assignment, playing second fiddle to Samuel Jackson's overpowering Jules. Next, the boss, Marsellus (Ving Rhames) has him chaperon his wife Mia (Uma Thurman) to the ultimate 1950s diner, "Jackrabbit Slim's." With Archie comic book decor and Fats Domino cheeseburgers, not a pop culture trick is missed. An Ed Sullivan impersonator acts as host, "Marilyn Monroe" is one of the waitresses, and "Buddy Holly" is bussing tables. The "date" is the most ongoingly funny segment of the film. But it, too, peaks with a darkly comic moment, to be examined shortly.

Tarantino affectionately spoofs Travolta's *Saturday Night Fever* persona at Slim's by having Mia demand that both she and Vincent enter a dance contest. Both before and during this date Vincent is nervous about getting romantically involved with Mia. And when they win the competition the viewer suspects this is going to happen. Indeed, when they return to her house he enters the bathroom to give himself a pep talk about no sex.

His bathroom exit has him flirting, however, with becoming the ultimate antihero. Mia has taken some drugs he had in his coat pocket and is near death. Vince rushes her to his dealer's (Eric Stoltz) house with a driving style befitting the Keystone Kops, topped off by piling into the house of his drug connection.

To save Mia's life (and Vincent's if she dies) she must receive an adrenalin shot in the heart. But neither Eric's character, Lance, nor Vincent has ever done this, or as Tarantino's script notes state, "Nobody knows what the fuck they're doing."[54] However, Mia has overdosed and they have to act. With the help of a red dot marker over her heart, Vincent must stab the needle through the breast plate in front of her heart. Once done, he must push down on the plunger and see what happens.

Mia's eyes pop wide open and she bolts up in a sitting position with a scream and the needle still stuck in her chest. It is a moment out of one's favorite Dracula picture . . . only more comically surprising due to its unexpectedness here. She is O.K., and Vincent has survived Marsellus turning him into a grease spot.

The viewer next sees the antiheroic Vincent briefly in the boxing segment. Butch has broken his promise to throw the fight and is ready to escape Los Angeles, when he realizes the gold watch is still at his apartment. Vincent is supposed to be staked out at Butch's, on the odd chance the boxer will return. Unfortunately, Vincent, like a 1990s sort of Walter Mitty, has a habit of taking adventure stories into bathrooms for lengthy stays. This time he even leaves his machine gun on the kitchen counter. Butch returns, finds the watch, and decides he has time for a pop tart. Then he notices the weapon just as Vincent, still on the toilet, opens the bathroom door. Each startled man stares at the other. Bang, the toaster pops up Butch's tarts and he instinctively fires the weapon, killing Vincent.

Following the boxer segment, the story goes back in time to Vincent and Jules's hit man assignment. After the previous scene the viewer is so pleased to have the antiheroic Vincent back that one forgives him anything, including accidentally blowing a colleague's head off. Resting his gun on the car seat as he turns to talk to the soon-to-be-accidental-backseat-victim (Jules is driving), a bump causes the gun to go off and suddenly the vehicle's interior is done over in basic red, as are Vincent and Jules.

Travolta's character responds just like a little child when Jules asks how this could have happened. It was an accident. He is sorry. But these things happen. . . . The rest of this segment plays like a movie from those pioneering antiheroes Laurel and Hardy, only with much more adult language. Jules is the dominating Oliver Hardy and Vincent is the wise fool Stan Laurel. And these spats range from an ongoing how-could-this-happen to an argument over who should be cleaning up the brain matter splattered in the backseat area. Tarantino embraces this in part when he observes *Pulp Fictions*'s characters are "a cross between criminals and actors and children playing roles."[55]

The childhood slant is especially apparent when the hit men look for a place to clean up the bloodstained car and themselves. Jules takes them to a friend's house, Jimmie (played by Tarantino), who is not happy to see their problem. But he reluctantly agrees to help if they can be out of there before his wife comes back from work. From that point on it is a race against time to clean up their mess before "Mom" gets home. But success will only come when they are clean, too. That accomplished, they have to wear mismatched clothes from Jimmie's Goodwill box. Vincent and Jules now look like nerd adolescents. One could further flesh out Vincent's schoolboy nature by his bashfulness around Mia, or his comic concern over petty points of honor while he is most casual about being a hit man.

Lastly, the antiheroic Vincent surfaces, with Jules, in the restaurant which opens the film. They have come directly from Jimmie's, and one expects their wardrobes to turn a few heads. It has been an unusually stressful day, even for their line of work. They are looking to relax and continue discussion of Jules' "miracle." Suddenly the robbery attempt happens and a changed (retiring) Jules manages to avoid a bloodbath. But the viewer sadly knows Vincent has fatally decided to stay in a business not suited for an antihero . . . and will die soon. Indeed, a Thurber moral for him might be, "He *really* got caught with his pants down." Antiheroic ranks are ever enlarging. And this film keys upon the most unlikely of sorts—Vincent Vega. But one could broaden this by saying that *Pulp Fiction* showcases every kind of antihero, best defined by just not caring. Or, as syndicated columnist Donald Kaul observed of his favorite 1994 film—"*Pulp Fiction* is about life-losers."[56]

If antihero seems too casual a term to apply to this "violent" film, the words of the staid *Commonweal* bear quoting: "*Pulp Fiction* has about as much to do with actual criminality or violence as *Cyrano de Bergerac* with the realities of seventeenth-century France or *The Prisoner of Zenda* with Balkan politics."[57] As *Commonweal* critic Richard Alleva goes on to say, "If gangsters really had this sort of wit, they'd be writing screenplays."[58] They have more the pop culture/couch potato film knowledge of the movie's writer/director. Tarantino, a high school drop-out, was raised on films (an American François Truffaut). Later, as an adult, he did further "study" as a video store clerk.

The actors playing their parts periodically remind the viewer it is just a movie. This is not unlike Jules's comment outside the room where he and Vincent have to kill three men. Prior to this they have been kidding around, but then Jules observes, "Let's get into character." When a viewer goes to see *Pulp Fiction* he or she gets into character for a witty dark comedy. The violence is more comic book, pulp fiction violence. People without the mindset have difficulty with Tarantino's film, and possibly black comedy in general. All this is not to say Tarantino does not make adjustments. The script originally had the accidental shooting in the car much more graphic. Now the viewer does not see the person actually being shot. Also the script detailed a bloody shoot-out during the restaurant robbery, whereas the scene avoids any sort of violence.

There is no correct "reading" to this film, or to the others addressed in this text. And each generation will bring its own angles of vision to such works. But at this time *Pulp Fiction* and the others seem best posed to meet the dark comedy needs of today.

NOTES

1. James Greenberg, "In Film Noir, the Past Is Present and Perfect," *New York Times*, February 6, 1994, Section 2, pp. 9, 15.

2. Mark Horowitz, "Fault Lines," *Film Comment*, November-December, 1990, p. 57.

3. Horowitz, p. 55.

4. Robert Emmet Long, *Nathanael West* (New York: Frederick Ungar, 1985), p. 49.

5. Peter Biskind, "The Low Road to *Chinatown*," *Premiere*, June 1994, p. 72.

6. Vincent Canby, *Chinatown* review, *New York Times*, June 21, 1974, p. 26.

7. Horowitz, p. 55.

8. Pauline Kael, *Reeling* (New York: Warner Books, 1976), p. 469.

9. Biskind, p. 72.

10. *Chinatown* file, citation incomplete, Billy Rose Theatre Collection, New York Public Library at Lincoln Center.

11. Kael, pp. 625-26.

12. Long, p. 131.

13. Jay Martin, *Nathanael West* (1970; repr. New York: Carroll and Graf 1984), p. 313.

14. Michael S. Reynolds, *The Sun Also Rises: A Novel of the Twenties* (Boston: Twayne, 1988), p. 15.

15. Fred Schruers, "The Rolling Stone Interview: Jack Nicholson," *Rolling Stone*, August 14, 1986, p. 48.

16. Bonnie Britton, "Film Takes Insidious Look at Hollywood," *Indianapolis Star*, May 1, 1992, p. D-1.

17. Leonard Maltin, *Movie and Video Guide: 1994* (New York: Penguin Press, 1993), pp. 991-92.

18. Diana Rico, "S.M.A.S.H.," *GQ*, May 1992, p. 95.

19. Gavin Smith and Richard T. Jameson, "The Movie You Saw Is the Movie We're Going to Make," *Film Comment*, May-June 1992, p. 23.

20. Ibid.

21. Rico, p. 99.

22. David Sterritt, "A Movie that Pokes Fun at Movies," *Christian Science Monitor*, April 10, 1992, p. 14.

23. Kenneth Turan, "*Player* Brings Altman Background with a Vengeance," *Los Angeles Times*, April 10, 1992, pp. 1-F, 6F.

24. Reynolds, p. 91.

25. Terrence Rafferty, "Killer," *The New Yorker*, April 20, 1992, p. 82.

26. David Ansen, "The Player," *Newsweek*, March 2, 1992, p. 61.

27. David Kehr, "A Teeming *Player*," *Chicago Tribune*, April 24, 1992, Section 7, p. 6.

28. Rafferty, p. 82.

29. Peter Travers, "Setting Up Hollywood for the Kill," *Rolling Stone*, April 30, 1992, p. 64.

30. Richard Corliss, "Critic Picks Slick Flick Pic," *Time*, April 13, 1992, p. 70.

31. Richard Blake, *The Player* review, *America*, May 30, 1992, p. 490.

32. Jack Kroll, "Robert Altman Gives Something Back," *Esquire*, May 1992, p. 89.

33. Sterritt, p. 14.

34. Mark Twain, "The Facts Concerning the Recent Carnival of Crime in Connecticut," in *Selected Shorter Writings of Mark Twain*, ed. Walter Blair (Boston: Houghton Mifflin, 1962), p. 149.

35. Todd McCarthy, *The Player* review, *Variety*, March 16, 1992, p. 3.

36. *Pulp Fiction* review, *Nation*, October 17, 1994, p. 434.

37. Richard Corliss, "A Blast to the Heart," *Time*, October 10, 1994, p. 78.

38. Owen Gleiberman, "Knockout Bunch," *Entertainment Weekly*, October 14, 1994, p. 35.

39. Quentin Tarantino, *Pulp Fiction* (Screenplay) (New York: Hyperion, 1994), p. 1.

40. Peter Biskind, "An Auteur Is Born, " *Premiere*, November 1994, p. 100.

41. Ibid.

42. Steve Pond, "Jerry Takes Shelter," *TV Guide*, February 4, 1995, p. 14.

43. Gavin Smith, "Quentin Tarantino," *Film Comment*, July/August 1994, p. 42.

44. Biskind, p. 100.

45. Gleiberman, p. 35.

46. Richard Blake, "Light and Dark," *America*, November 12, 1994, p. 23.

47. Biskind, p. 102.

48. See my *Populism and the Capra Legacy* (Westport, Conn.: Greenwood Press, 1995).

49. Ann Olderburg, "Golden Globes Show a Lot of 'Gump'tion," *USA Today*, January 23, 1995, p. 1-D.

50. Gleiberman, p. 34.

51. Anthony Lane, "Degrees of Cool," *The New Yorker*, October 10, 1994, p. 96.

52. Smith, p. 41.

53. Lane, p. 97.

54. Tarantino, p. 57.

55. Smith, p. 34.

56. Donald Kaul, "Of Course, Oscars Show Blew It Again" (syndicated column), appeared in *Muncie Star*, April 2, 1995, p. 13-A.

57. Richard Alleva, "Beaten to a Pulp," *Commonweal*, November 18, 1994, p. 30.

58. Ibid.

6

Conclusions

Madness is always fascinating, for it reveals the ungluing we all secretly fear: the mind taking off from the body, the possibility that the magnet that attaches us to a context in the world can lose its grip.

—Molly Haskell[1]

It has been stated that there is a parallel between modernism and madness. I thought of this when I came across author Molly Haskell's quote noted above. Modernism and madness are hardly strange bedfellows. As each chapter in the text suggests, though the madness that is black comedy has a long history, it moved to center stage in the modern age, fueled in part by the writings of Charles Darwin and Sigmund Freud. While Darwin's work destroyed belief in a rational, God-centered universe, Freud effectively called into question the possibility of even not being in control of one's own mind. Both represent fertile ground for dark humor.

The portion of the Haskell quote that notes the "ungluing we all secretly fear" also reminds me of Joseph Conrad's *Heart of Darkness* (1902), where the search for Kurtz represents the ease with which man's dark side can be released—the thin veneer of civilization. More specifically, the reference to "ungluing" brings to mind *Slaughterhouse-Five* (1972), where central character Billy Pilgrim becomes "unstuck" in time. In dark humor, characters sometimes time travel, or, as in the case of *Brazil* (1985), the lead character's madness gives him the gloriously ironic illusion that he is escaping.

Thoreau's observation that "most men lead lives of quiet desperation" has been an ongoing chorus in this book. But as dark comedy becomes more pervasive at every level of life, one is tempted to embrace novelist James Jones's reworking of the commentary: "Most men lead lives of desperate crappiness."[2] When the "lost generation" wrote their anti-war novels, such as Hemingway's *A Farewell to Arms* (1929, see Chapter 1), the dark comedy at least had a collapsed society upon which to focus. Later works, such as Heller's *Catch-22* (1961), are more desperate with their black humor because there is less sense of a structure upon which to start. Thus, while dark comedy continues to prick institutions like the church, the military, the government . . . the genre's movement seems as much about the disintegration of the individual as the disintegration of the society. As the frontispiece of Edvard Munch's *The Shriek* (1896) suggests, it is a disintegration based in lostness.

Dark comedy is about lostness, lostness even in the midst of crowds, whether it is the world of Kafka or Harold (of *Harold and Maude*, 1971) only having his suicides to fall back on in times of stress. This lostness is cradled in three black comedy themes: man as beast (echoes of Darwin and Freud), the absurdity of the world (inherently and sometimes assisted by man), and the omnipresence of death. If forced to select the most central of these three, it would be death, for nothing so rules the fears of mortal man. Indeed, the four pivotal lessons of death incorporate elements of the aforementioned black comedy themes.

First, there is the terrible absurdity of death. How can a living, passionate, thinking being turn into so much garbage in a split second? A second slant on absurdity is the casual randomness of death. In the ever-hopeful genre of populism, like Capra's *It's a Wonderful Life* (1946), all deaths have some purpose. In dark comedy just the opposite is true; witness the bump in the road which causes *Pulp Fiction*'s (1994) Vincent to accidentally blow off the head of a fellow passenger. Third, an additional perspective on absurdity involves the frequency with which death by suicide is employed in the genre. "To be or not to be" could be utilized as black comedy's axiom. As the theme song to *M.A.S.H.* (1970),

Suicide is Painless, ironically suggests, one of the few things modern man has under his control is the negation of his own being. And even here, the casual absurdity continues, such as when *M.A.S.H.*'s Painless Pole the dentist asks his buddies for suicide tips because "I'm kinda new at this." The fourth key lesson of dark comedy death, the callousness with which man can accept ever more gruesome shocks, speaks to the man-as-beast theme.

Despite this callousness, if this theme is recognized, pluses can come from it. First, provocative essayist and historian Paul Fussell has suggested that to make sense of the Holocaust (see Chapter 1), it must be seen not as a German crime but as a shared world atrocity—"Which means that if you can't imagine yourself an S.S. officer hustling the Jewish women and children to the gas chamber, you need to be more closely in touch with your buried self."[3] As repugnant as that statement was to this stereotypical bleeding-heart liberal, and while I initially was deeply offended, it represents a safety-valve device. I was reminded of the Mark Twain short story mentioned earlier in the text, "The Man that Corrupted Hadley-burg." Here was a morally smug town whose motto was: "Lead us not into temptation." A stranger (one of many dark strangers to populate the black humor of Twain's last decade) offered a subtle temptation to show just how hypocritical the town was. After this humiliating but educational experience, the town's revised moral became: "Lead us into temptation." Twain closes the story by observing: "It is an honest town once more, and the man will have to rise early that catches it napping again."[4] Fussell might very well have been influenced by Twain's short story.

If one is to guard against another Holocaust or a different crime against humanity, it is imperative to be aware of his/her dark side. Though not a black comedy, the title of Sinclair Lewis's last important novel, *It Can't Happen Here* (1935), catches perfectly the naive complacency that can lead to history repeating itself. Conrad's *Heart of Darkness* demonstrates a more focused look at the ease with which a single individual can be tempted. In the novel both Kurtz and the narrator in search of him are idealized characters—thus underlining even the best of men's vulnerability to the dark side. One of the rare flaws of director Francis Coppola's sometimes dark comedy screen adaptation of Conrad's novel, *Apocalypse Now* (1979), is that while Kurtz is initially a superior human being, the narrator is now a government assassin. Thus, his temptation to become like the now-lawless Kurtz does not offer as much dramatic tension . . . a fall from high ideals.

A second plus to black comedy's callousness, if it is recognized, is as a defense mechanism. This can vary from Holocaust victims and surrounding black humor as a day-to-day tool for survival, to the average person's ability to cope with the horrors of today's headlines. In the latter case, one can liken this to Freud's approach to humor. He saw comedy as the way in which people could comfortably address taboo subjects, especially sex. Dark comedy would merely transfer the focus from sex to the myriad of horrors which constitute today's news. Early twentieth-century author Salomo Friedlaender, sometimes known as the "Laughing Philosopher," used this technique in his famous books of "grotesque [dark humor] tales." Critic Jack Zipes stated, "To offset the chaos in the world around him, Friedlaender used the grotesque as the means for creating balance and sobriety."5 Of course, as one moves from Holocaust to headlines, an additional level should be noted in dark comedy's use. What about the private demons which plague so many individuals? As a personal footnote to this final development, the two years spent writing this book paralleled the most trying period of my life. Without black comedy to fall back on for relief and release, I doubt I would have been able to keep my sanity, let alone write a book. In speaking of private demons one remembers the poignant close to scholar/author Norman Maclean's short autobiographical novel *A River Runs Through It*. The book keys upon his charismatic brother Paul, and a family relationship tied to the river and fly-fishing as defining art. The boys were taught by their equally enthusiastic clergyman father that "there was no clear line between religion and fly fishing."6 When Paul was murdered as a young man, shortly after a masterful display of fishing, communication was never the same in the family. Maclean closes the book with the words, "I am haunted by waters."7

Although some use dark comedy to exorcise demons or headline horrors, the opportunity is unfortunately not for everyone. Some people's "need for order and surety [regardless of the reliability of the people or institutions concerned] . . . the drive that life does or should make sense, can make . . . [black comedy] seem trivial or uncomfortably subversive."8 But ironically, sometimes dark or sick humor is the best way to stay healthy.

Comedy theorist Jim Leach once observed, with humorous insight, "that a genre [comedy] which encompasses the visions of Jerry Lewis *and* [sophisticated] director Ernst Lubitsch is already in trouble."9 He went on to suggest a more ambitious examination of multiple comedy genres, noting what many film comedy enthusiasts have long believed—if a genre is defined too loosely [as in the case of comedy], it ceases to be of any value as a critical tool."10 This book has attempted to tighten things up by exploring a humor genre—dark comedy—that falls 180 degrees away from the feel-good populism of a Frank Capra.11 And black humor neither embraces the personality comedy genre of a Jerry Lewis nor parody as redefined by Mel Brooks. Lubitsch comedy falls in various genres, from dark comedy (see Chapter 2), to screwball comedy.12 While all of these genres are of invaluable importance, it seems that black humor has most often fallen through the genre cracks. When it did surface, it was most likely as a sometime characteristic of another genre, such as film noir (see Chapter 5). In the final analysis, this study asks one to rethink his or her approach to the genres of comedy, while paying particular attention to the one—dark humor—that seems the most contemporary of them all.

NOTES

1. Molly Haskell, *Love and Other Infectious Diseases* (New York: Citadel Press, 1990) p. 84.

2. Edmund Fuller, *Man in Modern Fiction* (New York: Random House, 1958), p. 13.

3. Paul Fussell, *Thank God for the Atom Bomb and Other Essays* (New York: Summit Books, 1988), p. 140.

4. Mark Twain, *Selected Shorter Writings*, ed. Walter Blair (Boston: Houghton Mifflin, 1962), p. 289.

5. Jack Zipes (ed), *The Operated Jew* (New York: Routledge, 1991), p. 119.

6. Norman Maclean, *A River Runs Through It* (1976; reprint, New York: Pocket Books, 1992), p. 1.

7. Ibid., p. 113.

8. Robert M. Polhemus, *Comic Faith* (1980; repr., Chicago: University of Chicago Press, 1982), p. 246.

9. Jim Leach, "The Screwball Comedy," in *Film Genre: Theory and Criticism*, ed. Barry K. Grant (Metuchen, N.J.: Scarecrow Press, 1977), p. 75.

10. Ibid.

11. See my *Populism and the Capra Legacy* (Westport, Conn.: Greenwood Press, 1995).

12. See my *Screwball Comedy: A Genre of Madcap Romance* (Westport, Conn.: Greenwood Press, 1986).

S H O C K

In the black comedy genre. . .

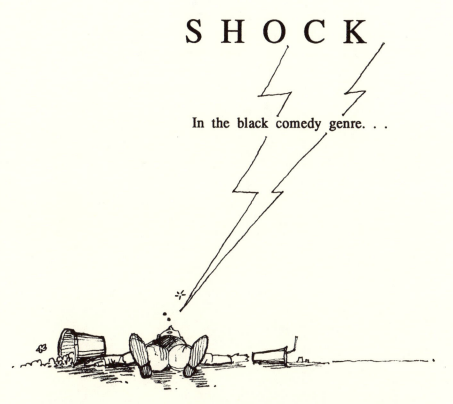

15. Shock college cartoon by J. David Hall. Courtesy of Mr. J. David Hall.

Appendix: Selected Filmography

PIONEERING AMERICAN BLACK COMEDIES

1933   *Duck Soup* (70 minutes).
        Paramount. *Producer*: Herman Mankiewicz. *Director*: Leo
        McCarey. *Screenplay, music and lyrics*: Bert Kalmar and Harry
        Ruby. *Cast*: Groucho Marx (Rufus T. Firefly), Chico Marx
        (Chicolini), Harpo Marx (Brownie), Zeppo Marx (Bob Rol-
        land), Margaret Dumont (Mrs. Teasdale), Louis Calhern
        (Ambassador Trentino).

1940   *The Great Dictator* (127 minutes).
        United Artists. *Producer/Director/Writer*: Charlie Chaplin.
        Editor: Willard Nico. *Cast*: Charlie Chaplin (Hynkel/Jewish
        barber), Jack Oakie (Napaloni), Reginald Gardner (Gar-
        bitsch), Billy Gilbert (Herring), Paulette Goddard (Hannah).

1942   *To Be or Not To Be* (99 minutes).
        United Artists. *Producer*: Alexander Korda/Ernst Lubitsch.
        Director: Ernst Lubitsch. *Screenplay*: Edwin Meyer. *Editor*:
        Dorothy Spencer. *Cast*: Carole Lombard (Maria Tura), Jack
        Benny (Joseph Tura), Robert Stack (Lt. Sobinski), Sig Ruman
        (Col. Ehrhardt), Stanley Ridges (Prof. Siletsky).

1944   *Arsenic and Old Lace* (118 minutes).
        Warner Brothers. *Producer/Director*: Frank Capra. *Screen-
        play*: Julius J. and Philip G. Epstein. *Editing*: Daniel Mandell.
        Cast: Cary Grant (Mortimer Brewster), Priscilla Lane (Elaine

Harper), Raymond Massey (Jonathan Brewster), Jean Adair (Martha Brewster), Josephine Hull (Abby Brewster), Peter Lorre (Dr. Einstein), John Alexander (Teddy "Roosevelt").

1947   *Monsieur Verdoux* (122 minutes).
United Artists. *Producer/Director*: Charles Chaplin. *Story/Screenplay*: Charles Chaplin (from an idea by Orson Welles). *Editing*: Willard Nico. *Cast*: Charles Chaplin (Henri Verdoux), Martha Raye (Annabelle Bonheur), Isobel Elsom (Maria Grosnay), Marilyn Nash (girl).

1953   *Stalag 17* (119 minutes).
Paramount. *Producer/Director*: Billy Wilder. *Screenplay*: Billy Wilder and Edwin Blum. *Editor*: George Tomasini. *Cast*: William Holden (Sefton), Don Taylor (Lt. Dunbar), Otto Preminger (Oberst Von Scherbach), Robert Strauss (Stosh).

1955   *The Trouble with Harry* (99 minutes).
Paramount. *Producer/Director*: Alfred Hitchcock. *Screenplay*: John Michael Hays, from the John Trevor novel. *Editor*: Alma Macrorie. *Cast*: Edmund Gwenn (Capt. Albert Wiles), John Forsythe (Sam Marlowe), Shirley MacLaine (Jennifer).

1959   *Some Like It Hot* (119 minutes).
United Artists. *Producer/Director*: Billy Wilder. *Screenplay*: Billy Wilder and I.A.L. Diamond, from a story by R. Thoeren and M. Logan. *Editor*: Arthur Schmidt. *Cast*: Marilyn Monroe (Sugar), Tony Curtis (Joe/Josephine), Jack Lemmon (Jerry/Daphne), George Raft (Spats Columbo), Joe E. Brown (Osgood Fielding).

BLACK COMEDY COMES OF AGE

1964   *Dr. Strangelove: Or, How I Learned to Stop Worrying and Love the Bomb* (93 minutes).
Columbia. *Producer/Director*: Stanley Kubrick. *Screenplay*: Stanley Kubrick, Terry Southern, and Peter George, based on Peter George's novel *Red Alert*. *Editing*: Anthony Harvey. *Cast*: Peter Sellers (Group Capt. Lionel Mandrake/President Muffley/Dr. Strangelove), George C. Scott (Gen. "Buck" Turgidson), Sterling Hayden (Gen. Jack D. Ripper), Keenan Wynn (Col. "Bat" Guano), Slim Pickens (Maj. T. J. "King" Kong), Peter Bull (Ambassador de Sadesky), Tracy Reed (Miss Scott).

1967   *The Producers* (88 minutes).
        Springtime/MGM/Crossbow. *Producer*: Sidney Glazier. *Director/Writer*: Mel Brooks. *Editor*: Ralph Rosenblum. *Cast*:
        Zero Mostel (Max Bialystock), Gene Wilder (Leo Bloom),
        Kenneth Mars (Franz Liebkind).

Jan. 1970 *M.A.S.H.* (116 minutes).
        20th Century-Fox. *Producer*: Ingo Preminger. *Director*:
        Robert Altman. Screenplay: Ring Lardner, Jr., based on
        Richard Hooker's novel. *Editor*: Danford B. Greene. *Cast*:
        Elliott Gould (Trapper John), Donald Sutherland (Hawkeye),
        Tom Skerritt (Duke), Sally Kellerman (Maj. Hot Lips), Jo An
        Pflug (Lt. Dish).

June 1970 *Catch-22* (121 minutes).
        Paramount and Filmways. *Producers*: John Calley, Martin
        Ransohoff. *Director*: Mike Nichols. *Screenplay*: Buck Henry,
        based on Joseph Heller's novel. *Editor*: Sam O'Steen. *Cast*:
        Alan Arkin (Capt. Yossarian), Martin Balsam (Col. Cathcart),
        Arthur Garfunkel (Nately), Buck Henry (Col. Korn), Jon
        Voight (Milo Minderbinder), Orson Welles (Gen. Dreedle).

Nov. 1970 *Where's Poppa?* (83 minutes).
        United Artists. *Producers*: Jerry Pokofsky and Marvin Worth.
        Director: Carl Reiner. Screenplay: Robert Klane, based on his
        novel. *Editors*: Bud Molin and Chic Ciccolini. *Cast*: George
        Segal (Gordon Hocheiser), Ruth Gordon (Mrs. Hocheiser),
        Ron Liebman (Sidney Hocheiser).

Dec. 1970 *Little Big Man* (150 minutes).
        National General/Cinema Center. *Producer*: Stuart Millar.
        Director: Arthur Penn. *Screenplay*: Calder Willingham, based
        on Thomas Berger's novel. *Editing*: Dede Allen. *Cast*: Dustin
        Hoffman (Jack Crabbe/Little Big Man), Fay Dunaway (Mrs.
        Pendrake), Martin Balsam (Allardyce T. Merriwhether),
        Richard Mulligan (Gen. Custer), Chief Dan George (Old
        Lodge Skins).

April 1971 *Bananas* (81 minutes).
        United Artists. *Producers*: Jack Rollins and Charles H. Joffe.
        Director: Woody Allen. *Screenplay*: Woody Allen and Mickey
        Rose. *Editor*: Ron Kalish. *Cast*: Woody Allen (Fielding Mellish), Carlos Montalban (General Vargas), Louise Lasser
        (Nancy).

Dec. 1971 *A Clockwork Orange* (137 minutes).
        Warner Bros. *Producer/Director/Writer*: Stanley Kubrick,
        from the novel by Anthony Burgess. *Cast*: Malcolm McDow-

ell (Alex), Patrick Magee (Mr. Alexander), Michael Bates (Chief Guard).

Dec. 1971   *Harold and Maude* (90 minutes).
Paramount. *Producers*: Colin Higgins, Charles B. Mulvehill. *Director*: Hal Ashby. *Screenplay*: Colin Higgins. *Editors*: William A. Sawyer, Edward Warschilka. *Cast*: Ruth Gordon (Maude), Bud Cort (Harold Chasen), Vivian Pickles (Mrs. Chasen), Charles Tyner (Uncle Victor).

1972   *Slaughterhouse-Five* (104 minutes).
Universal. *Producer*: Paul Monash. *Director*: George Roy Hill. *Screenplay*: Stephen Geller, based on Kurt Vonnegut, Jr.'s novel. *Editor*: Dede Allen. *Cast*: Michael Sacks (Billy Pilgrim), Ron Leibman (Paul Lazzaro), Valerie Perrine (Montana Wildhack), Eugene Roche (Edgar Derby).

1976   *Network* (121 minutes).
United Artists release of an MGM film. *Producer*: Howard Gottfried. *Director*: Sidney Lumet. *Screenplay*: Paddy Chayefsky. *Editor*: Alan Heim. *Cast*: Faye Dunaway (Diana Christensen), William Holden (Max Schumacher), Peter Finch (Howard Beale), Robert Duvall (Frank Hackett).

1980   *The Stunt Man* (129 minutes).
Melvin Simon Production. *Producer/Director*: Richard Rush. *Screenplay*: Lawrence B. Marcus, from the Paul Brodeur novel. *Editors*: Jack Hofstra, Caroline Ferriol. *Cast*: Peter O'Toole (Eli Cross), Steve Railsback (Cameron), Barbara Hershey (Nina Franklin), Allen Goorwitz (Sam).

June 1981   *S.O.B.* (121 minutes).
Paramount. *Producers*: Blake Edwards and Tony Adams. *Director/Screenplay*: Blake Edwards. *Editor*: Ralph E. Winters. *Cast*: Julie Andrews (Sally Miles), William Holden (Tim Culley), Marisa Berenson (Mavis), Richard Mulligan (Felix Farmer).

Dec. 1981   *Neighbors* (95 minutes).
Columbia. *Producers*: Richard D. Zanuck and David Brown. *Director*: John G. Alvidsen. *Screenplay*: Larry Gelbert, based on the Thomas Berger novel. *Editor*: Jane Kurson. *Cast*: John Belushi (Earl Keese), Dan Aykroyd (Vic), Cathy Moriarty (Ramona).

July 1982   *The World According to Garp* (137 minutes).
Warner Bros. *Producers*: George Roy Hill and Robert L. Crawford. *Director*: George Roy Hill. *Screenplay*: Steve

Tesich, from the John Irving novel. *Editor*: Stephen A. Rotter. *Cast*: Robin Williams (T. S. Garp), Glenn Close (Jenny Fields), Mary Beth Hurt (Helen Holm), John Lithgow (Roberta Muldoon).

Sept. 1982   *Eating Raoul* (83 minutes).
Independently made. *Producer*: Anne Kimmel. *Director*: Paul Bartel. *Screenplay*: Richard Blackburn, Paul Bartel. *Editor*: Alan Toomayan. *Cast*: Paul Bartel (Paul), Mary Woronov (Mary), Robert Beltram (Raoul), Buck Henry (Mr. Leech), John Parragon (Sexshop Salesman).

1983   *Reuben, Reuben* (101 minutes).
20th Century-Fox. *Producers*: Walter Shenson and Julius J. Epstein. *Director*: Robert Ellis Miller. *Screenplay*: Julius J. Epstein. *Editor*: Skip Lusk. *Cast*: Tom Conti (Gowan McGland), Kelly McGillis (Geneva Spofford), Cynthia Harris (Bobby Springer).

Feb. 1985   *Brazil* (131 minutes).
Universal. *Producer*: Arnon Milchan. *Director*: Terry Gilliam. *Screenplay*: Terry Gilliam, Tom Stoppard, Charles McKeown. *Editor*: Julian Doyle. *Cast*: Jonathan Pryce (Sam Lowry), Kim Greist (Jill Layton), Robert De Niro (Harry Tuttle), Katherine Helmond (Mrs. Ida Lowry), Michael Palin (Jack Lint).

June 1985   *Prizzi's Honor* (129 minutes).
20th Century-Fox. *Producer*: John Foreman. *Director*: John Huston. *Screenplay*: Richard Condon and Janet Roach, based on the Condon novel. *Editor*: Ridi Fehr and Kaja Fehr. *Cast*: Jack Nicholson (Charley Patanna), Kathleen Turner (Irene Walker), Anjelica Huston (Maerose Prizzi).

Sept. 1985   *After Hours* (97 minutes).
Warner Bros. *Producers*: Amy Robinson, Griffin Dunne, and Robert F. Colesberry. *Director*: Martin Scorsese. *Screenplay*: Joseph Minion. *Editor*: Thelma Schoomaker. *Cast*: Griffin Dunne (Paul Hackett), Rosanna Arquette (Marcy), Verna Bloom (June).

1986   *Crimes of the Heart* (105 minutes).
De Laurentiis Entertainment. *Producer*: Freddie Fields. *Director*: Bruce Beresford. *Screenplay*: Beth Henley, based on her play. *Editor*: Anne Goursaud. *Cast*: Diane Keaton (Lenny MaGrath), Jessica Lange (Meg MaGrath), Sissy Spacek (Babe

MaGrath), Sam Shepard (Doc Porter), Tess Harper (Chick Boyle).

March 1987 *Raising Arizona* (94 minutes).
20th Century-Fox. *Producer*: Ethan Coen. *Director*: Joel Coen. *Screenplay*: Ethan and Joel Coen. *Editor*: Michael R. Miller. *Cast*: Nicolas Cage (H. I. McDonnough), Holly Hunter (Ed), Trey Wilson (Nathan Arizona, Sr.), John Goodman (Gale).

Dec. 1987 *Throw Momma from the Train* (88 minutes).
Orion Pictures. *Producer*: Larry Brezner. *Director*: Danny DeVito. *Screenplay*: Stu Silver. Editor: Michael Jablow. *Cast*: Danny DeVito (Owen), Billy Crystal (Larry), Ann Ramsey (Momma).

Jan. 1989 *Heathers* (102 minutes).
New World Pictures. *Producer*: Denise Di Novi. *Director*: Michael Lehmann. *Screenplay*: Daniel Waters. *Editor*: Norman Hollyn. *Cast*: Winona Ryder (Veronica Sawyer), Christian Slater (J. D.), Shannen Doherty (Heather Duke), Lisanne Falk (Heather McNamara), Kim Walker (Heather Chandler).

Dec. 1989 *War of the Roses* (116 minutes).
20th Century-Fox. *Producers*: James L. Brooks and Arnon Milchan. *Director*: Danny DeVito. *Screenplay*: Michael Leeson, based on the Warren Adler novel. *Editor*: Lynzee Klingman. *Cast*: Michael Douglas (Oliver Rose), Kathleen Turner (Barbara Rose), Danny DeVito (Gavin D'Amato).

1992 *The Player* (123 minutes).
Fine Line Features. *Producer*: David Brown. *Director*: Robert Altman. *Screenplay*: Michael Tolkin, from his novel. *Cast*: Tim Robbins (Griffin Mill), Greta Scacchi (June Gudmundsdotti), Fred Ward (Walter Stuckel), Whoopi Goldberg (Detective Avery), Peter Gallagher (Larry Levy).

Aug. 1994 *Natural Born Killers* (119 minutes).
Warner Bros. *Producers*: Jane Hamsher, Don Murphy, Clayton Townsend. *Director*: Oliver Stone. *Screenplay*: David Veloz, Richard Rutawski, Oliver Stone, story by Quentin Tarantino. *Editors*: Hank Corwin, Brian Berdan. *Cast*: Woody Harrelson (Mickey), Juliette Lewis (Mallory), Robert Downey, Jr. (Wayne Gayle), Tommy Lee Jones (Dwight McClusky), Tom Sizemore (Jack Scagnetti), Rodney Dangerfield (Mallory's dad).

Oct. 1994   *Pulp Fiction* (153 minutes).
Miramax. *Producer*: Lawrence Bender. *Director/Screenplay*:
Quentino Tarantino. *Editor*: Salley Menke. *Cast*: John Tra-
volta (Vincent Vega), Samuel L. Jackson (Jules), Uma Thur-
man (Mia), Harvey Keitel (The Wolf), Tim Roth (Pumkin),
Amanda Plummer (Honey Bunny), Mariade de Madeiros
(Fabienne), Ving Rhames (Marsellus Wallace), Eric Stoltz
(Lance), Rosanna Arquette (Jody), Christopher Walken
(Koons), Bruce Willis (Butch).

SELECTED BIBLIOGRAPHY

Agee, James. "*Monsieur Verdoux*." In *Agee on Film*, vol 1. New York: Grosset and Dunlap, 1969. (Originally appeared in *Nation*, May 31, June 14, and June 21, 1947.)

Agee, John (unsigned). *Monsieur Verdoux* review. *Time* (May 5, 1947), p. 100.

Alleva, Richard. "Beaten to a Pulp." *Commonweal*, November 18, 1994.

Ansen, David. "*The Player*." *Newsweek* (March 2, 1992), p. 61.

Ansen, David. "Raw Carnage or Revelation?" *Newsweek* (August 29, 1994), p. 55.

Arsenic and Old Lace review. Credit citation missing, in the *Arsenic and Old Lace* film file, Billy Rose Theatre Collection, New York Public Library at Lincoln Center.

"Atomic Cafe" entry. In *TV Movies and Video Guide* (1987 edition). Editor Leonard Maltin. New York: New American Library, 1986, pp. 43–44.

Avisar, Ilan. *Screening the Holocaust: Cinema's Images of the Unimaginable*. Bloomington: Indiana University Press, 1988.

Beafort, John. "An Assault from Mr. Chaplin." *Christian Science Monitor* (April 19, 1947), p. 8.

Benchley, Robert. "Drama: Inventory." *Life* (December 7, 1922), p. 46.

Benchley, Robert. "How to Watch Football." *In Pluck and Luck*. New York: Henry Holt and Company, 1925.

Benson, Sheila. "*Heathers* Gets Lost in a Moral Thicket." *Los Angeles Times* (March 31, 1989), Section 6, p. 15.

Bergman, Andrew. "Some Anarcho-Nihilist Laff Riots." In Bergman's *We're in the Money: Depression America and Its Films*. New York: Harper and Row, 1972, p. 37.

Bergson, Henri. "Laughter." In *Comedy*, ed. Wylie Sypher. Garden City, N.Y.: Doubleday Anchor Books, 1956.

Bishop, André. "Preface." In Stephen Sondheim and John Weidman *Assassins*. New York: Theatre Communications Group, 1991.

Biskind, Peter. "An Auteur Is Born." *Premiere* (November 1994), p. 100.

Biskind, Peter. "The Low Road to Chinatown." *Premiere* (June 1994), p. 72.

"Black Humorists, The." *Time* (February 12, 1965), pp. 94–96.

Blake, Richard. "Light and Dark." *America* (November 12, 1994), p. 23.

Blake, Richard. *The Player* review. *America* (May 30, 1992), p. 490.

Blake, Richard A. "Stoned Again." *America* (September 17, 1994), p. 23.

Blessing, Lee. *A Walk in the Woods*. New York: New American Library, 1986.

Boggs, Joseph M. *The Art of Watching Films*. Mountain View, Calif.: Mayfield Publishing, 1991.

Bonadeo, Alfredo. *Mark of the Beast: Death and Degradation in the Literature of the Great War*. Lexington: University of Kentucky Press, 1989.

Borowski, Tadeusz. *This Way for the Gas, Ladies and Gentleman*. 1959; Reprint. New York: Penguin Books, 1986.

Britton, Bonnie. "Film Takes Insidious Look at Hollywood." *Indianapolis Star* (May 1, 1992), p. D-1.

Buñuel, Luis. *My Last Sigh*. trans. Abigail Israel. 1982; Reprint. New York: Random House, 1984.

Canby, Vincent. *Chinatown* review. *New York Times* (June 21, 1974), p. 26.

Canby, Vincent. "Hal Ashby's Comedy Opens at Coronet." *New York Times* (December 21, 1971).

Carl, Teet. "'Fun' working with the Marx Brothers? Horse Feathers!" *Los Angeles Magazine* (October 1978), p. 145.

Carlin, George. "Baseball-Football." On the album *An Evening with Wally Londo*. Los Angeles: Little David Records, 1975.

"Carole's Last Picture." *Fort Wayne [IN] News-Sentinel* (March 7, 1942), p. 11.

Carrol, Jerry. "Oliver Stone on His 'Natural Born' Overkill." *San Francisco Chronicle*, syndicated in the *Muncie Star* (August 28, 1994), p. B10.

Cather, Willa. *One of Ours*. 1922; Reprint. New York: Vintage Books, 1991.

Change, Chris. "Feed the Reaper." *Film Comment* (July/August 1994), p. 38.

Chaplin, Charles, Jr. (with N. Rau and M. Rau). *My Father, Charlie Chaplin*. New York: Random House, 1960.

Chaplin, Charlie. *My Autobiography*. 1964; Reprint. New York: Picket Books, 1966.

Chaplin, Michael. *I couldn't smoke the grass on my father's lawn*. New York: G. P. Putnam, 1966.

"Chaplin Says He Just Had to Make That Speech." *New York World-Telegram* (October 19, 1940), p. 7.

Chavance, Louis. "The Marx Brothers as Seen by a Frenchman." *The Canadian Forum* (February 1933), p. 175.

Chinatown file (citation incomplete), Billy Rose Theatre Collection, New York Public Library at Lincoln Center.

Clark, Alan. *The Donkeys*. 1961; Reprint. New York: Award Books, 1965.

Cobb, Humphrey. *Paths of Glory*. New York: Viking Press, 1935.

Cohen, Hennig. "Introduction to Herman Melville," in *The Confidence Man*. 1857; Reprint. New York: Holt, Rinehart and Winston, 1964.

Cohen, John. *The Essential Lenny Bruce*. New York: Ballantine Books, 1967.

Cohen, John S., Jr. "*Duck Soup*, a Marxian (Brothers) Burlesque That Is Below Their Standard." *New York Sun* (November 24, 1933). In the *Duck Soup* file, Billy Rose Theatre Collection, New York Public Library at Lincoln Center.

Corliss, Richard. "A Blast to the Heart." *Time* (October 10, 1994), p. 78.

Corliss, Richard. "Critic Picks Slick Flick Pic." *Time* (April 13, 1992), p. 70.

Corliss, Richard. "Stone Crazy." *Time* (August 29, 1994), p. 67.

Crawford, Deborah. *Franz Kafka: Man Out of Step*. New York: Crown Publishers., 1973.

Creelman, Eileen. *Arsenic and Old Lace* review. *New York Sun* (September 2, 1944). In the *Arsenic . . .* file, Billy Rose Theatre Collection, New York Public Library at Lincoln Center.

Creelman, Eileen. "Carole Lombard's Last Picture, the Somber 'To Be or Not to Be'." *New York Sun* (March 7, 1942). In the *To Be . . .* file, Billy Rose Theatre Collection, New York Public Library at Lincoln Center.

Crist, Judith. "Mirth and Murder." *New York Herald Tribune* (July 26, 1964), p. 27.

Crowther, Bosley. "Against a Sea of Troubles." *New York Times* (March 22, 1942), Section 8, p. 3.

Crowther, Bosley. *To Be or Not to Be* review. *New York Times* (March 7, 1942), p. 13.

Davis, Douglas M. *The World of Black Humor: An Introductory Anthology of Selections and Criticisms*. New York: E. P. Dutton, 1967.

Denby, David. "The Satirical *Heathers* Might Be Called Apocalyptic Sick Humor." *New York* magazine (April 3, 1989), p. 68.

Dickstein, Morris. Chapter 4, "Black Humor and History: The Early Sixties." In *Gates of Eden: American Culture in the Sixties*. New York: Basic Books, 1977, p. 117.

Durgnat, Raymond. "Four Against Alienation." In Durgnat's *The Crazy Mirror: Hollywood Comedy and the American Image*. 1969; Reprint. New York: Dell, 1972.

Ebert, Roger. "'Killers' a Biting Indictment of Society (Universal Press Syndicate)." Reprinted in *Cedar Rapids Gazette* (August 26, 1994), p .W–7.

Ehrlich, Eugene, Stuart Berg Flexner, Gorton Carruth, and Joyce M. Hawkins, ed., *Oxford American Dictionary* (1979; repr. November 1994), p. 100.

Epstein, Charles. *Heathers* review. *Films in Review* (September 1989), p. 424.

Eyles, Allen. *The Marx Brothers: Their World of Comedy*. New York: Paperback Library, 1971.

Eyman, Scott. *Ernst Lubitsch: Laughter in Paradise*. New York: Simon and Schuster, 1993.

Frank, Anne. *Anne Frank: The Diary of a Young Girl*. 1947; Reprint. New York: Pocket Books, 1958.

Frankl, Viktor E. *Man's Search for Meaning*. 1946; Reprint. Boston: Beacon Press, 1992.

Friedman, Bruce Jay, ed. *Black Humor*. New York, Bantam Books, 1965.

Fuller, Edmund. *Man in Modern Fiction*. New York: Random House, 1958.

Fussell, Paul. *Thank God for the Atomic Bomb and Other Essays*. New York: Summit Books, 1988.

Gardiner, Reginald. "*The Great Dictator*: Charlie Chaplin's Gift of Humor and Satire to the Totalitarian State." *New York Herald Tribune* (September 16, 1940). In *The Great Dictator* file, Billy Rose Theatre Collection, New York Public Library at Lincoln Center.

Gardner, Martin A. "The Marx Brothers: An Investigation of Their Films as Special Criticism." Ph.D. diss., New York University, 1970.

Gehring, Wes. "Chaplin's Film Pioneer Status in Black or Macabre Humor." In *His Reflection in Modern Times*, ed. Adolphe Nysenholc. New York: Mouton de Gruyter, 1991. pp. 139–49.

Gehring, Wes D. *Groucho & W. C. Fields: Huckster Comedians*. Jackson: University Press of Mississippi, 1994.

Gehring, Wes. *The Marx Brothers: A Bio-Bibliography*. Westport, Conn.: Greenwood Press, 1987.

Gehring, Wes D. *"Mr. B" Or Comforting Thoughts About the Bison*. Westport, Conn.: Greenwood Press, 1992.

Gehring, Wes. *Populism and the Capra Legacy*. Westport, Conn.: Greenwood Press, 1995.

Gehring, Wes. "Screwball Comedy." In my *Handbook of American Film Genres*. Westport, Conn.: Greenwood Press, 1988, pp. 105-24.

Gehring, Wes. *Screwball Comedy: A Genre of Madcap Romance*. Westport, Conn.: Greenwood Press, 1986.

Gehring, Wes. "Screwball Comedy: An Overview." *Journal of Popular Film and Television* (Winter 1986), pp. 178-85.

Gehring, Wes. *Screwball Comedy: Defining a Film Genre*. Muncie, Indiana: Ball State University Press, 1983.

Gleiberman, Owen. "American Psychos." *Entertainment* (August 24/September 2, 1994), p. 90.

Gleiberman, Owen. "Knockout Bunch." *Entertainment Weekly* (October 14, 1994), p. 35.

Gomery, Douglas. *Movie History: A Survey*. Belmont, Calif.: Wadsworth Publishing, 1991.

Graves, Robert. *Good-bye to All That*. 1929; Reprint, with revisions. Garden City, N.Y.: Doubleday Anchor Books, 1957.

"Great Dictator, The." *Sidney Morning Herald* (November 5, 1940), Woman's Supplement Section, p. 7.

Greenberg, James. "In Film Noir, the Past Is Present and Perfect." *New York Times* (February 6, 1994), Section 2, pp. 9, 15.

Guinness, Alec. Letter to the author (May 23, 1989).

Harold and Maude advertisement. *Village Voice* (December 23, 1971), p. 66.

Harold and Maude review. *Variety* (December 15, 1971).

Hasek, Jaroslav. *The Good Soldier Schweik* 1930; Reprint, New York: New American Library, 1963.

Haskell, Molly. *Love and Other Infectious Diseases*. New York: Citadel Press, 1990.

Heathers review. *Newsweek* (April 3, 1989), p. 67.

Heathers review. *Variety* (January 25, 1989), p. 15.

Heller, Joseph. *Catch-22*. 1961; Reprint. New York: Dell, 1968.

Hemingway, Ernest. *A Farewell to Arms*. 1929; Reprint. New York: Charles Scribner's Sons, 1957.

Hendra, Tony. *Going Too Far*. New York: Doubleday, 1987.

Hilfer, Anthony Channell. *The Revolt from the Village: 1915–1930*. Chapel Hill: University of North Carolina Press, 1969.

Hill, Hamlin. "Modern American Humor: the Janus Laugh." *College English* (December 1963), p. 174.

Hofstader, Richard. *The Paranoid Style in American Politics*. New York: Alfred A. Knopf, 1965.

Horowitz, Mark. "Fault Lines." *Film Comment* (November-December, 1990), p. 57.

Kael, Pauline. *Deeper Into Movies*. Boston: Little, Brown, 1973.

Kael, Pauline. *Heathers* review. *The New Yorker* (April 17, 1989), p. 115.

Kael, Pauline. *Reeling*. New York: Warner Books, 1976, p. 469.

Kael, Pauline. *State of the Art*. New York: E. P. Dutton, 1985.

Karl, Frederick R. *FRANZ KAFKA: Representative Man*. New York: Ticknor and Fields, 1991.

Kauffman, Stanley. "Apocalypse Now [Natural Born Killers]." *New Republic* (October 3, 1994), p. 26.

Kaul, Donald. "Of Course, Oscars Show Blew It Again" (syndicated column). *Muncie Star* (April 2, 1995), p. 13–A.

Kazin, Alfred. "The War Novel: From Mailer to Vonnegut." In *Viewpoint*, ed. Burton J. Fisherman. New York: St. Martin's Press, 1972.

Kehr, David. "A Teaming Player." *Chicago Tribune* (April 24, 1989) Section 7, p. 6.

Kehr, David. *"Heathers* a Corrosive Satire with a Weird Energy." *Chicago Tribune* (March 31, 1989), Section 7, p. 34.

Kirkley, Donald. *To Be or Not to Be* review. *Baltimore Sun* (March 12, 1942). In the *To Be . . .* file, Billy Rose Theatre Collection, New York Public Library at Lincoln Center.

Klawans, Stuart. *Heathers* review. *Nation* (April 17, 1989), p. 530.

Knickerbocker, Conrad. "Humor with a Mortal Sting" *New York Times Book Review* (September 27, 1964), pp. 3, 60–61.

Knight, Arthur. *The Liveliest Art: A Panoramic History of the Movies*. Revised. New York: Macmillan, 1978.

Kracauer, Siegfried *From Caligari to Hitler*. 1947 repr. Princeton, N.J.: Princeton University Press, 1971.

Kroll, Jack. "Robert Altman Gives Something Back." *Esquire* (May 1992), p. 89.

Lane, Anthony. "Degrees of Cool." *The New Yorker* (October 10, 1994), p. 96.

Lane, Anthony. *Pulp Fiction* review. *The New Yorker* (October 10, 1994), p. 96.

Leach, Jim. "The Screwball Comedy." In *Film Theory and Criticism*, ed. Barry K. Grant. Metuchen, N.J.: Scarecrow Press, 1977.

Lefcowitz, Eric. "'Dr. Strangelove' Turns 30. Can It Still Be Trusted?" *New York Times* (January 30, 1994), Section 2, p. 13.

"Life Imitates Cold War Art." *Newsweek* (October 18, 1993), p. 51.

Lifton, Robert Jay. "Beyond Atrocity." In *Viewpoint*, ed. Burton J. Fisherman. New York: St. Martin's Press, 1972.

Lipman, Steve. *LAUGHTER IN HELL: The Use of Humor During the Holocaust*. 1991; Reprint. Northvale, N.J.: Jason Aronson, 1993.

Long, Robert Emmet. *Nathanael West*. New York: Frederick Ungar, 1985, p. 49.

Lubitsch, Ernst. "Mr. Lubitsch Takes the Floor for Rebuttal." *New York Times* (March 29, 1942), Section 8, p. 3.

McCabe, John. *Charlie Chaplin*. Garden City, N.Y.: Doubleday, 1978.

McCarthy, Todd. *The Player* review. *Variety* (March 16, 1992), p. 3.

McGuinness, Richard. "Creatures Nosing for Crumbs." *Village Voice* (December 23, 1971), p. 66.

Macklin, Anthony. "Sex and Dr. Strangelove." *Film Comment* (Summer 1965), pp. 55–57.

Maclean, Norman. *A River Runs Through It*. 1976; Reprint. New York: Pocket Books, 1992.

Maland, Charles J. *Chaplin and American Culture*. Princeton, N.J.: Princeton University Press, 1989.

Maltin, Leonard. *Movie and Video Guide: 1994*. New York: Penguin Press, 1933, pp. 991–92.

Martin, Jay. *Nathanael West*. 1970; Reprint, New York: Carroll & Graf, 1984, p. 313.

Marx, Groucho. *Groucho and Me*. 1959; Reprint. New York: Manor Books, 1974.

Marx, Harpo (with Rowland Barber). *Harpo Speaks!* 1961; Reprint. New York: Freeway Press, 1974.

Maslin, Janet. "Getting Even." *New York Times* (March 31, 1989), Section C, p. 8.

Mast, Gerald, revised by Bruce F. Kawin. *A Short History of the Movies* (5th Edition). 1971; Reprint. New York: Macmillan, 1992.

Morella, Joe, and Edward Z. Epstein. *Gable & Lombard and Powell & Harlow*. New York: Dell, 1975.

"Mr. Chaplin Answers His Critics." *New York Times* (October 27, 1940), Section 9, p. 5.

Numasawa, Kōji. "Black Humor: An American Aspect." *Studies in English Literature*. University of Tokyo (March 1968), p. 177.

Obrdlik, Antonin J. "'Gallows Humor'—A Sociological Phenomenon." *American Journal of Sociology* (March 1942), p. 715.

Olderburg, Ann. "Golden Globes Show a Lot of 'Gump'tion." *USA Today* (January 23, 1995), p. 1–D.

Orwell, George. *1984*. 1949; Reprint. New York: New American Library, 1961.

Patrick, Corbin. "Comedy Is Serious: Lubitsch Film Seen with Mixed Emotions." *Indianapolis Star* (March 12, 1942), p. 13.

Pinsker, Sanford. Chapter 2, "The Graying of Black Humor." In *Between Two Worlds: The American Novel in the 1960s*. Troy, N.Y.: Whitston Publishing, 1980.

Poague, Leland A. *The Cinema of Ernst Lubitsch*. Cranbury, N.J.: A. S. Barnes, 1978.

Polhemus, Robert M. *Comic Faith*. 1980; Reprint. Chicago: University of Chicago Press, 1982.

Pond, Steve. "Jerry Takes Shelter." *TV Guide* (February 4, 1995), p. 14.

Pond, Steve. "Student Body Count." *Rolling Stone* (April 20, 1989), p. 38.

Price, Edgar. *To Be or Not to Be* review. *Brooklyn Citizen* (March 7, 1942). In the *To Be* . . . file, Billy Rose Theatre Collection, New York Public Library at Lincoln Center.

Pulp Fiction review. *Nation* (October 17, 1994), p. 434.

Raeburn, John. "The Gangster Film." In *Handbook of American Film Genres*, ed. Wes Gehring. Westport, Conn.: Greenwood Press, 1988, pp. 47–63.

Rafferty, Terrence. "Helter Skelter." *The New Yorker* (September 5, 1995), p. 106.

Rafferty, Terrence. "Killer." *The New Yorker* (April 20, 1992), p. 82.

Real, Michael R. "The Super Bowl: Mythic Spectacle." In *TELEVISION: The Critical View* (third edition), ed. Horace Newcomb. New York: Oxford University Press, 1982.

Remarque, Erich. *All Quiet on the Western Front*. 1928; Reprint. Greenwich, Conn.: Crest Books, 1964.

Reynolds, Michael S. *The Sun Also Rises: A Novel of the Twenties*. Boston: Twayne, 1988, p. 15.

Rico, Diana. "S.M.A.S.H.," *GQ*, (May 1992), p. 95.

"Robert Altman on *The Player*." *Film Comment* (May–June 1992), p. 26.

Robinson, David. *Chaplin: His Life and Art*. New York: McGraw Hill, 1985.

Rosenfield, John. "Nazis Can Be Had Even by Jack Benny." *Dallas Morning News* March 21, 1942. In the *To Be* . . . file, Billy Rose Theatre Collection, New York Public Library at Lincoln Center.

Scherle, Victor and William Turner Levy. *The Films of Frank Capra*. Secaucus, N.J.: Citadel Press, 1977.

Schiff, Stephen. "The Last Wild Man." *The New Yorker* (August 8, 1994), p. 52.

Schmitz, Neil. *Of Huck and Alice: Humorous Writing in American Literature*. Minneapolis: University of Minnesota Press, 1983.

Schruers, Fred. "The Rolling Stone Interview: Jack Nicholson." *Rolling Stone* (August 14, 1986), p. 48.

Schultz, Max F. *Black Humor Fiction of the Sixties*. Athens: Ohio University Press, 1973.

Shedlin, Michael. *Harold and Maude* review. *Film Quarterly* (Fall 1972), p. 51.

Smith, Gavin, "Quentin Tarantino." *Film Comment* (July–August 1994), p. 42.

Smith, Gavin, and Richard T. Jameson. "The Movie You Saw Is the Movie We're Going to Make." *Film Comment* (May–June 1992), p. 23.

Smith Julian. CHAPLIN. Boston: Twayne Publishers, 1984.

Sondheim, Stephen and John Weidman. *Assassins*. New York: Theatre Communications Group, 1991.

Sontag, Susan. *Against Interpretation: And Other Essays*. 1986; Reprint. New York: Anchor Books, 1990.

Spillman, Susan. "Taking Aim at the Mayhem and the Media." *USA Today* (August 26, 1994), p. D-1.

Stanbrook, Alan. "Invasion of the Purple People Eaters." *Sight and Sound* (Winter 1990), p. 49.

Sterritt, David. "A Movie that Pokes Fun at Movies." *Christian Science Monitor* (April 10, 1992), p. 14.

Stoppard, Tom. *Rosencrantz and Guildenstern Are Dead*. New York: Grove Weidenfeld, 1967.

Tarantino, Quentin. *Pulp Fiction* (Screenplay). New York: Hyperion, 1994.

Thompson, Leslie M., and William R. Cozart. "The Technology of Atrocity." *Forum* (Ball State University) (Autumn 1984), p. 64.

Thoreau, Henry David. *Walden and Other Writings of Henry David Thoreau*. ed. Brooks Atkinson. 1854 *Walden* Reprint. New York: Modern Library, 1965.

Thorson, James A. "A Funny Thing Happened on the Way to the Morgue: Some Thoughts on Humor and Death, and a Taxonomy of Humor Associated with Death." *Death Studies* (9, 3–4, 1985), p. 204.

To Be or Not to Be review. *Christian Science Monitor* (March 6, 1942). In *To Be . . .* file, Billy Rose Theatre Collection, New York Public Library at Lincoln Center.

To Be or Not to Be review. *Variety* (February 18, 1942). In the *To Be . . .* file, Billy Rose Theatre Collection, New York Public Library at Lincoln Center.

Tosches, Nick. *DINO: Living High in the Dirty Business of Dreams*. 1992; Reprint. New York: Dell, 1993.

Travers, Peter. "Movie's Blood from a Stone." *Rolling Stone* (September 8, 1994), p. 84.

Travers, Peter. "Setting Up Hollywood for the Kill." *Rolling Stone* (April 30, 1992), p. 64.

Turan, Kenneth. "*Player* Brings Altman Background with a Vengeance." *Los Angeles Times* (April 10, 1992), pp. 1-F, 6-F.

Twain, Mark. "The Facts Concerning the Recent Carnival of Crime in Connecticut." In *Selected Shorter Writings of Mark Twain*, ed. Walter Blair. Boston: Houghton Mifflin, 1962.

Twain, Mark. *Selected Shorter Writings*, ed. Walter Blair. Boston: Houghton Mifflin, 1962.

Tyson, Rae. "Radiation Testing Shown in Documents." *USA Today* (December 21, 1993), p. 2-D.

Van Doren, Carl. "The Revolt from the Village." *Nation* (October 12, 1921), p. 407.

"Veterans." *Time. February 3, 1947, p. 43.*

Vonnegut, Kurt, Jr. *Slaughterhouse-Five.* 1969; Reprint. New York: Dell, 1974.

Warshow, Robert. "*Monsieur Verdoux.*" In *The Immediate Experience.* 1962; Reprint. New York: Antheneum, 1972. (Originally appeared in the July–August 1947 edition of *Partisan Review.*

Waters, John. *Shock Value.* New York: Dell, 1981.

Weales, Gerald. "Duck Soup." In Weales's *Canned Goods as Caviar: American Film Comedy of the 1930s.* Chicago: University of Chicago Press, 1985, p. 80.

Weinberg, Herman. *The Lubitsch Touch: A Critical Study.* New York: E. P. Dutton, 1971.

Winsten, Archer. *To Be or Not to Be* review. *New York Post* (March 7, 1942). In *To Be . . .* file, Billy Rose Theatre Collection, New York Public Library at Lincoln Center.

Winston, Mathew. "Humor Noir and Black Humor." In *Veins of Humor,* ed. Harry Levin. Cambridge Mass.: Harvard University Press, 1972.

Zipes, Jack, ed. *The Operated Jew.* New York: Routledge, 1991.

INDEX

About the Author

WES D. GEHRING is Professor of Film at Ball State University. He is author of ten previous books: *Leo McCarey and the Comic Antihero in American Film* (1980); *Charlie Chaplin: A Bio-Bibliography* (1983); *W. C. Fields: A Bio-Bibliography* (1984); *Screwball Comedy: A Genre of Madcap Romance* (1986); *The Marx Brothers: A Bio-Bibliography* (1987); *Handbook of American Film Genres* (1988); *Laurel & Hardy: A Bio-Bibliography* (1990); *"Mr. B." or Comforting Thoughts About the Bison: A Critical Biography of Robert Benchley* (1992); *Populism and the Capra Legacy* (1995), all by Greenwood Press, and *Groucho and W. C. Fields: Huckster Comedians* (1994). His poems and humor pieces have appeared in numerous publications.

Recent Titles in
Contributions to the Study of Popular Culture